The Canary Islanders in Texas

The Canary Islanders in Texas

The Story of the Founding of San Antonio

ARMANDO CURBELO FUENTES

FOREWORD TO THE ENGLISH-LANGUAGE EDITION
BY FÉLIX D. ALMARÁZ JR.

Maverick Books ✣ Trinity University Press
San Antonio, Texas

Published by Maverick Books, an imprint of Trinity University Press
San Antonio, Texas 78212

ISBN 978-1-59534-845-6 paperback
ISBN 978-1-59534-846-3 ebook

Book design by BookMatters, Berkeley
Cover design by Anne Richmond Boston

The author thanks Francisco Navarro Quintana in the Canary Islands; Juan Leal, Rosario Aldana, and Adela Navarro in San Antonio, Texas; Pilar Lázaro at the Archivo General de Indias in Seville, Spain; Everett E. Larson, reference librarian at the Hispania Division, U.S. Library of Congress; and Donald A. Richie, historian emeritus at the U.S. Senate Historical Office.

Trinity University Press strives to produce its books using methods and materials in an environmentally sensitive manner. We favor working with manufacturers that practice sustainable management of all natural resources, produce paper using recycled stock, and manage forests with the best possible practices for people, biodiversity, and sustainability. The press is a member of the Green Press Initiative, a nonprofit program dedicated to supporting publishers in their efforts to reduce their impacts on endangered forests, climate change, and forest-dependent communities.

The paper used in this publication meets the minimum requirements of the American National Standard for Information Sciences—Permanence of Paper for Printed Library Materials, ANSI 39.48–1992.

CIP data on file at the Library of Congress

23 22 21 20 19 | 5 4 3 2 1

Trinity University Press gratefully acknowledges the support of these donors.

Alfonso and Mary-Alice Chiscano
Fundación Consejo España
Fernando Gil
Sheila and Joaquin Mira
Dr. and Mrs. Arturo Molina
Epitacio Resendez
John Daniel Rice
Dr. Mario Rodriguez
Hunter and Jesse Stanco

For Angeles, Marta, Elena, Luisa, Macarena, Luis, and Armando

History is not usually what has happened.
History is what some people have thought to be significant.

—IDRIES SHAH

Contents

Part Two

Foreword to the English-Language Edition

FÉLIX D. ALMARÁZ JR.

In 1402 the Canary Islands, located 823 miles northwest of the hump of Africa in the Atlantic Ocean, became an overseas possession of the Crown of Castile. During an interlude in hostilities between England and France in the Hundred Years' War (1337–1453), Enrique III, monarch of Castile, commissioned two French soldiers of fortune, Jean de Bethencourt and Gadifer de La Salle, to evict a motley cast of alien interlopers—Arabs, Portuguese, and a mélange of Europeans—from Lanzarote and Fuerteventura, the arid islands closest to the Sahara. Later in the fifteenth century Castilian adventurers gained control of four western islands in the archipelago: Gran Canaria, La Palma, La Gomera, and El Hierro. Even as late as 1492, the frequent eruptions of El Teide, the volcano on Tenerife, the largest island, discouraged explorers and soldiers from attempting that island's conquest via its northern shore.

Admiral Christopher Columbus, sailing on his epic voyage of 1492, docked at the harbor of Gran Canaria in late August to repair damaged maritime equipment and enlist additional mariners to replace inexperienced men whom he had recruited earlier at the jail in the port of Palos de la Frontera in southern Spain. Thus, from the beginning of Columbus's voyage of encounter with the New World, Canary Islanders (*isleños*) impressed their mark on the annals of America.

As time passed, Canary Islanders participated in reinforcing older Hispanic settlements in the western hemisphere: Caracas, Havana, Montevideo, Nombre de Dios (Isthmus of Panama), and Veracruz. Faraway Texas, the second-to-last province to be explored and occupied in North America during the transition from the seventeenth to the eighteenth centuries, possessed vestiges of governance in three frontier institutions: missions (ecclesiastical), presidios (military), and provinces (political). Still, as late as the second decade of the eighteenth century, Texas lacked any trace of municipal administration.

The marquis of Aguayo, a dynamic governor of Texas, whose vision and accomplishments reaffirmed Spain's claim to the province that lasted for a century, at the conclusion of his tenure in office in 1722, recommended to royal authorities in Mexico City and Madrid a program of initiating ten towns adjacent to missions and presidios he had either reestablished or newly founded. The viceroy of New Spain, the marquis of Casafuerte (1722–33), disapproved the petition as an extravagant drain on the royal treasury. For eight years, Aguayo's advocacy languished in dusty government archives. Finally, in 1729, after Aguayo's death, Gen. Pedro de Rivera, who had conducted a four-year inspection tour of the northern borderlands in New Spain, advised Casafuerte to review the merits of the Texas governor's report of 1722.

Acknowledging the value of frontier towns but still as tightfisted as ever, Casafuerte dispatched a copy of Aguayo's recommendation to Philip V, king of Spain, to which he appended an addendum for funding only one municipality. The monarch conveyed a royal *cédula* to the Canary Islands, authorizing a town government for Texas and soliciting settlers for the project. As an incentive to encourage volunteers to enlist, Philip V offered land grants, irrigation rights, horses, titles of minor nobility to heads of families (*hidalgos*, with the privilege of wearing spurs), subsistence allowances throughout the journey by sea and overland, tools for farming and construction of homesteads, and the opportunity to serve in the government (*ayuntamiento*) they were to initiate. Six of the seven islands recruited settlers; Lanzarote provided the vast majority; only El Hierro, the smallest, declined to participate owing to its few inhabitants.

En route to their destination, a few isleños died; other islanders, already residing in Havana and Veracruz, petitioned the dominant group for permission to join the Texas venture; some sojourners married in chapels along the royal road; and two women gave birth to infants, inspiring one to proclaim she was "The Mother of the Americas." Fifty-four travel-weary, but robust, pioneers finally trudged into the plaza of Presidio San Antonio de Béxar on March 9, 1731. An unknown sentinel, observing the hour of their arrival on the sundial, recorded: "Eleven o'clock in the morning."

Armando Curbelo Fuentes's translated edition of *Crónica Canaria* highlights the reversals and renewals of these spunky isleño settlers in their new homeland in Texas. In Spanish America, town-building required conferral of a royal *cédula.* The Canary Islanders were definitely in full compliance of the law. In their personal luggage, besides the viceroy of Casafuerte's endorsement of Philip V's decree, the isleños conveyed an image of La Candelaria, symbol of the Old World from which they had emigrated, together with another of Our Lady of Guadalupe, representing the New World in which they had arrived. They reserved these images for the dedication of the parish church of San Fernando they planned to construct. Their long-awaited contribution to Texas history commenced on August 1, 1731.

The stringent policies of Viceroy Casafuerte reluctantly compelled Franciscan pioneers, in 1730, to suppress three of their missions in the southern rim of the pine forest in east Texas. Slowly the refugees migrated westward, pausing briefly at the Colorado River, and continued to the San Antonio River, arriving four days ahead of the isleños. Shortly thereafter, the commander of Presidio de Béxar assigned land grants downriver for three new missions: Concepción, San José de los Nazonis (renamed San Juan Capistrano, to avoid confusion with San José y San Miguel de Ayuayo, founded in 1720), and San Francisco de la Espada. Altogether, five missions (including the first, San Antonio de Valero, inaugurated in 1718), one presidio, and Villa San Fernando de Béxar fortified the settlement pattern along a riverside frontier environment that, a century later, became the city of San Antonio, Texas.

Introduction

ANTONIO DE BÉTHENCOURT MASSIEU

There is no doubt that history is an increasingly wide-ranging science. It interrogates the past with an endless stream of questions in its search for explanations. Humankind, living in a world that is becoming more and more complex, has an overriding need to trace the source of its multiple problems.

At the same time, history is very much a human science, unlike other branches of learning that tend to express themselves in highly specialized, impenetrable language, and often need popular writers to help them reach their audiences. Historians, with a few exceptions, are able to connect easily with the general public, since they usually have at least a modicum of literary ability, and their writing follows more of a narrative style.

The growth in the production of historical works, and their great success in the market, is due both to humankind's increasing need to find answers, and to the ease with which this material can be disseminated.

As a consequence, not only are the ranks of professional historians, who learn detailed techniques at university, expanding, but a longstanding tradition is also continuing and growing: the entrance of late bloomers, coming from other professional fields or scientific areas, into the guild of historians. Some begin by delving into the history of the evolution of their specific field; others feel the call of history, the true vocation of a historian.

The author of *The Canary Islanders in Texas*, which I have the honor of presenting here, is a clear case of the latter. Armando Curbelo

Fuentes is a renowned practicing attorney who felt the call of history. The seeds of his vocation as a historian lay dormant, only to spring to life when an unusual event sparked his curiosity.

While working with the Gran Canaria Island Council Tourist Board, he was given the opportunity to visit the city of San Antonio, Texas, where he was astonished to meet a group of descendants from the handful of families who founded the city in 1731.

He discovered that, despite the passage of two and a half centuries, these people had preserved a sense of shared identity and pride as a social group, and some even shared his surname. They had maintained not only the language, the traditions, and the folklore, but also a deep, sincere love of the islands where their ancestors had once lived. He found this quite incredible, considering the massive upheaval involved in moving from a Hispanic community to an Anglo-Saxon one, and the vicissitudes of two centuries of evolution and progress.

Our author became interested in this experience, one of the thousands in which Canary Islanders played a key role across the length and breadth of the continent, both as individuals and in communities. The Canary Islands' contribution to American history, a historical subject of great magnitude, is yet to be written. This will be possible only through monographic studies like this one, which will help us embark on this important collective project.

Armando Curbelo Fuentes took a lively interest in this subject. He began to read everything that had been published about the history of San Antonio. He did not limit himself to those titles with direct references but rather examined any work that could enrich and explain the issues he was uncovering. On reading this book, evidence can be found of his extensive investigation. For the functioning of the *cabildos*,[1] or the regulation of property and use of irrigation water, see *La novísima recopilación* (Latest compilation of Spanish law). For the conflict-filled situation in the Canary Islands in the 1720s, and the tyrannical reign of the ill-tempered marquis of Valhermoso, see work by Viera y Clavijo. He also researched the exceptional organization of the Tlascala cabildo, and the organization of the postal service in the precolonial empires.

As a historian, he was unsatisfied with the available published evidence and turned eagerly to the archives. With dedication, enthusiasm, and tenacity, he went about gathering photocopies of everything he could find on this subject in the archives of the Canary Islands, Seville, and Madrid. His work did not stop there; he repeatedly crossed the Atlantic to do research in Mexican and North American archives. Much of what he recounts in these stories stems from his research at the University of Texas Libraries, in Austin.

The result of this tremendous effort has been the publication of two books, which, although very different in structure and narrative method, are at heart a single volume—the second book simply continues the story begun in the first: the founding of the town, and the descendants of the founders.

The first volume, *Fundación de San Antonio de Texas: Canarias, la gran deuda americana* (The Founding of San Antonio, Texas: America's Debt to the Canary Islands), was published in 1986 by the distinguished Las Palmas de Gran Canaria Royal Society of Friends of the Country. It was received with such accolade that in 1987 a second edition was released under the patronage of the Caja de Ahorros de Las Palmas (Las Palmas Savings Bank). A third edition was later financed by the municipal government of Teguise, on the island of Lanzarote, which was home to seven of the ten families who undertook the perilous expedition. The volume addresses the decade between 1722 and 1732, from the initial idea of colonizing the northern frontier of the Viceroyalty of New Spain with Canary Islanders, to the settlement of the Canarian community in San Antonio and the establishment of the cabildo, with all of the initial conflicts the islanders faced on that long, arduous journey.

The second volume is this very book, *The Canary Islanders in Texas*, in which he describes through a fictional historical lens the lives and fortunes of the Canary Islanders and their descendants. The author does not attempt a linear description of the history of the Canary Islanders in Texas; instead he extensively quotes original documents and uses a unique device—fictional memoirs of two historical women—to narrate the events of two different periods.

The author attributes the first section to María Curbelo Perdomo, born in Lanzarote, who writes her memoirs between 1800 and 1803, the year of her death at eighty. The events of the nineteenth century are written as the memoirs of her great-great-grandniece, María Jesús Curbelo Delgado, who finishes them in 1883 when she is seventy.

Both Curbelos were real women. The author chose them as narrators of the memoirs for well-considered reasons, and for the important historical moment in which each lived.

As Armando Curbelo describes the motives that impelled these two relatives to take up their pens, the narrative technique he uses gives their writing a sense of authenticity.

The aunt, María, is a witness to the events that occurred during the transition from the eighteenth to the nineteenth century. San Antonio, like the rest of the Spanish empire, was shaken by a profound crisis. Conditions were harsh, and were made worse by the waves of colonists ("from Germany, from Virginia, and from the rest of the northern states") settling in Texas, while Spain's weakness prevented it from sending the forces necessary to keep out these new settlers.

The last of the founders from the Canary Islands had died before her memoirs were supposed to have been written, and although their descendants continued to control the cabildo to some extent until 1831, they soon became absorbed into the culture of the Anglo-Saxon colonists. What moves her to write is the loss of the Canary Islands' culture. Her pages resonate with her love for the islands. She takes on the arduous task of keeping alive the memories of everything achieved by her compatriots.

In her great-great-grandniece, María Jesús, the sense of identity with the Canary Islands is more tenuous. The role of Canarian culture has declined. She laments the loss of Hispanic culture to a much greater degree, since she has suffered the trauma of integration into the Anglo-Saxon world. But María Jesús is not a woman living in the past. She marries a Methodist from Louisiana, and accepts the positive aspects of new customs; for example, she praises the Lancaster System used in schools. Endowed with a critical mind, she reflects negatively on aspects of the Catholic religion, and on Hispanic politics, administration, and behavior, to such a degree that it seems that the writings of the Black Legend[2] have penetrated her spirit.

Ultimately, the eighteenth-century memoirs are better-adapted to the traditions of the genre than those of the nineteenth century. They exude subjectivity, nostalgia, and even a degree of pride. However, the chapters dedicated to the fierce conflict between María's brothers-in-law, the solicitor and councilor, and the Gran Canarian Rodríguez Mederos, who introduced the Canarian system of irrigation to Texas, do not hold so true to this narrative style. The pages devoted to this conflict reveal more of the author's understanding of this process than the evaluation of an old peasant woman, whose education was probably limited.

When María Jesús writes, she relates the vicissitudes of the wars of independence sustained by Texas, first against Spain and then against Mexico. Although these events naturally affected the islanders, they were not the protagonists. At the same time, the abundance of preserved documents leads the narrator to quote long texts. This causes the memoirs to lose some of their intimate, personal tone, and turns them into more of a historical narrative in the style that Collingwood called scissors-and-paste.

While both sections are praiseworthy, as a Canary Islander, I was personally more interested in the material that dealt with the problems relating to the colonization by the Canary Islanders. Among these were the persecution by people already established in the area, such as Governor Perez de Almazán (the recovery of the sixty-one requisitioned horses; let's not forget the words of Inca Garcilaso, "my country was conquered by horsemen"), and the autonomy of the cabildo with respect to the military authorities; there were also problems with the Franciscans in the missions, their economic rivals for the labor force, the markets, and the water, and a strained relationship with "the other residents." The transformation of farmers into ranchers was also not without its difficulties. Special mention should also be given to the implementation of the irrigation system, the property regime and the use of water, which derived directly from the water board of Tenoya in Gran Canaria. Armando Curbelo wrote an intriguing article on this in the *Journal of the Canarian Forum* in 1984.

Finally, there is the arduous saga endured by Rodríguez Mederos for granting priority to the missions' irrigation canals rather than to the Canary Islanders' irrigation system, the origin of a long lawsuit that would not be resolved until 1747. The story of this process is a veritable adventure novel, particularly illuminating for the study of Spanish procedural law.

As I implied above, the vision of María Jesús Curbelo is more universal. She appears to be a more learned woman than her great-aunt. Through her memoirs and documents she narrates the story of the birth of the state of Texas, but she doesn't limit herself purely to the diplomatic and military developments that led to its independence, from its inclusion as part of Mexico, to the Alamo in 1835. She also covers other subjects, such as religious feelings (including the conflict over regalian rights, and the effect of the secularization of the missions), political policies (the reports by Aranda and Onís, for example), the population and the city of San Antonio, the exploitation systems (the Canary Islanders' branding irons), production, commerce, money and banking, and education (the new Lancaster System).

She also discusses the Indian attacks and the growing and often overwhelming presence of colonists from the United States (30,000 Yankees compared with 8,000 Hispanics in 1833), and devotes pages to describing the functioning of the irrigation system, identical to those implemented by the water boards on Gran Canaria.

Using a sequence of two fictional memoirs, Armando Curbelo offers us a well-documented piece of work, encapsulating two great chapters of Texan history, and at the same time discusses the mission of the Canary Islanders in America.

For Canarian readers, the first memoir is closer to home, since it refers to the founders of the city, who are present throughout the ten chapters that make up the first part of the book.

The second memoir is an authentic chronicle of an important period in the history of Texas. It is complete in its coverage, and uses historical events to explore how the descendants of the founders were affected as time passed.

In short, this book offers an indirect insight into the descendants and a very direct insight into the founders of this splendid and most welcoming city of San Antonio, where Hispanic people continue to play an active part in public affairs.

Ciudad Jardín, September 1991

PART ONE

Entry from the Journal of María Curbelo Perdomo

JULY 16, 1800

My name is María Curbelo Perdomo, daughter of Juan and Gracia, and I was born on a small island in the Canarian archipelago called Lanzarote.[3]

I left there with my parents and siblings on February 20, 1730, on a sloop heading for the island of Tenerife, and then on March 15 of the same year we set sail with nine other families for Cuba and Veracruz in the Viceroyalty of New Spain. From there, we traveled overland in a caravan, enduring all kinds of hardship and suffering, until we arrived at the fort of San Antonio, which would later become the capital of the province, and remains so to this day.

I am the last survivor of the fifty-five Canarian families who founded this city, and at my advanced age, in the solitude of my house on this hot summer afternoon, I feel great nostalgia for my Canarian homeland, to which I will never return. Perhaps it is because of the recent death of my husband, or that of the last Canary Islander who came with me on the expedition, or maybe it is the afternoon heat (which reminds me of my lost homeland), my age, or all of these things together. I feel, too, a pressing responsibility, when I see how today, July 16, 1800, the city that we Canarian families founded with such hard work and dedication is slowly losing its original identity, overrun as it is by Americans from the north who are pouring across the border into our town, the most desirable in all the territory.

These people, the majority ranchers like us, come from Germany, from Virginia, and from the rest of the northern states. The Canary Islanders who have governed the city through the cabildo, practically since its founding on March 9, 1731, have petitioned the viceroy for aid, asking him to send more soldiers to guard the border with Louisiana and thus impede the passage of so many foreigners, North Americans, who will doubtless one day take over these lands, which have cost so much Canarian blood.

Today, on this sad day, as I gaze through my window at the church that we built with such sacrifice for our blessed Virgin of Candelaria and her blessed Son, I realize that the Canary Islanders' achievements in America should be recorded for posterity. People should know what we Canary Islanders have done in San Antonio, from the founding of the city in 1731 to this year, 1800, when we have lost our power in the town council.

I am in a privileged position to tell this story, since my brother-in-law, Francisco Arocha, married to my sister Juana, was until his death in 1757 the secretary of the cabildo and notary public, and my other brother-in-law, Vicente Álvarez Travieso, married to my other sister María, was a councilor in the San Antonio cabildo until 1787. The documents that I describe in this modest diary have been obtained from these relatives.

The arrival of so many foreigners in these lands makes me think that here in San Antonio not only will the achievements of the Canary Islanders be lost in time, but also that these very lands will be lost to Spain. As the last living Canary Islander of the fifty-five people who left our island home, I am writing this diary as a testament for future generations here and abroad, so that they may know the truth of everything we humble Canary Islanders have done, after traveling from so far away to these promised lands.

CHAPTER 1

I. Taking Possession

The town of Villa de San Fernando de Béjar (today San Antonio, Texas) is located in the southwest of Texas.

It is flanked by two rivers or, more accurately, is between one river, the San Antonio River, and a stream, the San Pedro. In the eighteenth century, it was an expanse of fertile land, a perfect location for establishing a settlement. In fact, five Franciscan missions had already been built along the San Antonio River. Closest to the town of San Antonio was the San Antonio de Valero mission, later famous worldwide as the Álamo. Other missions included San José, San Juan de Capistrano, San Francisco de la Espada, and Concepción.

King Philip V of Spain was always particularly concerned with maintaining his sovereignty over this far northern territory located in the Viceroyalty of New Spain, whose capital was in Mexico City. This concern, which was in the back of the king's mind throughout his reign, resulted in his accession to the continuous petitions sent from this territory by the governor of the province of Texas and the New Philippines, as it was then called, asking him to send a group of families from the Canary Islands to populate the area. So it came to pass that we founded a city in accordance with the prevailing Law of the Indies, and in 1731 we established a municipal government in the form of a cabildo, between the San Antonio *presidio*[4] and the San Antonio mission, separated from the mission by the San Antonio River for greater protection against Indian attacks. The presidio, like all those of its time, was built as a square around a central plaza, encircled by a high wall of adobe and wood. A number of wooden buildings were constructed around the inside of the walls and housed the soldiers' quarters, the quartermaster, the stables, the kitchens, and other services. The fort had four large gates: two opening to the east, toward the San Antonio River, and two to the west, where the Canarian colonists, the founders of the town of San Antonio, lived. Ramps from the central plaza provided access to the upper part of the wall, and walkways were built along the walls and over the attached buildings for the sentries who were placed at the four corners of the fort, in tall towers for greater visibility.

After our arrival, the main entrance of the fort was always through the west gate, since this was the place we chose to establish the town. When we founded the town, we erected a small church in front of the gate of the fort, and the rest of the settlement was built around the church, leaving a plaza facing west, on the opposite side from the fort.

This was the town of San Antonio at the time of its founding. A handful of nearly illiterate farmers, with scarcely any protection, in an unknown land, living under the constant danger of unexpected attacks from savage Indians.

Apart from the Canary Islanders, the soldiers' families lived in the fort, making up a total population of around 300 people. However, when the cabildo was elected, all of its members were Canary Islanders. So, on the first of August, 1731, the following people passed into history as the first municipal government in Texas:

Juan Leal Goraz, First Councilor (Presiding Councilor and First Mayor)

Juan Curbelo, Second Councilor

Antonio Santos, Third Councilor

Salvador Rodríguez, Fourth Councilor

Manuel Ruiz, Fifth Councilor

Juan Leal Álvarez, Sixth Councilor

Francisco Arocha, Solicitor of the Public Council

Antonio Rodríguez, Treasurer

Vicente Álvarez Travieso, Sheriff[5]

After the creation of the first municipal government, much remained to be done. The houses, the streets, the plaza, the church—this was the great labor that had to be undertaken.

Juan Leal Goraz,[6] first president of the cabildo, summoned the councilors, the colonists from the Canary Islands, and the civilian members of the soldiers' families in the fort, and gave the following speech:

> We have come from far away. We have suffered many hardships on our journey here, until finally we reached the land promised by His Majesty, King Philip V, may God protect him. This land seems to be much better than we were told. There is abundant water. In our homeland we endured terrible droughts and were always crying out for water, while here we have a great river, the San Antonio, practically at our doors and our fields, and many streams, crucial for cultivating this exceptional soil. We have everything we need to get by and, much more importantly, to show ourselves worthy of the trust that our king has put in us. As subjects of His Majesty, who has granted us these lands, we are at his service, but as Canary Islanders we have even more of a responsibility. We all know that other Canary Islanders are depending on our efforts here, so they may leave behind the suffering and come to these magnificent lands. We must forget our personal problems, and must live together in peace in this extraordinary place. I know that many of you have not been in agreement with my decisions as leader of this expedition during our voyage since we left the island of Tenerife on March 27, 1730, but we must try to forget our difficult march through snow and deserts to arrive here. I know that some of our companions died on that arduous overland journey, and that none of us have fond memories of it, and will always remember our beloved friends who fell on the way.
>
> Someone had to make decisions. When faced with emergencies like those we endured, we needed a person who would make decisions which he believed to be for the common good. That great

> responsibility fell on me, ever since that afternoon in our beloved land of Santa Cruz de Tenerife, when you chose me to be leader of the expedition, a choice that you have ratified today by electing me as the first presiding councilor and first mayor during the first session of this town's cabildo.
>
> To you, the families who have been here many years longer than us, as I indicated when I was only another colonist, as first councilor of this cabildo I promise you that I will go to Mexico as soon as my office is confirmed by the viceroy. Once there, I will repeat the petition sent in my letter of July 29 calling on him to acquiesce to your request to be "other residents"[7] of this town, and to be conceded the same rights as ourselves, with respect to lands and other rights, for the comfort of all and, together with all of the families of this town, to banish the heathen Indians to some far-off land.
>
> Furthermore, I will make a first official petition to the captain of the presidio, J. A. Pérez de Almazán[8] as the military authority and the representative of His Majesty the King in these lands, asking him to return to the Canarian colonists the sixty-one horses that were delivered to us at the fort of San Juan Bautista before crossing the Río Grande, since without them we can neither farm nor transport stone and wood for our houses.

At the close of the speech, the silence in the small, newly built cabin outside the fort was complete. Leal's address was the first cry of independence by civil power in the face of the all-powerful military. It marked the first conflict between the recently designated president of the cabildo and the captain of the presidio. Juan Antonio Pérez de Almazán, until this point the supreme authority over all of the inhabitants for miles around, had never imagined that these humble colonists would petition him before the entire town. He was accustomed to military government, where he only needed to explain his decisions to his superiors. The silence seemed to go on forever, until it was interrupted, timidly at first, and then unanimously, by resounding applause.

Pérez de Almazán never forgave Leal for that public petition before all of the colonists. The following day he sent his aide Uribe to the settlement to instruct the president of the newly established cabildo, Juan Leal, to present himself at the fort.

II. Conflicts with the Captain of the Presidio

AUGUST 24, 1800

I remember word for word the account that Leal gave of his interview with the captain of the Fort of San Antonio, Juan Antonio Pérez de Almazán.

To these words, I should add that Leal's personality, demeanor, and behavior made it clear to the captain, right from the beginning, that he had found an enemy who, once invested as president, would not be easily cowed. As a consequence, he would need to act with care. Leal was a different person after being unanimously elected president of the cabildo. He now began to treat military officers as equals, rather than with the reverential fear with which he had held them since his arrival in Veracruz.

When Leal arrived at Pérez de Almazán's office, the captain told him that after hearing everything that Leal had said during the ceremony to establish the cabildo, he had summoned Leal to remind him that since their arrival in these lands, the colonists had always relied on his aid. When they were attacked by Indians upon leaving the fort of San Juan Bautista and crossing the Río Grande, he had defended them. When they settled next to the fort, he had provided them with tents. It had been he, as the supreme authority, who had distributed the parcels of land for farming and provided them with stones and wood to build their houses and fences, and, finally, it had been he, in the name of the viceroy, who had conferred upon them their offices after the cabildo was established. Despite all this, Leal had the temerity to ask him in front of all of the colonists to return the horses delivered to them at the fort of San Juan Bautista.

Leal politely but firmly answered that he had made the petition in the name of the recently constituted cabildo and that his mission as president was to care for and defend the interests of the civilian population whenever necessary. In this case it had been Captain Pérez de Almazán, the military leader, who had commandeered the horses that they so desperately needed to carry materials, to build their houses, and to work their fields. And at the end of the day, all of the aid that he had provided to the colonists had been part of his duties as representative of the viceroy in those lands, as set forth in the order of November 28, 1730, which named all of the Canary Islanders hidalgos and made no reference whatsoever to the seizure of the horses.

Pérez de Almazán reaffirmed the requisition, since he considered himself to be the supreme authority of the territory, and the establishment of the cabildo, although mandated by the viceroy in his order, was to him a mere formality, empty of any greater significance. In the Indies, he said, there was a saying: "You must obey the letter of the law, but not the spirit"; in other words, he would obey the order, but not comply with its intent.

Awaiting Juan Leal at the gate of the fort when he left the meeting were his trusted men from the newly elected cabildo: the solicitor Francisco de Arocha; the sheriff, Vicente Álvarez Travieso; the treasurer, Antonio Rodríguez Mederos; and his eldest son, Juan Leal el Mozo, the sixth councilor. They crossed the courtyard of the fort, walked along its north side, and soon reached the lands of Antonio Rodríguez Mederos, where they proceeded to hold a meeting in the only room of the newly built house.

Juana and María Curbelo and Josefa Niz, wives of Álvarez Travieso, Francisco Arocha, and Antonio Rodríguez respectively, prudently stepped out onto the porch when they saw the men arriving, leaving them alone in the house. They sat outside and settled back into their long-standing conversation that had begun when they left their individual Canary Islands. Juana and María spoke of Teguise on the island of Lanzarote, and Josefa Niz of her village, Tamaraceite, and of the great city of Las Palmas in Gran Canaria. She recounted, again and again, how she would walk down to the city on the most important festival days.

While the women dreamed of their Canary homelands, the husbands debated the problems that would need to be addressed in the newly founded cabildo.

"I think we are going to face enormous problems governing the town," said Juan Leal. "I thought that once we founded the cabildo it would be respected as the civil power, but I can see from the attitude of Captain Pérez de Almazán in this first and relatively minor problem of returning the horses, that he wants to continue ruling over soldiers and civilians alike. He intends to carry on as before, without acknowledging that there is a legally elected cabildo, and that according to the Laws of the Indies in these territories, it is the cabildo and not the military authority that must govern the civilian population. It is true that he has an advantage over the cabildo because he is a learned man and knows how to read and write, unlike us, with one or two exceptions. We only know that we are councilors of the Villa de San Fernando de Béjar cabildo."

They also needed to know, however, how to take legal action in the face of the arbitrary decisions of the captain of the fort. Some of them had been councilors in Teguise, on the island of Lanzarote, but that was a different case; here they were alone against a military power that up until then had been the supreme civil and military authority. In the Canary Islands, long before any of them had entered the municipal government of Teguise, there had already existed a separation between the two powers. When conflicts occurred, they could always travel to Tenerife, where there were higher authorities to appeal to, and as a last resort they were closer to the royal court.

Juan Leal told those present that as soon as he left his meeting with the captain, he had wished to hold this urgent meeting in order to propose that, in the face of recent events and the position expressed by Pérez de Almazán, they should agree that he would travel immediately to Mexico City, to denounce before the viceroy the seizure of the horses and to meet with the brigadier, Pedro de Ribero. The latter had treated them so well during his interview with the viceroy when they passed through the city on their way to San Antonio, and they should thank him for his kind attentions to all of the Canary Islanders. Secondly, he would request written instructions on their rights and obligations as a cabildo, in accordance with the relevant laws of the Indies in these lands, and finally, although as a Canary Islander he believed that this should come first, he would attempt to get the millstone that they had brought by sea from the Canary Islands sent to them. Unfortunately, their guide Duval had decided to leave this millstone in the city of Veracruz, against the wishes of all of the islanders. Juan Leal's proposal was unanimously accepted, and recorded in the minutes by the notary, Francisco de Arocha. When the meeting ended, Arocha and the others went home with their wives. Juan Leal walked slowly back to his own, accompanied by his son, Juan Mozo.

It was six o'clock, and the sun was setting behind the northwest tower of the fort. The main gate was open, and through it in the distance they could see the silhouettes of Captain Pérez de Almazán and his aide Uribe, climbing the south ramp up to the wall to inspect the four guard towers.

Leal, exhausted by the misfortunes suffered by the colonists, during which he had always acted as the leader of the expedition, having to make decisions that often caused harm to his friends and companions, many of whom he had known since his childhood on Lanzarote, asked his son if he had been right to convince so many people from his village of Teguise to leave the islands for these hostile lands, full of savage Indians. They were only simple farmers, not soldiers, and in these lands it was as necessary to know how to handle arms as it was to farm the earth, as they had seen during the attacks they had suffered during the journey to San Antonio. He wondered if they would ever be safe there. The Indians would continue to attack, since the colonists were occupying their lands. More than once he had thought of returning to the Canary Islands, but he dismissed the idea as impossible. He feared that their sacrifices and deaths on the journey would be in vain if the aid promised by the king was not forthcoming, and that perhaps their fate was to die of hunger, or at the hands of the Indian infidels. Was it worth making such an effort? Was it worth the sacrifice of dying in a foreign land? He felt overwhelmed by the huge responsibility that he and his countrymen had taken on from the day they set sail from Santa Cruz de Tenerife. As I mentioned earlier, their situation had been different in the Canary Islands. There they had been better protected against injustice, not only by the island authorities but also by the royal court, which was much closer.

Here, in the middle of these territories, surrounded by Indians, it was almost impossible even to travel to Mexico to see the viceroy. Moreover, the Canary Islanders were not warriors or conquistadors, like those his grandfather used to see when he lived in Las Palmas and repaired their boats in the bay of Confital, in the northern part of La Isleta. More than once, his grandfather had offered them chunks of sandstone taken from the reefs that protected the bay. The conquistadors valued the stone highly and brought it back to America in boats to make basins for filtering the water. The Canary Islanders were farmers, and had not come to kill or to be killed; they had come to farm the land.

There was good soil and there was water, but if they had no help, they could do nothing.

CHAPTER 2

I. President Juan Leal's Journey to Mexico

SEPTEMBER 3, 1800

After August 9, when the cabildo made the decision to send Leal to Mexico City in an urgent, extraordinary session with only five of its members present, the Canarian colonists continued to work hard in the fields and on completing their houses. Even Captain Pérez de Almazán, no close friend of the Canarian colonists (as we have seen, after the contentious transfer of power to the elected cabildo), wrote to the viceroy, the marquis of Casafuerte, on September 29, 1731, indicating his satisfaction with their labors: "The Canary Islanders have worked with determination, with every individual pitching in, and they have planted twenty-two *fanegadas*[9] with corn, gourds, many different green vegetables, and watermelons. It is most noteworthy that the grapevines they have planted in the town, transported from the province of Coahuila, are already showing fruit for this year, despite the long journey and the very scarce rain we have had so far this year."

The first piece of news that cast a ray of hope over the Canary Islanders in Texas was received by the cabildo on November 4, 1731. By decree on October 24, 1731, the viceroy, the marquis of Casafuerte,[10] affirmed that "having scrutinized the elections held in the town of Villa de San Fernando de Béjar for the constitution of the cabildo of said town, the elected members are considered to be legally invested in their offices as counselors of said cabildo." This decree of investiture was the second time in three months that the Canary Islanders in San Antonio had upset the captain of the fort, Pérez de Almazán. Nevertheless, he continued to believe that he, as representative of the viceroy in the area, was the supreme authority. He did not understand how there could be a civil government led by a bunch of lowly, ignorant colonists, no matter what kind of cabildo they had established. If they didn't know how to read, how could they govern? However, he wasn't aware of the determination and tenacity of these Canary Islanders. They had not made such a long and arduous journey to be governed by the captain of a fort.

The captain sent the decree to the cabildo in the hands of his aide, Uribe, and on receiving it, Leal immediately called a session in his house. All of the members attended, and he read them the viceroy's decree confirming their offices as councilors of the cabildo. Although everyone considered this to be excellent news, Francisco de Arocha, the solicitor who recorded the minutes of the meeting as secretary, reminded them that on the day of the election they had agreed to ask the viceroy for an audience; this request had been sent to Mexico on August 1, but they still had not received a reply. As solicitor, he recorded in the minutes that they needed to know how the cabildo worked, what their rights and obligations were, how to keep the accounts when they had money, and how and where to record their decisions.

A few days after receiving the decree, Captain Almazán called President Juan Leal and told him not to worry about the laws that regulated the functions of cabildos in the Viceroyalty of New Spain, and that they should not trouble themselves by going to Mexico City, which was so far away; they should also not bother His Excellency with a matter of so little importance. He, as representative of the viceroy in these territories, would happily offer his services in clearing up any doubts they might have about governing, since this was his duty.

He insisted that they never forget, as he had said before, how as representative of the viceroy of New Spain, he had so far helped them with everything. He was the viceroy's highest representative, and thus was also King Philip V's representative, in these remote lands. Just as he had distributed the parcels of farmland to them, and had instructed them on how and where to build their houses, and how and where to lay out the streets and erect the church, he should similarly be made aware of all decisions made in the cabildo, which should be sent to him for approval.

Leal did not answer him, but simply took his leave, giving the impression that he had accepted Almazán's words. Uribe, the captain's aide, who was present during the conversation, did not share the optimism with which his superior described Leal's submission. He could not forget the Canarian's proud bearing the first time he went to fetch him from the town for a meeting with the captain.

Uribe continued to believe that behind the proud gaze was an indomitable character which did not correspond to the submission that the captain claimed he had shown in the face of his pretensions as supervisor of the cabildo's decisions. But the aide preferred to remain silent. Time would tell if he were right or not. After this meeting with Almazán, Juan Leal met with his councilors, and explained his fear that Captain Pérez de Almazán had interfered with their petition for an audience with the viceroy, since he had spoken of it without officially knowing anything about it. Francisco Arocha, the cabildo's solicitor and the man who had come up with the idea of the petition, did not agree. According to his information, the postal service in the viceroyalty was very good; in fact it had already been excellent in the time of the Aztecs, when messages were carried by Indians on foot. Today it was carried by men on horseback.

Finally, on November 6, they received an answer from the viceroy. The response was addressed to Juan Leal as first councilor of the cabildo of Villa de San Fernando, and granted them the requested audience on December 31.

Juan Leal prepared himself for the long journey. As it was the first he would make to Mexico City, he hired the services of the guide, Francisco Duval, who had led the caravan of Canarian colonists on their first journey. Leal paid only a modest sum for the guide's company, since Duval had not found employment in the town since arriving with the caravan in March and wished to return to the capital of the viceroyalty.

After crossing the Frio and Hondo Rivers, where the expedition of the Canary Islanders had suffered Indian attacks on the way to San Antonio, they reached El Saltillo where they rested for three days. This was the most important city for miles around. It reminded Juan Leal of his Canarian homeland—not of his village of Teguise, but rather of Santa Cruz de Tenerife, a city he had twice visited. On the first occasion he had traveled with his companion, Juan Curbelo, for an interview with Bartolomé de Casabuena, superintendent of the Court of the Indies for all the islands, in which they were informed of the details of the royal order of February 14, 1729, sent to the municipal government of Teguise, on Lanzarote. When he arrived on Tenerife for the first time, Leal had been surprised by the large bay that served as a port. The bay of Anaga was a magnificent natural refuge that had transformed the island into a great port for mooring all of the boats crossing the Atlantic, both outbound and inbound. The central plaza of El Saltillo reminded him of the central plaza of Santa Cruz de Tenerife, La Candelaria, surrounded by buildings with long, wooden balconies.

The three days he spent in El Saltillo were nostalgic days for Leal, since the city brought back memories of his Canary Islands, and this served to remind him of the importance of the task invested in him by his companions when they elected him president of the first cabildo of Villa de San Fernando, near the San Antonio presidio. He had faith that one day people would talk about how the Canary Islanders had arrived in San Antonio with nothing, and had labored hard to build a city comparable in beauty to El Saltillo and even, why not, to Santa Cruz de Tenerife. His interview with the president of the city's cabildo had encouraged him to continue with his struggle, and to propose to the viceroy, through his great friend the brigadier Pedro de Ribera, that there must be independence between the cabildo and the military power of the captain of the San Antonio presidio, Pérez de Almazán.

From El Saltillo, Leal and his guide set out for the city of Quaticlán, where they had met many people during their two months there with the caravan of Canarian colonists on the way to San Antonio. They also spent several days there. On the morning of December 15, they left for Mexico City, arriving at noon on the same day.

Faced with the immediacy of his interview with the viceroy, Leal lost heart, and worries began to consume him. He was overwhelmed by the enormous responsibility he felt toward all of his Canarian countrymen, and dwelled on the influence he had over all his companions from the island of Lanzarote, who made up the majority of the expedition of colonists in San Antonio. He had convinced them all to leave their homeland with his passionate words after his meeting in Santa Cruz de Tenerife with the superintendent of the Court of the Indies, Bartolomé de Casabuena.

What he had promised them in the beginning, little more than a pleasure cruise across the sea to settle in a promised land, had been converted by unforeseen circumstances into an unprecedented adventure, in which they had crossed the entire Viceroyalty of New Spain from Veracruz to the San Antonio presidio. They had traveled over mountainous territory, where several died from the snow, the cold, and the altitude of Mexico's highest mountain, the Pico de Orizaba, and then across hostile desert lands, populated by savage Indians who attacked them on a number of occasions. What hurt him most was not only that the Canarians blamed him for this, but also that they reproached him for convincing them to come to these lands; that they thought his promises were false and would force them to die in this far-off place, without being able to return to see their parents and loved ones left behind in the Canary Islands.

What would happen to him if everything turned out badly, if the cabildo were unable to act without the supervision of the captain of the presidio? What would happen to them if the town they had so recently founded could not coexist with the soldiers, independent of their authority, if they did not have the means to advance their town?

Leal later recounted to the cabildo how he had first set eyes on Mexico City, and how he had wandered its streets, lost in his thoughts, until he finally reached the Alameda and the viceroy's palace.

The first person he met was his friend, Pedro de Ribera,[11] who received him immediately in his office.

It was a large room that looked out over the Alameda, with a ceiling of finely worked wooden beams and a wooden floor, almost completely covered by magnificent handcrafted indigenous rugs and presided over by an immense table with candelabras, also of Mayan craftsmanship, and a large panel of embossed silver. At the far end of the room, two great windows with wooden internal doors opened out onto a balcony. The sun shone through the glass and emphasized the eagles woven into the rugs.

Before anything else, Leal solemnly thanked Ribera as a Canary Islander and, in the name of all of the colonists, for "the considerable help that you have given us since the beginning of our long journey from the city of Veracruz to our final destination, near the San Antonio presidio." He described how this assistance had been invaluable, all the more so because the brigadier had taken pity on them and added horses, carriages, clothes, tools for working the earth, and soldiers who protected them and helped them to bridle and harness the animals. He also acknowledged that the captain of the presidio, Pérez de Almazán, had diligently followed his instructions with respect to settling them, distributing the land, and building the town, its streets, its plaza, and the church. The brigadier replied that he had recently sent the confirmation of the elections for the establishment of the cabildo to the town, addressed to Leal, and that the speed with which the captain of the presidio had carried out his orders had greatly pleased both the viceroy and himself. Despite this, Leal continued, there were a few small unresolved questions that were not related to the specific orders given to the captain (since he had allotted the plots of farmland to each family and had complied with his written orders to the letter). These unresolved questions had brought him to the city and had moved him to request an audience with the viceroy so that, as great protector of the Canarian families, and considering the enormous sacrifice that they had made in coming from so far away to inhabit these lands, he could advise them on the best possible way to solve the issues.

Ribera, who had been so impressed with this man during the first interview he had granted him as leader of the expedition of Canarian colonists, watched him attentively. At this time, Juan Leal was around fifty-five years of age, tall, with gray hair and gray eyes. He explained matters passionately and firmly. His face clearly showed the deep preoccupation and sense of responsibility that assailed him, burdens that had been present when the brigadier first met him as leader of the expedition, and were now even more profound: firstly because Leal was a Canary Islander like the other residents of the town, and secondly because he was president of the newly founded cabildo.

Evidently Ribera found this situation to be quite distinct from the other occasions when representatives from towns had come to ask him for solutions to their problems. Leal was different. He understood the town's problems because he was not just another political civil servant who had arrived from the peninsula to take up office. He was also a colonist, and had been voted into his office by the unanimous decision of all of the inhabitants of Villa de San Fernando.

The first problem they had encountered, explained Leal, was that the captain of the presidio, Pérez de Almazán, had confiscated the sixty-one packhorses given to them by the captain of the San Juan Bautista presidio to aid the colonists in crossing the Río Grande. Without the horses they could not survive, as they needed them both for agricultural labor and to carry stones. The brigadier, better than anyone, would understand the daunting task that faced them in those lands, since he had traveled them widely, long before the colonists arrived, on a reconnaissance expedition for the viceroy.

Pedro de Ribera was surprised at Juan Leal's words. He assured him that this action on the captain's part had not been ordered by the viceroy and was surely due to the captain's personal interpretation of the royal ordinances. The captain probably believed that if the army had given them sixty-one horses to cross the Río Grande and reach the San Antonio presidio, then once they had arrived, the horses should be returned to the army. He had clearly not considered the particular characteristics of the group of Canary Islanders that Leal represented, colonists under royal orders to found and build a town. The brigadier would inform the viceroy of the situation, so that he could issue an order for the immediate return of the horses. "My thanks, sir; I expected no less of your generosity and understanding," said Leal. In the face of such a fast and favorable resolution of this problem, Leal quickly brought up another resource issue which, although not the reason for his journey, was nevertheless crucial for any colonist, and even more so for the Canary Islanders who had endured its scarcity since birth.

"The second problem," continued Leal, "concerns water. While this is a necessity for all colonists, it is even more important for us, since we grew up on our Canary Islands hearing our parents and our neighbors complaining of the lack of water, not just for the fields, but also for drinking." He explained that, as Ribera already knew, the town of Villa de San Fernando was established next to the San Antonio River, and that the missionaries were opposed to the colonists channeling its waters to irrigate their lands. The captain of the fort had ordered them to water their fields from a meager stream, the San Pedro, on the other side of the town. Leal informed the brigadier that one of the town councilors, Antonio Rodríguez Mederos, from the island of Tamaraceite on Gran Canaria, had worked from a young age with his father on the Tenoya Water Board. As Ribera knew, this consisted of a system of trustees who had been set up around the islands, practically since the time they were conquered, in order to manage the problem of water scarcity in the fields and population centers. This water board transported water from the mountain peaks down to the lowlands and the coasts. Antonio Rodríguez was therefore well qualified to take charge of the work necessary to build an irrigation channel from the mighty San Antonio River to the fields and the town.

Forbidding the Canarians from using the San Antonio River to water their fields was tantamount to bringing them here from so far away only to die of hunger or, as the missionaries wished, to take refuge in the missions established along the length of the river. There they would be divided into small groups to work the mission estates with no hope of leaving, like the infidel Indians whom the missionaries indoctrinated as they worked in the fields.

Although he had provided an immediate solution to the first problem, the brigadier did not hold out much hope for resolving this second one. He did offer to consult the viceroy on the subject, but the enormous power of the church meant that a solution for the Canarian cabildo might not be forthcoming. Leal insisted that he would take the situation to the viceroy himself, since it represented the most important issue currently facing the Canarian community in Villa de San Fernando.

Finally, Leal mentioned to the brigadier that before the Canary Islanders had arrived in the area, there was already a number of civilians living in the San Antonio presidio, mainly families of the soldiers from the garrison, who had been established there for almost seventeen years, farming lands that were not their property. There was no recognition of their rights to the land, and so they had not received the same consideration from the authorities as the Canary Islanders, who had been granted title to the land. These residents complained, he continued, that as they did not have the title of first inhabitants like the Canary Islanders, and were considered to be merely "other residents," they were not able to take part in the formation of the first cabildo, and after living there for seventeen years they suddenly found themselves governed by a pack of newly arrived Canary Islanders.

Leal explained that it would be better to begin the founding of the town with unity between all of the civilians and the soldiers instead of discord, particularly in a region as remote as Villa de San Fernando, near the San Antonio presidio. He believed that the spheres of responsibility of each power in the community should be clearly defined from the start; to do otherwise would give rise to problems that would only heighten with time.

"This is a difficult problem," answered Pedro de Ribera, "considering that the other residents of Villa de San Fernando, no matter how long they have been living in the territory before the town was founded, cannot be given the same treatment as the Canarian colonists; the colonists were sent to these lands by royal order, as His Majesty King Philip V made clear to the viceroy of New Spain, the Marquis of Casafuerte. You, the Canarian colonists, arrived with titles of nobility, which are valid not only while you live in Villa de San Fernando, but also in any other part of the Indies, so that you will always be recognized as men of nobility, with known name and lineage, with all of the honors and rights that this entails for all of the knights and hidalgos of the Kingdom of Castile according to the charters and laws of Spain."

Ribera continued that in the absence of a governor in the province of Texas and the New Philippines, the establishment of the cabildo and the subsequent election of its members was presided over by the captain of the fort, Pérez de Almazán, who affirmed with his presence the legality of the election and the process the cabildo should henceforth follow. This same election had been recently confirmed by the viceroy.

Leal saw that there was no hope for his petition for equal rights for the other residents and the Canarian colonists. He dropped the issue but saw an opportunity to introduce the true motives for his visit to Mexico. "How should we organize the future functioning of the cabildo as a civil entity independent of the military authority?" he asked. "Captain Pérez de Almazán insists that he must ratify the decisions of the cabildo with his military authority—is this true?"

Leal went straight to the heart of this crucial matter, asking whether Captain Almazán really had the right to instruct them on how the cabildo should function as an institution.

The brigadier was categorical in his solution to the problem, and promised to provide Leal with an exhaustive report setting out the governing regulations of cabildos in the utmost detail, which, once approved by the viceroy, he could take back with him.

While Juan Leal searched for lodging in the grand capital of the viceroyalty, Ribera considered how to present to the highest authority the issues Leal had raised, although perhaps the most immediate problem was how to persuade the viceroy to bring forward the audience granted for December 31.

The day after this meeting, Ribera went to the viceroy's office on ordinary business; once this was completed, he casually mentioned the matter to the viceroy, pretending it was of little importance. The viceroy replied that he remembered the problems of the Canarian expedition[12] very well, and that it was for this reason he had granted them an audience on December 31.

As preparation for Leal's audience, Ribera informed the viceroy of the issues Leal had brought to him, observing that he was able to solve all of them himself save one, which was of vital importance to the Canary Islanders. It placed them in conflict with the interests of the missionary fathers installed along the length of the San Antonio River, and Ribera felt that the viceroy should be aware of all of the details of the matter before meeting with Leal, and could take advantage of Ribera's personal knowledge of those lands from his previous expedition. Once the audience was over, Leal felt rejuvenated, calmer, and less pessimistic. He did not know what the report from the viceroy on the regulations and procedures of the cabildo would contain, but from Pedro de Ribera's tone of voice, he understood that it would surely be something favorable for the Canary Islanders. He had always had faith in his protector, ever since the nearly two months of negotiations while the caravan was on the way to San Antonio. Time would prove Leal's hunch to be true. Thanks to the brigadier's understanding and appreciation of the situation, the cabildo of San Antonio would be able to function completely separately from the military authority right from the start: a crucial factor in the development of the modern city of San Antonio.

FEBRUARY 15, 1801

I cannot resist recording a transcript in this diary of Ribera's conversation with the viceroy, and Leal's interview. I remember word for word what he recounted to my brothers-in-law in my house, just after he returned from Mexico. I remember it perfectly. I was struck by Leal's strong personality, which had impelled him to speak in such a way to the viceroy.

Ribera began by explaining to the viceroy how on September 2, 1730, the father superior of the Franciscans, Friar Miguel Sevillano, had sent him a letter that he wished to discuss with the viceroy. In this letter, he asked that the Canarian colonists who would soon be arriving with the intention of settling next to the presidio of San Antonio de Béjar be divided instead among the missions established along the San Antonio River. This letter was written after the friar had already requested this in an interview, and had been verbally informed that this was impossible since these colonists were coming to the territory under a royal decree from His Majesty King Philip V, which established that they should settle next to the presidio and found a cabildo. Notwithstanding this, he wrote to the viceroy with the same request that the brigadier had denied.

As soon as the Canarian colonists had elected the members of their cabildo and begun to work their farmland, the missionaries appeared before the cabildo and the captain of the presidio as representative of the viceroy to energetically oppose the colonists' use of the water from the San Antonio River to irrigate the lands granted to them by royal decree. Ribera continued, explaining to the viceroy that "the Canarian colonists have an expert among them from the island of Gran Canaria, named Antonio Rodríguez Mederos, who worked with his father from a young age on the Tenoya Water Board, near the town they lived in. Your Excellency, this man is an expert in the art of channeling water through canals for irrigation and for supplying towns. He has undertaken a project that the missionaries are well aware of, since they were informed by the captain of the presidio, who is great friends with them."

Ribera noted that the viceroy's interest was piqued, and so he decided to continue. "Father Friar Gabriel de Vergara, the superior of the missions of Texas, as you know, is opposed to the Canary Islanders using water from the San Antonio River for irrigation and insists that these waters belong solely to the missions," he said. "Captain Pérez de Almazán has thus prohibited the Canary Islanders from watering their lands from the river, and has ordered them to use only water from the San Pedro stream, whose flow is clearly insufficient. The missionaries have brought judicial proceedings against the Canary Islanders before myself and the judge Juan de Oliván Revolledo."[13]

"A difficult matter, to be sure, Ribera," the viceroy said. "Let us not forget the saying that you cannot fight the church . . . although I seem to remember that in the latest edition of the Laws of the Indies."

"Indeed, Your Excellency," Ribera said. "Law 11, Title 17, Book 4, page 113 onward of volume two declares that 'each person shall attain in turn the water that they require, so that it be removed from those who seek to take possession and control, and for their authority to prevail, until all those beneath them have watered the lands they have been granted.' I believe that this precept is sufficiently clear, sir, and that this is the line of reasoning you should use in the resolution you dictate."

"And with respect to the request that the Canary Islanders should live in the missions," the viceroy said, "what is your opinion? You lived in those lands during the reconnaissance expedition that we sent you on before the Canarian families arrived. I believe that in your exploration report, you spoke of the lands near the San Antonio River, and of how the forces camped in the presidio would afford them protection against attacks from the Apache Indians who inhabit that territory.

"And I seem to remember you saying," he continued, "that while there are different tribes of Apaches, such as the Mescaleros, the Lipanes, the Chiricaquis, and the Laneros, they are all allied. I also believe that you told me they were cannibals, and I distinctly remember that the Indians of Texas are different from other tribes, since they hold great festivals where they activate their victims' blood circulation with whips or friction, and after this they are roasted, while the multitude of men and women dance in a circle giving off whoops of glee. But the most horrifying part was that each one in turn took bites from the victim, entranced by the savage frenzy evoked by the shouting, the dancing, and the wild movements."

"Very frequently, Your Excellency," Pedro de Ribera said, "the missionaries request protection from the captain of the presidio when they leave the missions. It seems that during an Indian attack, one of the fathers of the Order of San Francisco was captured and put to death in the most horrifying manner. First they scalped him, cutting off his skin and exposing his skull. Then they speared his skin on a lance and danced around it, after which they tied him to a stake, all the while enjoying the torture with barbaric glee, mocking his profession, and telling him that this was but minor revenge for the rivers of Indian blood spilled by the Spaniards. After they had quenched their thirst for vengeance with this lamentable spectacle, they built a great bonfire around their victim and continued dancing around the fire until his body was reduced to ashes."

He continued: "I believe that if the missionaries are asking for such constant protection from attacks like this, then you cannot send women and children to live in the missions; on the contrary, as His Majesty the King said, they should be settled next to the presidio where they will be better protected by the forces camped there."

"So be it, Ribera," the viceroy said, "but I would like to know in more depth the other problems faced by the community of Canarian colonists, particularly if the captain of the presidio has, as you say, been involved."

On December 18, three days after speaking with Brigadier Pedro de Ribera, the viceroy received Juan Leal and the brigadier in an official audience. Leal was not intimidated by the viceroy's impressive office. He had already been there on two previous occasions. The viceroy received him warmly, as before.

"I understand perfectly the matters that have forced you to make the long journey to this city, in particular the opposition of the missionaries to the Canarian colonists watering their lands from the San Antonio River," the viceroy said. "Before we proceed, however, I would like to hear your personal account of the state of affairs between the newly constituted cabildo and the captain of the presidio, Pérez de Almazán, who is, as you know, my personal representative in the absence of a governor for those territories."

"Your Excellency," Leal responded, "while it is true that our main problem is the opposition of the missionaries to our use of the San Antonio River for watering our fields, it is no less certain that, as I mentioned to Brigadier Pedro de Ribera a few days ago, the recently established cabildo has faced great resistance from the captain of the presidio in recognizing and allowing us to act as a municipal institution, independent of his military authority.

"This, sir," he continued, "will have grave consequences for the development of the town. I know this from my experience in our homeland, the Canary Islands, where the general commander of the islands, Lorenzo Hernández de Villavicencio y Cárdenes, marquis of Vallehermoso, allowed his tyrannical behavior to permeate every aspect of his governance, to the extent that he brought thirty military officers from the peninsula and granted them great power over the islands, thus converting them into thirty tyrants. He decreed that no religious or lay person could move from one island to another without his written permission, and, through personal enmity, refused to allow the chief superintendent of commerce with the Indies, whom I met during our preparations for the voyage from Tenerife to these far-off lands, to carry out his office. After the terrible hurricane that battered the Canary Archipelago on October 25, 1722, causing death, hunger, and misery, he refused to take any measures to alleviate our suffering, and instead seized the remaining grain supplies and harassed the city administrators until the city fell into bankruptcy and insolvency. I mention this now, Your Excellency, as a way of showing what can happen in a far-off land such as the Canary Islands, whose great distance from the peninsula allowed these events, and far graver ones which I will not relate here, to occur. In the distant lands of the viceroyalty, alone with the captain of the presidio, we could find ourselves in the same predicament if Your Excellency does not redress the situation from the inception of the cabildo."

The viceroy listened attentively. "I met the superintendent of commerce with the Indies in the Canary Islands," he said, "when I passed through the island of Tenerife in August 1722 on my way to take possession of this viceroyalty. He received me at the city's port and we spoke of the hunger and sickness afflicting the islands, and how in the calamitous year of 1721, over 7,000 people had died on the island of Gran Canaria alone, since many inhabitants of Lanzarote and Fuertaventura had fled to the city as a last hope. I remember how he told me that in a village called El Sauzal, on the island of Tenerife, 300 people had landed at once, in search of refuge and shelter. He spoke of the terrible corruption that existed among the authorities of the peninsula who held offices on the Canary Islands, and he showed me a report, a copy of which I still possess, in which the Superintendent General of the islands, Juan Antonio de Cevallos,[14] wrote, upon taking office 'of the strenuous opposition of the captains general to separating them from their commissions and thus from their dependents and other ministers,' for which he recommended removing the captain general from the island of Tenerife, since his business interests were the source of tremendous fraud, such as the arbitrary confiscation of merchandise proceeding from the Indies. This led to enormous profits and the serious abuse of power, and motivated the captains general to live on the island of Tenerife and to take over the supervision of the islands, as a pretext for leaving the island of Gran Canaria, home to the Royal Audience of which they were presidents."

The viceroy continued: "I also remember walking around the main plaza, with its splendid houses, and visiting the three castles that defend the city of Santa Cruz de Tenerife. I am familiar, Mr. Leal, with the peninsula. I know what it feels like to be a peninsular governor, since I was governor of Messina, in Sicily, before coming to this viceroyalty, which was my life's ambition. By becoming viceroy of these lands, I am also viceroy of the Indies, the land of my birth. I came into this world in Peru, and although I moved to the peninsula at the age of thirteen, I am still creole, and so I understand your sentiments of being governed by men from the peninsula. In my viceroyalty, I try to prevent the manifestation of these sentiments against those who come from Spain to take up offices in the Indies, and I therefore assure you that I will nip in the bud any problem that may arise between the community of Canarian colonists or their cabildo, and the captain of the San Antonio presidio, Pérez de Almazán."

The viceroy turned to his brigadier and said, "Ribera, please provide Mr. Leal with a written document addressed to the captain of the San Antonio presidio, which clearly specifies and defines the functions of the cabildo and those of the captain. Perhaps he is overzealous in carrying out his obligations as my representative in these far-off lands. I can assure you that in this viceroyalty, the only exception is the cabildo of Tlaxcala, which enjoys the unique privilege, conceded by Cortés for aiding him in his fight against Montezuma, that no Spaniard, either Creole or European, may form part of the cabildo, only Indians. For this reason it is of the utmost importance that their decisions are ratified by the viceroy's representative, since they are simple people, much given to errors due to drunkenness, a vice which even the friars have not rid them off, despite their conversion. All of the cabildos may govern themselves independently of the military."

As Juan Leal left the interview, there was a spring in his step. He now had the means to turn his dream into reality: an effective cabildo, run exclusively by Canary Islanders, through which they could lay the foundations for a great city, founded and ruled by Canary Islanders. As their pride and joy, the city would be an inspiration for all those who had remained on the islands and who could, one day soon, come and cultivate these magnificent lands.

II. The Triumphant Return

OCTOBER 1801

Leal's return journey to San Antonio was much faster. He hastened his march on several occasions in order to accompany the post headed for San Luis Potosí. Once there, he rested for two days until another postal service passed through on the way to the San Antonio presidio.

His return was triumphant, both among his friends and in particular among the councilors of the cabildo. They met immediately in the adobe hut that his compatriots had built in his absence to act as the town hall, and it is recorded in the minutes from December 27, 1731, how Juan Leal informed them of his interview with the viceroy and the brigadier, Pedro de Ribero, and how he read to them the directive sent to Captain Pérez de Almazán from the viceroy ordering him to return the horses he had requisitioned.

He then read them the rules by which the cabildo should be governed, also addressed to Captain Pérez de Almazán.

"In general terms," Leal said, "the cabildo governs the population through six councilors. One of them is a sheriff, one is a solicitor, and one is the treasurer of public goods, with the power to name two magistrates who serve as ordinary judges of first instance in civil and criminal matters, and have the right to attend cabildo meetings together with the councilors."

Next he read the dispatch in which the responsibilities of each position were detailed. These magistrates would be first instance judges in whichever city or town they were elected, and for fifteen leagues around, in accordance with the Laws of Kingdoms of the Indies, Law 3, pages 2, 5–6. At times there might be jurisdiction conflicts with the hearings, in which case they would have to submit to the governor of the province in order to resolve the matter in question. They should never judge cases involving the Indians, since these were reserved for the viceroy.

The sheriff would be charged with the enforcement of final rulings and sentences, and would also be responsible for payment orders, seizing objects to be sold, imprisoning criminals, and recovering money. He would be the superintendent of the prison and, together with the lieutenant of the presidio, would make public announcements and would visit public areas, both night and day, to prevent immoral activities and disputes. Failure to fulfill these duties would result in his suspension from office and the payment of any damages resulting from such negligence. He would also have the obligation to accompany the magistrate on visits to the prisons.

The treasurer would be the administrator of the cabildo's property, and the director of the cabildo's works.

The councilors would have multiple responsibilities, among which were the overseeing of security and provisioning of the towns, the implementation and monitoring of public works, visits to the jails, administration of hospitals, and action on behalf of the magistrates when necessary.

The solicitor would maintain the public records and the book in which the city accounts were detailed; he would record and sign the minutes of the cabildo meetings, together with the other members; he would sign legal documents and make declarations in legal cases before the ordinary magistrates or judges of first instance; he would distribute news and notifications around the town; and he would ensure the safekeeping of the cabildo's archives by maintaining an inventory of all of the documents, which he and the other councilors would sign. He would also keep the municipal accounts and would oversee the archives, submitting both to an audit at the end of every year.

"Our cabildo meetings," Leal said, "are to be either closed cabildo (or municipal council), in which the magistrates, councilors, and a few other officials will be required to attend, or open or extraordinary cabildo, whereby the ordinary cabildo summons the governor or his representative and convenes an open cabildo, in which the whole town may participate, including some residents, principal figures, and captains, to deal exclusively with matters of war, problems with taxes, prices, disasters, and so forth."

He continued:

> The Law of the Indies allows us to draw up our own ordinances for the better governance of the city, as stated in Number 32, Title 1, Book 2. And according to Laws 1 and 2, titles from Book 4, at the same time we must build a town hall for the cabildo, which should be the only place where meetings are held.
>
> As we can see, the cabildo of San Fernando has complete independence. In fact, under Laws 7 and 9, Title 9, Book 4, and Law 2, Title 3, Book 5, it is forbidden for any other authorities, presidents, judges, etc., to interfere in the elections that the cabildos hold for their magistrates.
>
> The cabildo will also serve as an appeals court, in accordance with the Laws of the Indies, Law 1, Title 3, Book 5, which specifies that "appeals to its decisions and sentences will be heard by the audiences and governors or by municipal governments, as ordered

> by the laws of these bodies and kingdoms." In such cases, appeals for matters involving up to 60,000 *maravedís* may be presented before the cabildo, and the competent cabildo will be that of the city where the case was initiated, under Laws 17 and 18, Title 12, Book 5. Furthermore, we will hear appeals filed for errors in sentencing for amounts no greater than thirty ducats. (Law 19, Title 12, Book 5.)
>
> Finally, we must keep a book in which all of our decisions are recorded; there shall be three keys to the municipal archives, and these shall be in the possession of one ordinary magistrate, one councilor, and the solicitor respectively, as stated in Laws 16 and 131, Titles 1, 9, Books 2 and 46.

When his reading of the detailed document came to an end, Leal asked if anyone had any comments. Those present congratulated him on his skillfulness in solving the seemingly insurmountable problems surrounding the creation of the first cabildo formed entirely of Canary Islanders, in this land that would years later become the most powerful nation of the world, the United States of America. After the initial elation had died down, the first to speak was the solicitor, Francisco de Arocha, who noted in the minutes: "I believe we should inform Captain Pérez de Almazán of both reports, in order to recover the horses for building our houses and ploughing our fields. This notification will serve to clarify once and for all our responsibility for governing the city, and will give us grounds for requesting from the captain the property titles for the lands which were granted to us, and the other decrees that refer to our arrival and establishment in these lands, so that all of the documents may be deposited in the municipal archives, as stated in the Laws of the Indies."

With these historic decisions, the third session of the cabildo of San Fernando de Béjar ended, on January 17, 1732.

Encouraged by Leal's meeting with the viceroy of Mexico, the cabildo of San Antonio presented the governor with this petition:

Juan Antonio de Bustillo y Zevallos, Governor, Captain General of the province of Texas and New Philippines.

Petition made by the Canary Islanders with respect to their rights. The following, Juan Leal Goraz, Juan Curbelo, Antonio Santos, Manuel de Niz, Salvador Rodríguez, and Juan Leal Álvarez, members of the Cabildo of Villa de San Fernando, and Vicente Álvarez Travieso, by mutual agreement and as the law provides, and in accordance with their rights, make the following petition.[15]

Captain Juan Antonio Pérez de Almazán retains in his power the dispatches, decrees, and documents pertaining to the Canarian colonists, and the property titles granted them by His Excellency the Viceroy. With the intention of avoiding any future conflicts that may arise, we hereby ask Your Honor that these papers be deposited in the office of the solicitor of our cabildo, Francisco Arocha, together with a list of the dates and page numbers. Said list of documents shall be compiled in the Captain's archives, and the dispatches and documents placed in the custody of a person determined by Your Honor. The key shall be held by the person whom custom dictates in this kingdom.

In accordance with our petition, we hereby request that Your Excellency deliver the documents into the possession of the aforementioned solicitor of our cabildo, and we hope that Your Honor will accede to this petition in the furtherance of justice.

The governor responded with the following message:

In the light of your petition, and considering that no Canarian colonist is in possession of a strongbox with three keys in which to deposit the relevant documents, and that the existing houses in the city have no special place to hold a strongbox containing said documents, I hereby decree and order that they remain in the hands of the captain of the presidio, Juan Antonio Pérez de Almazán, who is captain and judge of the town. For this reason, the

> Captain will deliver a list of the relevant instruments to the notary of the municipal council, so that he may begin a permanent archive.
>
> Signed Juan Antonio de Bustillo y Cevallos

The struggle between the civil and military powers in the town was in full swing. Pérez de Almazán could not give way again. The municipal government of those semi-illiterate Canary Islanders was beginning to irritate him. After considering the matter with care, he replied to the previous missive, a copy of which had been passed to him by the governor, this way:

> Governor, having examined the petition presented before Your Honor by the municipal government of Villa de San Fernando, and the decree passed for its provision, I hereby offer the following considerations:
>
> It is evident to Your Honor that none of the Canarian councilors has in his house a strongbox with three keys, nor is there a house where the documents requested could be kept safe from fire, since their houses are made of dry wood and grass.
>
> For this reason, I beg Your Highness to order that the councilors leave the documents they are requesting in the box in my house for the moment, and that the key be placed in the hands of the learned José Rodríguez Díaz, vicar and ecclesiastical judge of Villa de San Fernando, so that the councilors may consult them when necessary. The following is a list of the documents deposited there:
>
> > A dispatch from His Excellency, dated November 28, 1730, in which His Excellency the Viceroy orders that the fifteen families be received and provided with all that they need for their survival and comfort. The dispatch consists of seven written pages.
> >
> > A second dispatch that lays out the area where they are to be settled and the limits and boundaries of the lands to be delivered to them (farmlands). This consists of thirty-two

pages. Another dispatch of the same date with a list of the fifteen families and ordering the election of the public offices for the municipal government. This consists of twenty written and several blank pages.

These are the only documents relevant to the aforementioned members of the municipal council.

Signed Pérez de Almazán

The Canarian colonists could not even begin to imagine the tremendous opposition that they would face from the Franciscan missionaries in those lands.

The Franciscan order had been established long before the Canary Islanders arrived, and spanned the length and breadth of the Viceroyalty of New Spain, from Mexico, Mérida al Sur, to northwest Chihuahua and Coahuila, Mazatlán, Sambrete, Zacatecas, and Tampico. The Franciscans had five missions along the San Antonio River: San Antonio de Valero, near the San Antonio presidio where the Canarian colonists founded the city of San Fernando, and the missions of Concepción, San José, San Juan, and Espada. Each one was surrounded by large estates where the missionaries' herds grazed, tended by Indians. The smallest mission had 2,000 head of cattle, while the largest, Espíritu Santo, had 10,000.

CHAPTER 3

I. The Intrigues of the Missions against the Canarian Colonists

OCTOBER 30, 1801

Long before the events I have recounted, on the morning of September 2, 1730, when the Canary Islanders had only just reached Veracruz on their way to San Antonio, the Superior of the Franciscans in the Viceroyalty of New Spain, Friar Miguel Sevillano de Peredes, arrived at the office of Brigadier Pedro de Ribera in a state of high agitation, requesting an urgent interview. Although he did not have an appointment, he was seen immediately.

The friar informed him that he had recently become aware of the arrival in the port of Veracruz of a group of Canarian colonists who were to settle next to the presidio of San Antonio, Texas, and that they were to found a town and a cabildo to govern it.

He informed the brigadier that the Franciscans had established a series of missions in the area, with large estates and herds of cattle, and that the order had charged him, as the superior of these lands, with requesting, for the good of the kingdom and the royal treasury, and of course, for the poor families of Canarian colonists, that groups of five or six colonists be settled in the missions of San Antonio and San José, and in the Espada mission, which was currently under construction. In this way, these poor Canary Islanders, who had come from so far, would have shelter and water from the San Antonio River to cultivate their land, while at the same time helping to care for the cattle on the estates.

"This seems to me to be a noble and selfless offer, Friar Miguel," said Ribera. "As Your Excellency is aware, I am well-acquainted with those lands, since I traveled across them before the Canarian colonists arrived, on the orders from the viceroy. The report from that voyage was delivered to His Excellency His Majesty the King, who then decreed that the Canarian colonists would come and establish themselves in those lands under the conditions indicated in the Order of November 28, 1730. However, when the colonists reached Veracruz, I informed the viceroy that it would be impossible for them to travel by sea to the places that His Majesty the King had ordered, since the lands were most inhospitable. He therefore decided, on the basis of my report, that the ideal location was alongside the San Antonio presidio, where there were fertile lands that could be watered, just like the estates of your missions, by the San Antonio River. So I fear that it will be difficult to agree to your request. Nevertheless, I will inform the viceroy of your offer."

Leaving the brigadier's office, Father Miguel de Paredes understood perfectly that his request would not be well received. He needed to act quickly and astutely. He knew only too well the influence that Pedro de Ribera had over the viceroy.

He hurried back to the monastery and, once in his office, wrote the following letter to the viceroy:

> To the honorable Juan de Acuña, Marquis of Casafuerte, Knight of the Order of Santiago, Commander of Adelfa in the Order of Alcántara, member of the Council of His Royal Majesty, Supreme War Leader and Captain General of the Royal Audience and Viceroy of New Spain.
>
> It has come to the attention of this Royal Franciscan Order that Canarian families have arrived in this viceroyalty, and are to be established as colonists in the lands around the San Antonio presidio. This order proposes that these Canarian families be housed in the three missions that are to be built on the banks of the San Antonio and Median rivers, where they can work the earth and water their lands from the San Antonio River. This would avoid further strains

> on the Royal treasury, which has already invested in their food and clothing, and would prevent much misery and suffering for these families.
>
> Signed, the superior of the Franciscan Order in the Viceroyalty of New Spain, Friar Miguel Sevillano de Peredes.

His next act was to write another letter to the superior of the monastery of San Antonio de Valero, Friar Gabriel de Vergara, instructing him that when the Canarian families arrived at the San Antonio presidio, he should inform the captain of the presidio of their opposition to the settlement of the Canary Islanders on those lands and should, above all, fiercely oppose their use of the water from the San Antonio River, since this water source was to be used exclusively by the estates belonging to the missions. And so, even before the Canarian colonists arrived in San Antonio, a battle for water began with the missionaries.

On December 25, 1731, the viceroy the marquis of Casafuerte dictated a missive addressed to the captain of the San Antonio presidio, Juan Antonio Pérez de Almazán, in which Casafuerte informed the captain that it was

> imperative that the Canarian colonists continue living close to the presidio and in no other location, for their protection from the enemy Indians. This decision is based on the continuous requests from the reverend missionary fathers for escorts of soldiers to act as bodyguards, for which the Canarian families in possession of the lands and water that have been distributed to them should have equal rights.
>
> To this end, you, Sir, should divide and distribute the water, sharing it in equal measures between the missions and the Canary Islanders. Although it may appear that the legal provisions instituted by their reverences the fathers (he refers to Friar Gabriel de Vergara, presiding father of the missions) should be applied solely in favor of the missions, this provision should not be a motive for

profit in favor of one or the other when the motive is the scarcity of supply, particularly when dealing with water. After His Majesty has spent a considerable sum of money from his Royal Treasury to bring these families here from the Canary Islands, it would be lamentable if they were to be abandoned and left without water, which would be tantamount to bringing them here to die (here the viceroy uses Juan Leal's words from their interview of December 15, 1731). Furthermore, it was the king himself who assigned them the place in which to settle.

This document reached Captain Almazán on January 20, 1732. That same day, the cabildo of Villa de San Fernando gave him a copy of the order from the viceroy to return the sixty-one horses that he had confiscated; a copy of the document signed by Brigadier Pedro de Ribera laying down the laws governing the cabildo; and a request addressed to the captain from the cabildo, calling on him to deliver the documents, property titles for the lands granted to the Canarian colonists, and decrees on the establishment of the city so that, in accordance with the Laws of the Indies, they could be deposited in the municipal archives.

Pérez de Almazán headed straight to the San Antonio mission to see the superior of the Franciscan order in the viceroyalty, Friar Miguel Sevillano de Peredes, and to show him the demands he had received from the cabildo.

The friar made no comments on the cabildo's request for their documents for the municipal archives. He was disturbed, however, by the order to distribute the water from the San Antonio River between the missionaries and the Canary Islanders. This implied what both the military and the missionaries had feared: that the Canary Islanders would live close to the presidio, as a town and with a cabildo, and not split up among the missions. In other words, they would govern themselves. The missionaries needed to fight back. If matters followed their normal course, as shown by examples across the viceroyalty, there would soon be great competition for selling cheese, fruit, grains, hides, and more to the presidios. If the viceroy was ordering that the Canarians' settlement be established as a town, it was logical to assume that he would also authorize the sale of agricultural products from their harvests. This would be very harmful to the missions. They needed to establish a plan. It was too late to fight against the establishment of the cabildo, since this had already been accomplished. They had to fight back against the Canary Islanders using the water from the San Antonio River for their fields. In this battle they had the captain and the army of San Antonio, and the influence of the church in Mexico. But they had to delay the Canary Islanders' irrigation works.

Friar Miguel asked Captain Almazán to invite Rodríguez Mederos, the canal builder, to stop by the mission to speak with him.

Rodríguez presented himself at the San Antonio mission and accepted the task that the superior of the Franciscans asked of him: to build a canal for the missions to irrigate the Concepción estate with water from the San Antonio River.

Antonio Rodríguez did not realize that his acceptance of this undertaking favored the missions over his companions, the Canarian colonists, since it meant that for a while he would not be able to direct the cabildo's building projects.

With this strategy, the missionaries thus divided the Canary Islanders, which would have grave consequences for our history, as we shall see.

Antonio Rodríguez's acceptance not only separated the cabildo and the missions for good; it also converted Rodríguez into a figure of scorn for the Canarian cabildo. They would never forgive him for agreeing to direct the construction of the Concepción canal, even though he would later make another for the Canarian colonists, not only to water their fields but also to supply water to the town.

The conflicts between the cabildo and the missions would not end until 1823, with the secularization of the missions.

II. Antonio Rodríguez Mederos Builds the Concepción Canal for the Missions

DECEMBER 3, 1801

Excited after his interview with Captain Almazán, Rodríguez immediately called together his companions in an urgent session of the cabildo to announce what he thought was wonderful news.

When he had finished explaining what Friar Benito and Captain Almazán had told him, there was a heavy silence in the small hut that housed the newly established cabildo. First to speak was Juan Leal el Viejo. His response, which follows, is taken straight from the minutes of the cabildo, dated August 10, 1732:

> I cannot believe that it is not obvious to you that this proposal for construction has been put to you by our enemies. They have been our enemies ever since we arrived from the Canary Islands. As member of this cabildo, you must know of whom I speak: the Superior of the missionaries in Mexico, Friar Miguel Sevillano de Paredes, who petitioned the viceroy, the marquis of Casafuerte, to prevent us from founding this town, and consequently, this cabildo. He wanted us separated and distributed among the missions along the San Antonio River, in order to thwart our plans to found a town under the Laws of the Indies, which state that a settlement can be founded by more or less than thirty freemen, but no fewer than ten persons.
>
> This would have stopped us from competing against the missions in the sale of agricultural products to the presidios. The missions have opposed our use of the San Antonio River to water our farmland, and they continue to fight us through legal action against the cabildo, which is still awaiting judicial resolution. They have sent a petition on behalf of the other residents, the families of the soldiers who settled on these lands before us, and who are neither founders of the town, nor members of this cabildo, so that they might also

> be granted land. This petition in itself would seem just, if I did not know that the true intention is none other than to create an illusion of conflict for the viceroy, which is magnified by the distance and exaggerated in Mexico in our absence. They want us to fail in our governance of the town, so that we end up living in the missions, as they wished from the beginning. Obeying their orders, like the Indians. And as you know, we have all been named hidalgos by His Majesty King Philip V and you, treasurer of the cabildo, the only one of us who understands irrigation works, and whose mission is to oversee the construction works of this institution, propose to go and work for our enemies?
>
> Gentlemen, I propose that we agree here to prevent the member of this institution, Antonio Rodríguez Mederos, from abandoning his obligations as councilor and, even worse, from using his knowledge to improve the irrigation works of our enemies the missionaries, when this cabildo is in grave need of construction works for bringing water to the town and the lands of our Canarian companions who, at great risk to their lives, accompanied us on this long journey.

Leal continued, glaring at Antonio Rodríguez: "If you accept the missionaries' proposal, you will be failing to carry out the obligations laid upon you by His Majesty the King, to cultivate the lands that he has given you from his royal treasury."

When Leal had finished, Antonio Rodríguez asked to speak. "My fellow councilors," he said, "I understand my obligations as a Canary Islander, but I also understand that as a Catholic, I have the obligation to help our Holy Mother Church, which has been accomplishing such great works of evangelism and assistance among the savage Indians of these lands, ever since they were incorporated into the Crown of Castile. You do not need to remind me of my obligations as a colonist, since the missions will send me three Indians to work my lands while I am directing the construction of the Concepción canal."

"But your obligation as a councilor," answered Leal, "is to aid the cabildo, to direct our planned construction projects, to build a canal, to bring water to the town, and to irrigate Canary Islanders' farmland. If you do not, you must cease to be a member of this cabildo."

Captain Pérez de Almazán, who was also present, said: "If you will permit me, as the highest military authority and representative of the viceroy in the absence of the governor, and having lived here for many years, I am perhaps more familiar with the region than you gentlemen. I would like to suggest that there could be a positive side to the missionaries' proposal. The fact that they have chosen such a prominent member of the cabildo for this important project could perhaps lead to a solution to the problems between the cabildo and the missions. By authorizing Antonio Rodríguez to help the missions with this project, we could end their opposition to the Canary Islanders establishing a town and a cabildo."

Juan Leal quickly saw that the captain's proposal was the solution the cabildo had been looking for. "I accept your reasoning," he said, "and would be willing to modify my proposal if, as soon as Antonio Rodríguez finishes the missions' canal at Concepción, you will promise, by virtue of the office you hold, to intercede in our unresolved petition to the viceroy regarding the construction of a canal and irrigation channels to water our lands and bring water to the town."

Pérez de Almazán accepted Leal's proposal, not because he cared about the Canary Islanders' canal, but because he wanted to resolve the missions' problem with the canal at Concepción.

On September 12, 1732, Antonio Rodríguez Mederos presented himself at the Concepción mission, to the south of the town and on the other side of the San Antonio River, and informed Friar Bartolomé García de Paredes of his requirements for a project of this size.

To begin with, he needed some twenty Indians with tools to work as laborers, as well as two pairs of oxen and a sledge for removing the rocks they would dig up. He would also need around ten soldiers to

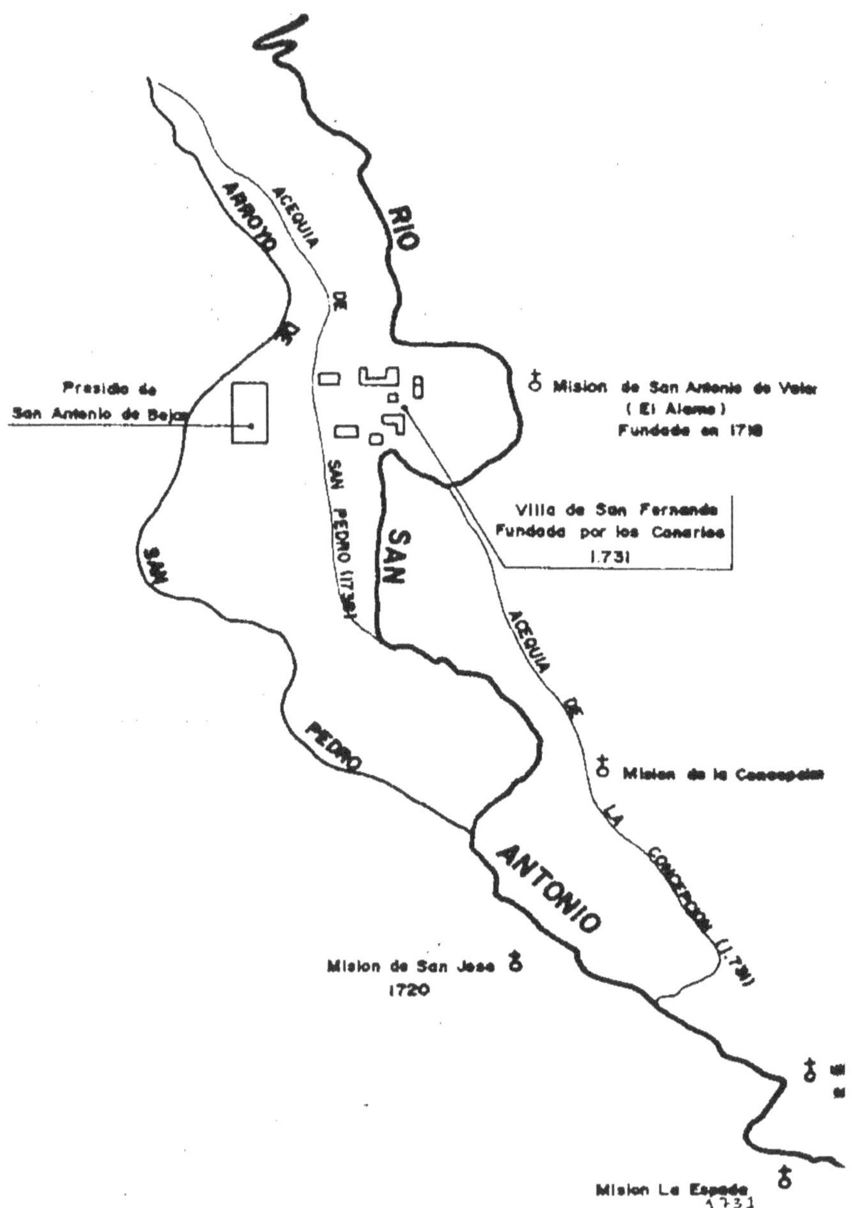

RIO
SAN
ANTONIO
ARROYO DE SAN PEDRO
ACEQUIA DE SAN PEDRO
Presidio de
San Antonio de Bejar
Mision de San Antonio de Valer
(El Alamo)
Villa de San Fernando
Fundada por los Canarios
1.731
ACEQUIA DE LA CONCEPCION
Mision de San Jose
1720
Mision La Espada
1731

protect the laborers from Indian attacks and, more importantly, to keep watch during the night so that the Indians who were working on the project did not run off with the tools.

From the moment the project began, Rodríguez saw how difficult it would be. His plan involved cutting and digging a long tunnel at a depth of forty-five meters before emerging at the surface.

The work was ceaseless; Rodríguez had to struggle against the apathy and indolence of the Indians, which meant that he was working double. When they had finished more than half of the canal, he traveled by boat from one end to the other, inspecting the work.

Although Leal had accepted through sheer opportunism that Rodríguez would direct the canal project for the missionaries, the community of Canarian colonists never forgave him for what they considered to be an act of betrayal: working for their enemies the missionaries, and building them a canal that the Canary Islanders desperately needed. They could also not forgive the fact that while they labored in their fields, wresting forth their crops through great sacrifice, Antonio Rodríguez's fields were not even worked by his wife or his family members, but by four Indians sent by the missionaries.

When the canal builder arrived home at night, tired after a hard day's work, he would sit on his porch with his wife, and she would tell him the news of the town, which inevitably revolved around him. His father-in-law, Manuel Niz, the fifth councilor, gave him direct news of the intrigues against him by his main enemies in the town and in the cabildo, the solicitor Francisco de Arocha and the sheriff Vicente Álvarez Travieso. These two Canary Islanders had not left with the rest of the colonists from Santa Cruz de Tenerife but had joined them during their two month stay in Quanticlán, and were never fully accepted by the other members of the expedition. They said they had arrived in 1729.

When Vicente Álvarez Travieso joined the expedition in Quanticlán, he said that he was from the island of Tenerife, and was twenty-five years old, while Francisco de Arocha was from Lanzarote, and was twenty-seven years old. They had been living in Mexico City for a year, and had learned of the Canary Islanders' expedition the day they arrived in Quanticlán, from an officer under orders from Pedro de Ribera who had been charged by the viceroy with all matters relating to transporting the expedition to Texas. They introduced themselves to Juan Curbelo, who was leader of the expedition at that time.

What the Canarian colonists most disliked about both Francisco de Arocha and Vicente Álvarez Travieso was their actions following the disclosure that in order to join the expedition and to have the same rights as the rest of the Canary Islanders in terms of access to land and so forth, it was necessary to be the head of a family, either by marrying a widow or a single woman from the group. On learning this, they immediately asked my father, Juan Curbelo, for the hands of my sisters, María Ana, eighteen years old, and Juana, fourteen years old, in marriage. María Ana was to marry Vicente, and Juana was to marry Francisco.

The day after the wedding, both couples traveled to Mexico City to affirm that both Álvarez Travieso and Francisco de Arocha were now heads of families, and so the viceroy decreed on September 18, 1730, that both were to be admitted into the expedition with the same rights as the other Canarian colonists.

While Arocha and Álvarez Travieso were always great friends, now they were also brothers-in-law. I must admit that, although we are relatives, they were very ambitious men, and from the beginning they wanted to take charge of the expedition. When the cabildo was established, Vicente Álvarez Travieso was elected sheriff and Francisco de Arocha solicitor, positions that they were to hold for many years. They were practically the masters of the council, since the presidents came and went but these two remained in their offices.

On one of those nights when Antonio Rodríguez was sitting on his porch after a long day directing the construction of the Concepción canal, his wife María told him that her father had heard in the cabildo that Álvarez and Arocha had sworn vengeance on him for betraying the Canary Islanders and working on the canal at Concepción.

He was not worried; his conscience was clear, and they could do nothing against him as he was protected by the missionaries.

As sister-in-law to Arocha and Álvarez, I must say something in their defense, which is perhaps not general knowledge. Both men knew my sisters in Lanzarote, before they came to America, and for this reason they married them as soon as they found them again in Quanticlán.

While Antonio Rodríguez was certain that he was morally right, and that the correct course of action was to help the missionaries build the canal at Concepción instead of helping his Canarian companions, the other councilors thought differently. As his wife had mentioned, Álvarez Travieso and Francisco Arocha took every opportunity in the cabildo meetings, which Rodríguez could not attend because of his work on the canal, to discuss his betrayal with the other colonists. So throughout the town there was a growing sense of anger toward Rodríguez. Everyone blamed him for their inability to water their lands, since he was directing the construction of the canal for Concepción instead of their own. This increasingly isolated him from his friends and neighbors during the years that the missionaries' project lasted, and drew him closer to the missionaries, who considered both the cabildo and the colonists as their enemies, and not without reason.

As we have seen, the first great obstacle that Antonio Rodríguez encountered when beginning construction was the height of the terrain opposite the bend of the river, where the canal would begin. In the end, after studying the situation for a week, he decided to begin at that point, but to dig inward at a depth of forty-five meters.

The twenty Indians he had been given to help with the construction were instructed in the building techniques he had learned on Gran Canaria, and which were unknown in these lands. Meanwhile

Provincia de los Texas.

Estado que Manifiesta el Numero de Vasallos, y Habitantes q.e tiene el Rey en esta Probincia, Con distincion de Clases, Estados, y Castas de todas las Personas de Ambos Sexos Ynclusos los Parbulos.

Nombres de las Poblaciones.	Hombres.	Mugeres.	Niños.	Niñas.	Esclavos.	Esclavas.
Pres.o de San Antonio de Bexar, y Villa de S.n Fern.do	331	311	321	264	8	13
Mision de S.r San Jose	41	31	26	25	—	—
Ydem de San Juan Capistrano	53	26	13	7	—	—
Ydem de San Francisco de la Espada	32	28	8	6	—	—
Ydem de Nuestra S.ra de la Concepcion	32	29	18	8	—	—
Ydem de San Antonio Balero	49	35	56	29	—	—
Presidio de la Bahia del Sp.tu S.to	193	147	68	45	1	—
Mision del Sp.tu S.to	75	66	33	4	—	—
Ydem de Nuestra S.ra del Rosario	—	—	—	—	—	—
Pueblo de N.ra S.ra del Pilar de los Nacodoches	129	104	52	50	8	6
Totales del Presente Año	935	777	597	474	17	19
Totales del Año Anterior	947	786	597	474	17	19
Diminucion	12	9	—	—	—	—
Resumen Gral de Españoles	488	373	376	340	—	—
Ydem de Indios	290	241	70	75	—	—
Ydem de Mestizos	43	38	32	12	—	—
Ydem de Color Quebrado	114	125	119	46	—	—
Ydem de Esclabos	—	—	—	—	17	19
Totales	935	777	597	474	17	19
Resumen Gral de Eclesiasticos Seculares	3	—	—	—	—	—
Ydem de Regulares	8	—	—	—	—	—
Ydem de Casados	655	655	—	—	—	—
Ydem de Viudos	61	122	—	—	—	—
Ydem de Solteros	208	—	—	—	—	—
Totales	935	777	597	474	17	19

Real Pres.o de San Antonio de Bexar, y Dic.e 31. de 1783.

Dom.o Cabello

the soldiers kept watch for possible attacks from wild Indians, and ensured that the Indian workers did not steal the horses or tools.

The innovations Rodríguez implemented were enormous, not only in terms of the materials used in the construction of the irrigation channels, but also in his modifications to the plan that had been developed initially by the missionaries. Due to their lack of knowledge of this kind of project, the missionaries believed in avoiding obstacles and following the path of least resistance, skirting around higher ground. Rodríguez applied the techniques he had learned on Gran Canaria, and opted instead to cut through the heights, taking advantage of the change in elevation to create a greater drop and a more direct route for the water, which was more efficient in both time and effort. During the years that it took to complete the canal at Concepción, there was an intense drought in Texas. This brought much despair to the Canarian colonists, who saw with anguish how they lost harvests for lack of rain while the mission estates, located along the finished portions of the canal, had plenty of water thanks to the help afforded by Antonio Rodríguez. This, in the eyes of the colonists, was a violation of his duty as treasurer of the cabildo of San Antonio, the office to which he had been elected.

III. Are We Canary Islanders Prisoners?

DECEMBER 12, 1801

I would now like to transcribe the reports written by my brother-in-law, Vicente Álvarez, in November 1734, while he was suffering from a serious illness. During the same period that the Canary Islanders were struggling to build the town, a matter of huge significance arose that would affect the whole community in a most particular way.

The events begin with a note added to some special reports that read:

> In the presidio of San Antonio de Béjar within the jurisdiction of Texas and the Kingdom of New Philippines, on November 2, 1734,

the following petition was presented to me, Manual de Sandoval, Captain of the Spanish Infantry, Governor and Captain General of this province, its presidios, and its borders, and commander of the Governor of Coahuila and Penzacola, by order of His Majesty:

> Petition: I, Vicente Álvarez Travieso, chief sheriff of the town of Villa de San Fernando, hereby appeal to Your Excellency, since I have been seriously ill for two years and have been unable to find a cure in this land. As there is no medicine for my illness for many miles around, I would ask Your Excellency's permission to travel to Mexico City or at least to Saltillo to seek a cure before it is too late. We understand from Your Excellency that there is a higher order to the effect that no Canarian colonist may leave Villa de San Antonio, and that Your Excellency cannot grant us this permission, but I sincerely believe that I must be exempted from this order since my life is in danger.
>
> The aforementioned order has been filed and therefore cannot remain in force, and we know perfectly well that we are not banned from leaving the town, and are even permitted to travel to Mexico to purchase what we need, if we have just cause. To the contrary, our liberty would be restricted, and if we are granted permission for other smaller matters, there is even more reason to do so in this case. This irrational measure is an attack against the freedom of all of the Canarian colonists. In light of this, I hereby ask Your Excellency for permission to travel at least to the town of Saltillo to find a cure for my illness, as I can no longer continue living without hope of ridding myself of this sickness, which grows steadily worse. In Saltillo I would visit a doctor who recently cured the reverend father Friar Miguel Sevillano, president of the Río Grande mission. I have been unable to work, and will remain so until I am cured.

> If necessary I am prepared to provide a deposit as a guarantee that I will not abandon the town and will return as soon as I have recovered from my illness. In the event that Your Excellency does not allow me to leave and seek a cure, I will bring a lawsuit before the pertinent authorities for damages, of which my wife and children will be the beneficiaries, if my death is caused by Your Excellency's failure to grant me permission in time to cure myself.
>
> Vicente Álvarez Travieso
>
> DECREE. Having read the text presented by Mr. Álvarez Travieso and having verified his illness, I hereby authorize him to leave to find a cure. The prohibition stems from a higher order, by virtue of which the Canarian colonists may not leave the town whenever they wish.

The Canary Islanders' discovery that they could not leave the town without the governor's permission, even in the event of illness, was the cause of great disappointment and indignation, since they had arrived as free citizens and wished to continue living as such. But years would pass before they were allowed to leave the town freely. It was not until 1770 that the viceroy of New Spain, the Baron of Riperdad, authorized the free movement of the Canary Islanders throughout the viceroyalty.

CHAPTER 4

I. The Construction of the San Pedro Canal

JANUARY 1802

The discontent that bubbled up over the years generated pressure from the townspeople, which was reflected in the decisions made by the cabildo in 1738. In particular, they demanded the immediate fulfillment of the promise made by the then-captain of the presidio of San Antonio de Béjar, Juan Antonio Pérez de Almazán: that as soon as the Concepción canal was completed, Antonio Rodríguez would begin construction of the San Pedro canal, starting from the San Pedro stream, to irrigate the lands of the Canarian colonists.

Work on the Concepción canal had finished, and Antonio Rodríguez continued on excellent terms with the missionaries and had returned to his job as treasurer of the cabildo.

Representatives of the cabildo therefore went to the fort to visit the new captain, José de Urrutia, who had replaced Juan Antonio Pérez de Almazán,[16] to show him the minutes of the meeting in which his predecessor had pledged to intercede with the governor and, if necessary, with the viceroy, so that construction of the San Pedro canal could begin, as granted by the Crown to the Canary Islanders. A commission had been elected, presided over by the president of the cabildo, Ignacio Lorenzo de Armas and, of course, the ever-present members, Francisco de Arocha and Vicente Álvarez Travieso.

Captain Urrutia received them in his office—not in the fort but in the newly built governor's palace, which he occupied in the absence of a governor.

Upon seeing the needs of these poor people and understanding the reasoning behind their arguments, he took charge of the situation and gave orders for the construction work to begin immediately.

Antonio Rodríguez Mederos, now back in his position as treasurer of the cabildo, was unanimously elected to direct the work. Three weeks later, the commission met the captain once again to inform him of the plans for building the canal. Antonio Rodríguez Mederos, author of the project, explained that the canal would begin at the source of the San Pedro stream, and would run in a straight line down through the center of the town, supplying both the presidio and the town, and would come to an end near the Concepción mission. In this way they would irrigate about four hundred acres of land on either side of the canal. The canal would be about six feet wide and two feet deep. All of the Canary Islanders offered to work on the project as long as the soldiers protected them from Indian attacks.

The cabildo clearly specified in the minutes that they had unanimously approved Antonio Rodríguez Mederos as director of the construction of the San Pedro canal. This was due to his vast experience in this kind of irrigation engineering, as demonstrated not only in smaller projects for the cabildo, but also, much more importantly, in the project he had carried out for the Concepción canal.

It was stipulated that Antonio Rodríguez "should oversee the digging and construction of the canal to ensure that it has the appropriate width and depth, and that the sluice gates are wide enough to water the land located on either side, with absolute fairness, and without benefiting some people at the expense of others. He should also ensure the fair distribution of water as it passes through the town."

The cabildo, or more accurately, my brothers-in-law, the solicitor Francisco de Arocha and the councilor Vicente Álvarez Travieso, never fully trusted Antonio Rodríguez, and proposed that two supervisors be named to watch over the project. So it was that, unsurprisingly, Vicente Álvarez Travieso and Francisco de Arocha were chosen, and with a very specific mission: "To keep watch over the tools and to ensure that Antonio Rodríguez Mederos follows the planned excavations and measurements of the canal and the irrigation channels which will water the adjoining fields on both sides."

On hearing of the agreement, Rodríguez Mederos requested the materials necessary for implementing the project: three pairs of oxen, twenty-five picks, eight axes, three large pots for the workers' meals, four bulls per week for the duration of the construction works to feed the workers, troops for protection, and three handfuls of tobacco, a half mule load of salt, and some ninety kilograms of the toasted and milled corn that the Canary Islanders called *gofio.*

The workers were to be divided into gangs, each led by a trusted Canary Islander named personally by Rodríguez.

The horses belonging to the Indians who worked on the project were to be guarded by soldiers so that they did not run away with tools and supplies as had occurred during the construction of the Concepción canal. The captain of the fort would send enough soldiers every day for the Indians to respect them. These soldiers would also stand guard throughout the night to prevent the Indian laborers from fleeing and to repel possible attacks.

Rodríguez included all manner of details in the report. He wrote of the way the canal and the irrigation channels would be built, saying that "they should be built whenever possible with slabs laid one after another where the canal has a natural surface of rock, because the salts and the lime, transported by the water, will make the joins more consistent." Another part of the canal would be built with small stones, although Rodríguez would try to avoid doing this at all costs, since in his experience, both in the Canary Islands and in the Concepción canal, this kind of construction required frequent repairs. For this reason, he preferred to build with stones and mortar as much as possible.

According to the stories of the Indians who had worked on the construction of the Concepción canal (tales that quickly spread by word of mouth around the town), the mortar prepared by Antonio Rodríguez, which he mixed personally without allowing anyone else to watch, was so good because he made it with hundreds of eggs and lots of goat's milk.

In his study, Antonio Rodríguez had also foreseen that "when plots cannot be irrigated because they are too high, we will use waterwheels, which will elevate the water above the level of the canal."

After three years of intense work by everyone, but particularly by Antonio Rodríguez, the canal finally reached the center of the town, where it supplied water to all of the houses, to the fort, and to the adjoining farmlands, through small irrigation channels.

In 1741 the town unanimously elected Antonio Rodríguez Mederos as president of the cabildo of Villa de San Fernando de Béjar, in recognition of his huge contribution to the community. His enemies, my brothers-in-law Francisco de Arocha and Vicente Álvarez Travieso, who were still solicitor and councilor respectively, never forgave this choice.

Francisco de Arocha, as solicitor and secretary, was responsible for taking the minutes of the meetings, managing the municipal and other accounts, and keeping the archives in order.

Vicente Álvarez Travieso's responsibilities as councilor were the enforcement of final rulings and sentences, payment orders, seizing objects to be sold, imprisoning and punishing criminals, and recovering money. He was also the superintendent of the prison and, together with the lieutenant of the presidio, would make public announcements and would visit public areas, both night and day, to prevent immoral activities and disputes. Failure to fulfill these duties would result in his suspension from office and the payment of any damages resulting from such negligence. He also had the obligation to accompany the magistrate on visits to the prisons.

These key figures in the town government never forgave Antonio Rodríguez for building the Concepción canal for the missionaries before the canal for the Canary Islanders. But more importantly, as we shall see, they were unable to forget that he had been unanimously elected president of the cabildo in recognition of his work on the San Pedro canal. Over their years in the cabildo, these two loyal members had proved themselves to be staunch defenders of the

Canary Islanders' interests, particularly in their role as supervisors of the construction of the San Pedro canal, and yet Antonio Rodríguez was president, while they were still simple councilors.

As the years passed, this envy they felt toward Antonio Rodríguez slowly transformed into hatred, and unconsciously gave rise to what would become the cabildo's most important legal battle against one of its members and the most implacable persecution between Canary Islanders that I believe has ever existed. It began with a lawsuit filed by the cabildo of San Fernando de Béjar, composed entirely of Canary Islanders, against one of its members: Antonio Rodríguez Mederos.

II. Construction of the First Church of the Holy Virgin of Candelaria and Her Holy Son Jesus Christ

JANUARY 1802

The residents of San Fernando de Béjar continued making improvements through the cabildo. In 1738, they not only petitioned the governor (with the aid of the new captain of the presidio) to allow them to build the canal for irrigation and to bring water to the town, but also petitioned him, "as devoted Christians, for a church where we can worship with honor and dignity our most holy Virgin of Candelaria and her most holy Son, our Lord Jesus Christ."

On February 18, 1738, the cabildo of San Antonio met to discuss whether to build a church. Although the councilors expressed different points of view, in the end they agreed that a church would indeed be built. However, problems arose when deciding to which virgin to dedicate the church. Everyone had an opinion, proposing one virgin after another. Finally, it was my brother-in-law, Vicente Álvarez Travieso, a devotee of the Virgin of Candelaria, who convinced them. In the face of the opposition of the entire cabildo, he explained how he had brought with him from the Canary Islands two keepsakes from Tenerife, given to him by his mother: a painting of the Virgin of Candelaria and a book titled *On the Origin and the Miracles of the*

Holy Image of Our Lady of Candelaria, Who Appeared on the Island of Tenerife, with a Description of This Island. The book was written by the Dominican father Alonso de Espinosa, a devotee of this virgin, and printed in Seville in 1594.

To convince the rest of the Canary Islanders on the cabildo to accept the Virgin of Candelaria as their patron, he read a portion of the second chapter, describing how she appeared before a few Guanche[17] shepherds, and their actions when they saw that she did not move:

> The shepherd was displeased and turned to his customary weapons, which were stones, and taking one in his hand he raised his arm to threaten her or to throw it at her. And as he raised his arm, preparing to draw it back to make his throw, it remained stiff, rigid and extended, unable to move. When his companion saw this, he was unchastened and emboldened by the fact that she neither moved nor spoke and that, when they called to the image or body, she did not respond. He resolved to try another way of ascertaining whether she was a living being, even if it meant risking his life. He approached her with more fear than shame, and picked up a *tahona*, a smooth, jet black stone that when struck with another stone makes slivers as sharp as a knife, used for cutting and slicing. Taking up this stone, he approached the holy image with the intention of cutting one of her fingers, to satisfy his ignorance and see if she could feel. Placing the image's finger over his own, he began to cut, and the foolish man soon found himself outwitted as he saw that he had cut his own hand, leaving the hand of the holy image undamaged. And being obstinate and stubborn (because he was a fool), he tried again, and once again he failed. His fingers ran with blood from the wounds that he had unintentionally inflicted on himself, and the holy image's hands remained clean and whole, with no sign of injury. These were the first two miracles that this Lady performed for the good of these lands, and they were upheld later, as we shall see.

When Álvarez Travieso observed the silence that followed his reading, he realized that it was the right moment to read chapter thirteen, which contained a description of her image. And so he continued reading:

> The Virgin of Candelaria is so named for the stump of green candle she holds in her hand, and for the ornate candles and lights that surround her; for this reason her main festival is the Purification.
>
> This image is perfectly carved and finished, the like of which I have never seen in all my life. It is nearly five hands tall, including the plinth on which it stands, which has a thickness of two fingers. It is of an unknown colored wood, not very heavy, and solid.
>
> The face is in harmony with the perfect proportions of the long body, and has large, oval eyes which appear to follow one no matter where one stands. There is so much solemnity and majesty in those eyes and in her face that no person can gaze upon her without their hair standing on end and their shoulders tensing.
>
> She is dark-skinned with beautiful rosy cheeks, although her coloring is difficult to comprehend, since it is very common (as we shall see below) for the face to change color, and to appear one day with one coloring and the next with another.
>
> She has thick hair, without veil or mantle, and it is golden, and perfectly arranged in six braids hanging down her back. To her right is a beautiful naked boy holding a little golden bird in each hand. This boy is seated on the right arm of the image, and she holds him in her hand. In her left hand she has a stub of green candle made from the same wood, about the size of a *jeme*,[18] with a hole in the top to hold a larger candle. Her garments are old-fashioned, and she is dressed from her throat to her feet in golden clothing. Inscribed upon the gold of her low collar are the following Latin letters, written in colors:
>
> TIEPFSEPMERI

The gold is so perfect, so well placed and polished, that no scribe could do it so well, and I say this because I understand the work involved. On the border or hem of her clothes are the following letters:

EAFM • IRENINI • FMEAREI

Some of the letters are missing, as I believe that pieces of the skirt have been removed, together with the base, to be used as relics. A small part of her left foot can be seen outside the skirt, gracefully encased in a colored slipper, and on the cuff at her left hand, which holds the candle, are written these letters:

IMAGELPVRINENIPEPNEIFANT

Her clothing is girded beneath her breasts (which from all sides gives her an exceedingly graceful form) with a blue belt, with golden letters that read:

IMAGENARMPRLMOTARE

Her mantle is draped about her shoulders and attached at her breast with a colored cord as long as a jeme, tied in a bow at her left hand. This mantle is a perfect blue, bestrewn with large golden flowers on both sides, and its border is of polished gold, printed with old Latin letters in color. On the right side it reads:

IMAGEOIM • INRANFR • IAEBNPFM • RFVEN

IMAGENVINAPIMLFINVIPI • NIPIAN

The letters on the left side are:

IMAGEFVPMIRNA • ENVPMTI • EPNMPIR • VRVIVNRN

IMAGEAPVIMFRI • PIVNIAN • NTRHN

At the back of the mantle, along the bottom of the border it reads:

IMAGENBIMEI • ANNEIPERFMIVIFVF

This is the description of the holy image which appeared on this island so many years ago. One hundred and ninety years have passed since she appeared, and she has been carried from one headland to another and taken out a thousand times in processions. She has been dressed and undressed, and touched and stroked by many (and I have seen her naked), and yet today, October 25, 1590, she is still as beautiful, as lovely, and the colors, the golden hues, are as perfect as if she had been made only a few days ago. One thing that I revere in this holy image, which is worthy of admiration and marvel in all who behold her, is that even without clothing and without repair, just as she first appeared, her face is so well-proportioned (according to geometry) in relation to her height that nothing more could be asked. When dressed in her habitual clothing, she is almost three hands greater in size and stature (which is worthy of admiration), and is so perfect that all who see her cannot but take it as a miracle.

The meaning of the letters and characters written on the borders should be addressed by one who is more qualified than myself, who can exercise his genius upon them and unlock their mystery. This would be no small accomplishment since until now nobody has understood them, although they have been sent to several lands and kingdoms, and many men learned in the universal languages have studied them. While some have argued that they are meaningless, inscribed merely for their beauty and decoration, this is only because they do not wish to fail by admitting that they do not understand them. For myself, I have surrendered to the unknown, and believe that they do have a meaning, and refer to some hitherto unknown merits of this virgin, not yet ours to understand as we do not deserve them. As ornate decorations, there are so many other patterns that are easier and perhaps more beautiful than letters, and if they did not mean anything, they would not be divided into sections with periods, but would simply flow continually. Nor would there have been any reason to place certain letters together, as can be seen. This mystery is an exercise in good judgment.

When he finished reading, there was a deep silence. As the residents looked around at each other, Álvarez Travieso knew that his proposal had triumphed. As I was later told by those present, the feeling was unanimous. The story had transported them back to the Canary Islands, each to his own. They were reminded of their families, their customs, and their homeland, and this was powerful enough for them to overcome the rivalries between islands, unspoken but latent in every decision they had taken as a group since we left the Canary Islands.

Vicente Álvarez's story had united them all, and they were able to put aside those rivalries and make the decision that the future church would be consecrated to the Holy Virgin of Candelaria.

At this time, Ignacio Lorenzo de Armas was president of the cabildo, and Juan Leal Goraz, Juan Curbelo, Antonio de los Santos, Juan Leal Álvarez, Vicente Álvarez Travieso, Francisco de Arocha, and Antonio Rodríguez Mederos were councilors. Vicente Álvarez Travieso and Antonio Rodríguez Mederos were elected as collector of money for the construction of the church and director of the construction works, respectively.

After seven days, the collections were as follows:

Prudencia Orobio Basterra, governor, 200 pesos

Juan Recio de León, priest, 25 pesos

José de Urrutia, captain of the presidio, 100 pesos

Manuel Cruz, ten cartloads of stones

Ignacio Lorenzo de Armas, 10 pesos

Juan Leal Goraz, councilor, a one-year-old lamb

Antonio de los Santos, 10 pesos

Juan Curbelo, councilor, 10 pesos

Juan Leal Álvarez, councilor, 10 *fanegas*[19] of corn and 20 pesos

Vicente Álvarez Travieso, 20 pesos

José Arocha, 10 pesos

Antonio Rodríguez Mederos, councilor, twenty cartloads of stones

José Leal, 20 fanegas of corn, a six-month-old lamb and 4 pesos

Patricio Rodríguez, 10 pesos

Juan Delgado, 10 pesos

José Antonio Rodríguez, 20 pesos

Martín Lorenzo de Armas, a young calf and 4 pesos

Toribio de Urrutia, 4 pesos

The troops from the fort contributed with a series of donations that totaled 664 pesos and two reals. The king of Spain also appears on the list with 400 pesos.

Construction began and was riddled with difficulties from the start, due to the problems that arose between the two enemies, Álvarez Travieso and Rodríguez, who were the head of the committee controlling the funds and the director of construction, respectively.

Lack of money and poor management caused the work to drag on, and only ten years later did the project actually begin to take shape. Years of unfinished construction work passed, until finally on January 13, 1748, the administrator of the money, my brother-in-law Vicente Álvarez Travieso, wrote to the viceroy, Francisco de Guemes y Horcasitas, asking that "the Royal Treasury provide 12,000 pesos for the purchase of materials for the construction and decoration of the town's parish church." In this letter, Álvarez Travieso, as administrator of the money, mentions that "certain amounts of money were diverted for another project, and for this reason I request that the aforementioned 12,000 pesos be stored in a strongbox with three keys, one in the possession of the cabildo, one with the priest, and one with the captain of the fort."

The viceroy, aware from other reports of the issues that had arisen during the construction of the town church over the past ten years, answered promptly on January 26, accepting Travieso's proposal and going one step further by instructing him that "the church will be built, but the construction should not be a simply crafted house, but rather a church to last through the ages, even though this will increase the cost due to the town's remote location.

"As the Canary Islanders have no money and therefore cannot cover the costs," continued the viceroy in his letter, "His Majesty will finance the bills, to be paid by the priest, the captain, and the cabildo. The funds should be used as soon as possible for the construction of the church, and every year the amounts paid by the captain of the fort, the priest, and the cabildo will be verified, together with the actual work carried out."

As soon as they received this letter from the viceroy, Francisco de Arocha and Vicente Álvarez Travieso met and decided to propose in the next meeting of the cabildo that Antonio Rodríguez Mederos be replaced as director of construction by Álvarez Travieso, so that it would appear to the viceroy and the governor that Antonio Rodríguez was guilty of mismanagement, even though he had nothing to do with administrating the money.

The replacement of Rodríguez Mederos intensified the enmity between these men. He clearly saw the handiwork of his enemies in his removal. This was the spark that ignited the bitterest dispute faced by this group of Canarian colonists in the state of Texas. Antonio never accepted that after directing practically all of the construction works in the town, he had been removed from what he considered to be the most important project of all: the town's church.

The missions were never happy with the idea that the Canarian colonists were to build a church. They had lost the initial battle over the founding of the town to these stubborn islanders, seeing that the settlement of the colonists would create competition for selling agricultural products to the surrounding presidios, the town itself, and the neighboring city of El Saltillo. As we have seen, the town was founded despite their opposition, and the missions continued to fight with the Canary Islanders to prevent them from watering their lands from the San Antonio River. So far, they had been successful in this endeavor, although the Canary Islanders had managed to build a canal from the San Pedro stream. After this victory for the Canary Islanders, the missions saw that they were losing power, since they had governed almost the entire territory before the arrival of the colonists and the foundation of the town and the cabildo.

Despite this, they still had some influence over the Canary Islanders, who were fervent Catholics and depended on the San Antonio de Valero mission for religious services on Sundays and during Catholic festivals. With the construction of the town church, the inhabitants would no longer need the mission, and would attend religious services at the new church, with a parish priest independent of the Franciscan order. So, when Antonio Rodríguez Mederos mentioned to Friar Benito Fernández de Santa Ana that he had been replaced in the construction of the new church, the friar showed him how his enemies in the cabildo had done him a great injustice by making the governor, the viceroy, and the Canarian community in general believe that he was entirely responsible for the delayed construction and the mismanagement of funds.

The conversation between the friar and Antonio Rodríguez was recounted to me by Rodríguez's wife, Josefa Niz, who, due to my relationship with his enemies Francisco Arocha and Vicente Álvarez, consulted me on what her husband should do, since I was the person she trusted most in the community of Canarian colonists. I remember her words as if I heard them only yesterday, and I recount them here.

"There is no doubt," Friar Benito told him, "that your enemies Álvarez Travieso and Francisco Arocha have told the viceroy that you are to blame for the failure to finish the construction after ten years, and of course they are also saying the same to the Canary Islanders. You are clearly also being blamed for diverting the donated money to other projects, since they continue in their positions while you have been removed."

"That is impossible," answered Rodríguez, visibly upset. "I was only in charge of directing the construction—if it has not been completed in all this time, it is due precisely to mismanagement by Álvarez Travieso, who caused us to run out of money."

These conversations continued over several weeks, with the superior of the missions emphasizing how Rodríguez Mederos had been incriminated.

One fine day, taking advantage of the emotional turmoil that Rodríguez Mederos had been plunged into, the missionary told him: "I think that your good name and that of your family demand public recognition in the face of the infamy they have committed against you by replacing you as director of the construction of the church. If I were you, I would inform the viceroy of all of the irregularities that you believe Álvarez Travieso has committed when managing the church construction funds."

"I could never do that to a fellow Canary Islander, and even less so to a member of the cabildo."

"I agree, but they have done exactly that to you by replacing you as director of the project."

"My replacement was not a direct accusation against me, because if that were the case they would have said so explicitly in their letter to the viceroy."

"Yes, but it is certain that you appear to be guilty. It seems to me and to the whole community like an indirect accusation, to keep them from having to take responsibility."

During his walk home after his meeting with Friar Benito, and all through the night, the friar's words resounded in Rodríguez Mederos's head. The following morning, what had before seemed unthinkable was now nothing more than defending his honor and that of his family.

The next day he headed to the San Antonio mission so that Friar

Benito, a man of letters, could write to the viceroy denouncing Vicente Álvarez Travieso and Francisco de Arocha. On the way he ran into his father-in-law, who asked, "Where are you going so early in the morning, Antonio?"

"To the San Antonio mission, so that Friar Benito, to whom I spoke last night, may write me a letter denouncing Vicente Álvarez Travieso and Francisco Arocha for unjustly removing me as director of the construction of the church. Their actions have caused the townspeople, the governor, and the viceroy to believe that I am the person responsible for the delays, while, as you know, they were the result of mismanagement of the money, which deprived me of the resources necessary to cover the expenses and carry out the work at the speed I had originally planned."

When they parted, his father-in-law, who had never actually spoken to his son-in-law about the rumors in the town surrounding his replacement and the general opinion that he was guilty, headed to the cabildo, where he severely rebuked Vicente Álvarez Travieso and Francisco de Arocha.

"You have removed my son-in-law as director of the construction of the church," he said, "and you have made him seem guilty in the eyes of the town and all of the authorities of this viceroyalty; but take care, as the truth will always come out in the end, and he will denounce both of you to the viceroy, since you are the guilty parties who mismanaged the funds for the construction of the church."

"That is untrue," answered Álvarez Travieso. "He is entirely responsible, since he didn't know how to direct the construction and took ten years to build a church that could have been done in four."

Juan Niz left without deigning to respond. He knew them well and understood what cowards they were. He only needed to mention his son-in-law's complaint, and they would surely return him to his position as head of construction.

How far he was from imagining the repercussions of this conversation.

Francisco de Arocha turned to his comrade and said, "Do you

think that as well as removing him for his incompetence, we should also remove him as a member of the cabildo? At the end of the day, such an incompetent man is not fit to be councilor. This way, we will seem more credible to the viceroy, if he does actually denounce us."

"Remember that he is a particularly dangerous man—he has the missionaries' protection, and removing him would imply open war, not just against him, but against the missionaries, who would surely support him."

"I don't think that fear should stop us from finally putting an end to the negative influence that Antonio Rodríguez has in the cabildo and in the town. It's absurd to be scared of the missionaries, as they will never confront us just for removing Rodríguez."

"I think they will," said Álvarez Travieso, "because with his removal they'll lose their only point of contact in the cabildo, and their source of information on what we are doing with respect to the missions."

"All the same," said Arocha, "I believe that the time has come to decide once and for all to remove Antonio Rodríguez as councilor. But it is of the utmost importance that we do so as soon as possible, and we should consider very carefully how to propose it to our companions in the cabildo so that it does not reach his ears and give him time to present his complaint against us or prepare his defense; for this reason his father-in-law, Manuel Niz, should not be told of our proposal."

And so it was that their proposition for the removal of Antonio Rodríguez from the cabildo was put only to José Martín Lorenzo, first councilor or mayor, and to Antonio Santos, and, of course, to the notary public and secretary of the cabildo.

In truth there was little to debate. Everything had already been decided by Álvarez Travieso, and he proposed it as a done deal. The rest of his companions assented, and on June 21, 1749, they presented the document, signed by each of them, that would give rise to the longest and most important judicial proceeding that the Canarian colonists would face throughout all Canarian-American history.

CHAPTER 5

I. The Cabildo of San Fernando de Béjar versus Its Councilor, Antonio Rodríguez Mederos

MARCH 1802

The document containing the allegations was addressed to the governor and captain general of the province of Texas or the New Philippines, Pedro del Barrio Junco y Espinilla. It explained how the colonists had arrived in San Fernando de Béjar from the Canary Islands, by order of His Majesty the King Philip V, and then described how they presented themselves to the captain of the San Antonio presidio, Juan Antonio Pérez de Almazán, who called on them to form a cabildo to govern the town, in accordance with a dispatch from the viceroy of New Spain, Juan Acuña, marquis of Casafuerte.

"During the establishment of the cabildo," the text read, "Antonio Rodríguez Mederos, one of the Canarian colonists, specifically from the Island of Gran Canaria, was elected as a councilor and as treasurer, whose responsibility was to manage public moneys and supervise public works within the town."

The following is a list of the main charges against Antonio Rodríguez. The first entries essentially gave rise to the rest of the problems among the Canarian colonists in San Antonio.

1. That he was in contact with the opposition (the missionaries and the other residents).

2. That the cabildo had previously formulated a complaint against Rodríguez, but when the two attorneys were on their way to Mexico to present it directly to the viceroy, they found Antonio Rodríguez at an inn in the town of El Saltillo, gravely wounded. Both councilors, as Canary Islanders so far from their homeland, took pity on him and decided to help him, despite the complaint. During the time they spent together he convinced

them not to abandon him there alone and wounded, far from his family in San Antonio, whom he had not contacted so as not to alarm them. Over the days they spent in his company at the inn in El Saltillo, he spoke to them of his village of Tamaraceite on the island of Gran Canaria, where his mother lived.

He told them of his childhood memories, and how he saw his father die there while attempting to save his neighbors during a flood in the Tenoya ravine. Rodríguez made a solemn promise that he would help them and would collaborate more in the future with the cabildo and not with the opposition. He so convinced them that once he was cured, the three men returned together to Villa de San Fernando without presenting the complaint against him in Mexico City. "Once back in town," continued the text, "and fully cured of his wounds, Rodríguez broke his word, and once again betrayed the Canary Islanders by presenting a complaint against the cabildo, calling himself councilor and the town's attorney; a complaint that to all appearances was drafted by the missionaries to seek revenge on the cabildo."

3. Politically, Antonio Rodríguez was impossible to work with. His words always had a double meaning. In the cabildo, they could never reach any agreement during the normal sessions unless they held them in secret so that he didn't attend, since he always tried to impose his opinion and to select whomever he liked to fill positions within the cabildo.

The fourth charge was almost as crucial as the first.

4. Antonio Rodríguez was to all intents and purposes the town's mayor, despite being only the treasurer, because the other members of the cabildo were poor and often had to leave the town to tend their fields, while he remained in the town and acted as mayor, by replacing his absent superiors.

Francisco de Arocha and Vicente Álvarez could not tolerate

the fact that Antonio Rodríguez had a higher economic status than the rest of the Canarian colonists in San Antonio. This stemmed firstly from the money that he earned directing the construction of the Concepción canal, and secondly from the fact that he did not have to tend his fields, since the missionaries sent Indians to help him.

5. "In exercising the functions of town judge he committed grave injustices; if he was a bad mayor, he was a worse judge. By way of example," continued the text, "it is said that on one occasion when the parish priest refused to marry one of his friends, he told him not to worry, that as a judge he would perform the marriage rites."

According to Francisco de Arocha, whose idea it was to include this accusation, it was such a grave invasion of the sacred ministry of the church, that it would convince the Franciscans not to support Antonio Rodríguez in his defense against these serious allegations by the cabildo. However, this was not the case, and the Franciscans supported Rodríguez against the cabildo throughout the proceedings.

Finally, the document stated that not only could they prove these charges, but that they could also demonstrate that Rodríguez mistreated his family, a fact that was well known in the town. It ended by requesting "that Antonio Rodríguez be removed from his position in the cabildo and from the title that he so unworthily displays," and that he be banished from the town in the name of peace and justice. Additionally, that "the cabildo be forgiven for presenting this document on common paper, since there was no official stationery showing proof of payment of His Majesty's tax."

That same day, July 21, 1749, the governor of the province of Texas and the New Philippines, Pedro del Barrio Junco y Espinilla, issued a decree accepting the document and requesting that an investigation be opened and witnesses be questioned.

Upon receiving news of the admission of their complaint and the opening of proceedings, my brothers-in-law Francisco de Arocha and Vicente Álvarez Travieso were jubilant.

"We should be very careful," said Francisco de Arocha, "because the governor has forgotten what we agreed with him, before we submitted the complaint. He has not decreed Rodríguez's imprisonment and this could cause problems because with his influence in town he will surely pressure the witnesses and destroy the evidence we have against him. We must prepare an urgent document that you will deliver by hand to the governor, informing him that we will prove the charges immediately, and asking him to decree the swift imprisonment of this undesirable person."

Álvarez Travieso took the document explaining the cabildo's fears straight to the governor.

This document read: "The cabildo is willing to provide information on the scandalous lifestyle of Antonio Rodríguez, both at his home and in public, and we herein request that you imprison him immediately. If he remains at liberty, it will be impossible for the cabildo to prove the accusations due to the influence of the missionaries, who are Antonio Rodríguez Mederos's protectors."

Villa de San Fernando was abuzz with the news of the charges presented by the cabildo against one of its members, especially such a distinguished councilor as Antonio Rodríguez, who had done so much for the town that the townsfolk themselves had recognized his contributions by naming him president of the cabildo. That day, July 23, 1749, would never be forgotten by the Canary Islanders, and the events that took place from then on, as a consequence of the lawsuit presented by the cabildo against Rodríguez Mederos, would become a story that every parent told their children as an example of something that should never occur between brothers.

From that day forward, the Canarian community of San Antonio was divided into two irreconcilable camps: the friends and the enemies of Antonio Rodríguez Mederos and the friends and the enemies of the cabildo—although others knew that the true instigators of the persecution were Francisco de Arocha and Vicente Álvarez Travieso, rather than the entire cabildo.

The same division could also be found among the soldiers of the fort, the other residents, the military authorities, and even among the missionaries, although as a whole the missionaries were always in favor of the accused man.

The governor, Pedro del Barrio, decreed the imprisonment of Antonio Rodríguez, making Juan Sierra, the commanding officer of guards at the presidio, responsible for his capture in order to avoid problems between the captain of the San Antonio presidio and the residents who supported the prisoner.

He was taken into custody and placed in the so-called royal houses, or the governor's palace. He was imprisoned in a room of around six square meters. It held a single table of dirty, rough-hewn wood, a stool, and a pallet in the corner. Half of the roof had caved in. At night he could contemplate the stars in the dark, clear, Texas sky.

His faithful wife, Josefa Niz, brought his meals to the prison, three times a day. This was the only contact with the outside world that he was allowed, apart from the guards. Antonio Rodríguez awaited her arrival with anxiety, in case she brought news of his imminent release. He never imagined that his confinement would last for long, especially in light of who he was, a man who had done so much for the people of the town and who had a strong friendship with the missionaries.

As soon as his father-in-law heard of his son-in-law's imprisonment, he went straight to the cabildo to interrogate Arocha and Álvarez. He found them in Arocha's office in the cabildo.

"What's going on with my son-in-law?" he said. "Why is he in prison? Why has the cabildo filed complaints against him, without calling all the councilors to a meeting to discuss the matter?"

"Those are a lot of questions all at once, my dear Juan," they said. "The complaints were made against him because the Canarian community was fed up with your son-in-law's betrayals by constantly taking the side of our enemies, the missionaries. As we are members of the cabildo, the body elected by the community to represent it, we filed the suit to protect the interests of the community from a traitor in our midst. As it was an urgent issue, only the members present at that moment signed the document, with no time to advise the others."

This answer did not convince Juan Niz, especially as he was well aware of the enmity between the men.

Two days after the arrest, Arocha and Álvarez, obsessed with the possibility that Rodríguez would escape, convinced the governor-judge to send soldiers to search the prison, claiming that the prisoner had in his possession "a blunderbuss, and bad intentions."

The judge ordered Corporal Sierra, head of the guards in charge of the prisoner, "to go immediately and without delay to the royal houses and search all corners of the room occupied by the councilor Antonio Rodríguez Mederos, as well as his clothing and other places, and to verify the owner of any weapon and bring it before the judge."

After the search, Corporal Sierra found "a Spanish pistol with a length of one hand, made in Madrid by Matías Baeza in 1713, as stated on the butt of the pistol and on the left-hand side, while in the center of the silver body, the initials A.R.M. are engraved. The pistol is nineteen inches long, and has a caliber of 60. A nine-inch powder horn was also found, with a three-inch base, decorated with floral and animal engravings." On confirming the accusation, the judge dictated a ruling which declared him "unworthy of the great consideration in which he has been held by housing him in such an honorable prison," and ordered that he be asked the following questions: if he recognized the pistol; his purpose in having said pistol; if he was carrying it when he was arrested and, if so, why he had not declared it.

Antonio Rodríguez recognized the pistol as his own and confirmed that it was in his pocket when he was arrested. He had not declared it because "it is the privilege of the office of councilor, and by order of His Majesty and royal law, which permits councilors to carry offensive and defensive weapons." He added that he also carried the pistol to use in defense of his person, since the region had been declared a war zone, as his accusers, his enemies, knew very well.

II. Complaints to the Viceroy

APRIL 1802

This humiliating search was the final straw, and caused Antonio Rodríguez to react at last, and to snap out of the depression he had sunk into. In an instance he understood that he had to fight back and defend himself: this was clearly not a simple lawsuit and a hasty decision to imprison him by the judge, which would soon be revoked. No, they wanted to ruin him as a councilor and as a man. This search clearly demonstrated the hatred that his enemies, Arocha and Travieso, held for him.

When his wife arrived on July 1 to bring him his lunch, Rodríguez told her, "You must go at once to the San Antonio mission and ask to speak to the father superior. Give him these notes and these blank pages signed by me, so that he can draw up two complaints, one against Vicente Álvarez Travieso, and the other against the governor, Pedro del Barrio, and can send them to the viceroy. But be sure to tell him that he should not send them to Mexico in the normal way but should instead send a horseman to ensure that they reach the viceroy's palace safely."

Josefa Niz did as her husband asked, and on July 25 the document, dated July 19, 1749, and signed by Antonio Rodríguez Mederos, arrived in Mexico City and was delivered to the viceroy of New Spain himself, de Güemes y Horcasitas.[20] It was a counterattack against Álvarez Travieso, and contained the following points:

1. That his companion, Álvarez Travieso, should without further delay provide the cabildo with the dispatch from his Excellency

the viceroy of New Spain, and the letter which the governor and captain general, José Antonio Bustillos y Ceballos, sent to the cabildo. On receiving these documents, the cabildo should oblige the aforementioned Travieso to give an exact account of how the money for the construction of the San Antonio church had been spent.

2. With respect to the mismanagement of the money for the construction, it stated that "Travieso allocated two pesos per day for his own meals." Similarly, it alleges that "1,000 pesos were spent on royalties, but it is unknown who received the payment of 800 pesos for personal work, or 2,500 pesos for two images, one of Our Lady of Candelaria and another of San Fernando: this amount is particularly difficult to believe, since the most it should have cost him was 200 pesos. Furthermore, said images were purchased following his own criteria, without consulting the cabildo." It continues: "Álvarez Travieso should be thoroughly audited, and his accounts for 12,000 pesos should not be accepted, since in San Antonio this money is worth 30,000 pesos, and Señor Travieso wants to keep the profits."

Rodríguez makes frequent references to this claim in his defense against the accusations made by the cabildo.

The other document, presented to the viceroy on the same day, is directed against the judge who ordered his imprisonment—the governor of the province, Pedro del Barrio, who, according to Rodríguez, conspired against him with the two councilors, Arocha and Álvarez.

This document does not seem to be written by him as a councilor—since on its date, July 19, he was still in prison—but rather in the name of the cabildo, although he alone signs it. It attacks the governor, Pedro del Barrio, and alleges that "on being named governor, he did not visit San Antonio in the manner of other governors, but rather arrived without warning, and was particularly rude to some of the councilors of the San Antonio cabildo, although the poverty of the town was evident from the outset. The Canary Islanders who live there have been able to survive thanks to the goodwill of the captain of the presidio and to the Franciscan missionaries, who took pity on us from the beginning and helped us, giving us supplies in moments of crisis. For this reason, it was most surprising to the Canarian colonists that as soon as the governor arrived, he was so unjust to the captain of the fort and to the reverend Franciscan fathers, abusing his office and refusing to provide them with certifications and copies of the complaints that they presented to him."

In this paragraph we can clearly see the hand of the Franciscans, defending the captain of the fort, their ally, and at the same time attempting to solve their own problems with the governor.

The text continues, explaining that "he himself was summoned for exceeding his area of jurisdiction, by sending me a legal instrument which removed me from the cabildo as councilor, thereby annulling the vote of the people of San Antonio. It was not within his power to do this, since his business is military, and the governance of the community belongs to the freely elected cabildo. His fantasies lead him to believe himself the governor of the kingdom."

He did not forget his enemies Arocha and Álvarez Travieso, and in this complaint against the governor he included a request that he had not covered in his claims against Álvarez Travieso, "that your Excellency order Vicente Álvarez Travieso, sheriff of the cabildo, and Francisco Arocha, secretary and notary public, to leave this town, since they are indecent, seditious, and disturbers of the peace and tranquility."

With these two accusations, Antonio Rodríguez thus responded to his enemies.

A few days after the viceroy had received the letters, the governor, Pedro del Barrio, met with Arocha and Álvarez Travieso in San Antonio.

"Gentlemen," the governor said, "I must inform you that I have received news by special post from Mexico, informing me that the prisoner, who is in the royal house itself, has inexplicably been able to send written complaints to the viceroy, surely through his friends the Franciscans, accusing me of a series of irregularities. These documents will be sent to me shortly so that I may respond, but they are not only against me but also against the two of you. Gentlemen, Antonio Rodríguez is kept in solitary confinement, and the only person who visits him is his wife, who brings him food. In future, the guard will take the prisoner his meals, in order to avoid direct contact between him and his wife, and to prevent Rodríguez from directing his defense from his cell. You should deliver the list of interrogation questions to be used by the cabildo in the proceedings against Antonio Rodríguez, and do so as quickly as possible in order to justify his imprisonment. This prisoner is no common enemy: he has the backing of the missionaries, not only in the town, but more importantly, and much more dangerously for us, in Mexico with the viceroy."

"I warned you," Arocha said to Francisco Álvarez Travieso, "that we should not proceed against him, because he was a dangerous enemy."

"Let's not worry, as this has only just begun. We should continue proceedings as soon as possible, as the governor said," answered Arocha.

"Once you present the interrogation questions, as governor and judge of the proceedings, I can suspend them in the face of more important issues without pronouncing on his imprisonment. This will mean that we can keep him in captivity for several months, so that you can calmly gather your proof, while he cannot."

While still in the governor's office, they proceeded to write out the list of interrogation questions. It begins by explaining that in accordance with the proceedings initiated by the cabildo against the councilor, Antonio Rodríguez Mederos, they were presenting this document containing thirteen written interrogation questions "so that the governor is more clearly informed and can consider the truth of the declarations made by our companions from the Canary Islands, as well as the other residents of this town."

The first is concerned with general law.

The heart of the matter begins from the second question onward. While it is true that the cabildo's complaints are only against Antonio Rodríguez, they also attempt to involve other parties who, although not directly involved against the cabildo in these proceedings, had confronted it on other issues, both intimately related with Antonio Rodríguez. These of course were the cabildo's age-old enemies, referred to in the text as "the reverend fathers and the captain of the fort." This question reflects the general discontent in the cabildo against the power of the military and the church in the town. These two conflicts arose, as we have seen, during the founding of the town by the Canarian colonists and the constitution of the cabildo by election, with its corresponding legislative, executive, and judicial power over the civilian population of the town. Until that point, these powers had been exercised by the captain of the fort and the missionaries, who were the true rulers, even over the captain. We should not forget that in the eighteenth century, more than 7,300 missionaries lived in the Viceroyalty of New Spain.

The question reads as follows: "It is true, and the witness knows or at least has heard, that while the cabildo and the community were involved in lawsuits, one of which was against the reverend fathers of the missions and the captain of the San Antonio presidio, Antonio Rodríguez isolated himself from the Canary Islanders, turned traitor and opposed us, and went to Mexico where he schemed against us, and presented false, unjust accusations and charges, which were most damaging to us poor men. And then, after causing us all this damage, he retracted his accusations."

In another question, to highlight only the most important ones, they ask about the immoral lifestyle of Antonio Rodríguez, his mistreatment of his family, and the persecutions he enacted upon the inhabitants of the town, "as well as election campaign promises of positions in the cabildo in exchange for money."

In the tenth question, cloaking themselves in the prestige and pride of being Canary Islanders and founders of the town, the cabildo states that "it is certain that during his journeys to Mexico, he speaks disparagingly of the Canary Islanders, even outside the borders of the province."

There are two other very interesting questions that are closely connected to the second one and that once again address the main underlying issue present right from the start: the struggle between the missions, the cabildo, and the military. The eleventh question reads: "It is certain that while visiting the town, Governor Francisco García Larios wished to remove Antonio Rodríguez from the office of councilor as a result of the charges already enumerated in this proceeding, which have been proved to be true. However, the reverend missionary fathers and the captain of the presidio used their strong influence to defend him to the governor, so that Antonio Rodríguez kept his position as councilor, and the proceedings were run as they desired." This question highlights the fact that Antonio Rodríguez was not only supported by the missionaries, but also by the captain of the presidio.

The thirteenth question reads: "It is certain that the reverend missionary fathers and the captain of the presidio aided Antonio Rodríguez against the cabildo, manifesting in public that whatever the results of this proceeding, they would ensure that Rodríguez retained his position."

This help from the missionaries could be seen as contradicting the eighth question, in which they accuse Rodríguez of mistreating a priest, when the priest asked Rodríguez to free an honest Spaniard unjustly imprisoned. This is not so, however, since they distinguish between a simple priest, like the injured party, and a priest who was a member of the missions, and was therefore protected by the power of the order.

On July 28, 1749, the same day that the interrogation questions were drawn up, the judge and military governor, Pedro del Barrio, issued a decree to Arocha and Álvarez in which he accepted the presentation of the document and suspended the proceedings, saying, "I have no option but to suspend proceedings in order to perform other duties for my royal service. As this matter cannot be delegated to any other person, it will remain suspended until my royal obligations have been concluded."

This deferral surprised Antonio Rodríguez and the missionaries who were organizing his defense. It could quite well be an indefinite, *sine die* suspension, with the added frustration that they could not communicate with Antonio Rodríguez in prison in order to prepare his defense. In light of this situation, Friar Benito Fernández invited the captain of the presidio, Toribio de Urrutia, to call on him at the San Antonio mission. The captain later told me their conversation, which I recount below.

"Captain," Friar Benito began, "you have always been a great friend of the missions, not only in the office you now hold as captain of the San Antonio presidio, but also in other capacities during your service to His Majesty in this Viceroyalty of New Spain. I have been reliably informed of this by members of my order in places you have been stationed before. I therefore requested your presence here because I would like you to be aware that in this lawsuit so unjustly brought by the cabildo against our friend, Antonio Rodríguez Mederos, we missionaries are practically managing his defense, although we cannot officially take on that role.

"As you know," the friar continued, "the governor and judge of the proceedings, Pedro del Barrio, has suspended them for an unknown length of time, during which our friend will remain in prison. This great injustice will prevent him from defending himself, since he cannot communicate openly with us, beyond the occasional message that his wife brings. For this reason, we need someone external to the proceedings who can intervene, by filing a complaint against the cabildo and the governor. Somebody courageous, who does not fear reprisals. With the understanding, of course, that the influence of the missions, both here and in Mexico with the viceroy, will strongly defend this brave man.... We thought that perhaps you could be that person."

Urrutia saw how they wanted to draw him into the conflict. While it would be bad to confront his governor, it would be even worse to be in conflict with the missions. In a fraction of a second, he calculated the risks and decided that anything would be better than going against the church. "I don't know what to say, Friar Benito," he said. "Of course I am always in favor of a just cause, and you are clearly correct to defend Antonio Rodríguez Mederos, so I will do whatever is necessary. Just tell me what I should do."

At this point, Friar Benito handed him a document addressed to the viceroy, which he only needed to read and sign. The text stated: "The governor of Texas, Pedro del Barrio, has arrested Antonio Rodríguez Mederos on the basis of a lawsuit filed by the cabildo, thus subjecting him to a cruel and most severe confinement more fit for a common traitor to the Royal Crown."

Dramatizing the situation even more, it continued: "He was moved to the royal houses under a guard of eight soldiers. Rodríguez is so highly thought of among the Canary Islanders that they entrusted him with the administration of justice in the town, so it is most strange that these same Canary Islanders would proceed in this way against a compatriot, simply because he has different opinions from the governor of the province."

> If he had not opposed the cabildo's judgments, then today he would be considered among the governor's favorites, as are his formal adversaries, the secretary of the cabildo and the town's notary public, Francisco de Arocha, and the councilor, Vicente Álvarez Travieso.
>
> Antonio Rodríguez is only permitted to speak to his wife when she takes him meals, and it is through her that he was able to send

> me a message asking me to intercede in his favor before Your Excellency, so that you will restore his honor and his office of councilor, to which he was elected by the vote of the entire town, and endorsed by Your Excellency.

Of course, the clear hand of the missionaries once again appears toward the end of the document, where they could not resist mentioning:

> The true enmity between the other members of the cabildo and Antonio Rodríguez arose when, driven by his conscience, he appeared before the captain general, Pedro Del Barrio, to put an end to the unjust lawsuits filed by the cabildo against the missions, the other residents, and the captain of the San Antonio presidio, and declaring his support of the missionaries. From that moment on they have been his enemies, and they have taken advantage of this opportunity to imprison him.
>
> Finally, in addition to the above, the cabildo's hostility toward Antonio Rodríguez was heightened because he tried to persuade them to make judicious and appropriate use of the sum of 11,000 pesos that Your Excellency granted them for the construction of a church, as you can see from an inquiry that they sent Your Excellency.
>
> The missions had not forgotten to include the accusation of possible irregularities in the management of the 11,000 pesos, since they understood perfectly that the construction of the town church would mean that the townsfolk would worship there, and not at the mission.

When he finished reading, Captain Urrutia realized the seriousness of the accusations contained in the document that he had promised to sign. He was not just worried about accusing the cabildo. What made him most concerned was the clear attack on the governor, who was his direct superior. But he was soothed by the protection promised by the missions.

III. Escape from Prison and Refuge in the San Antonio Mission

JULY 1802

Despite the news of the *sine die* suspension of the case without an order to release him, Antonio Rodríguez was relieved when he learned through his wife of the document signed by Captain Urrutia, and his spirits rose when he saw that not only was he protected by the missionaries, which he already knew, but also that he had the support of the captain of the presidio. This ray of hope did not last long, and as the days went by he was cast into a deep depression that lasted the entire month of August and brought his thoughts back again and again to his island of Gran Canaria.

Meanwhile, back at the cabildo, Francisco Arocha and Vicente Álvarez were secretly gathering testimonies from witnesses and working on their preparation of the evidence to back up their accusations against Antonio Rodríguez during the trial.

Once they had found all of the witnesses they could rely on, they convened them to make declarations on September 11, 1749. Antonio Rodríguez had been in prison since July 23.

The first witness to make a declaration was Juan Banul,[21] who stated that "Antonio Rodríguez went to Mexico, and during the legal proceedings of the cabildo against the missions he presented evidence against his companions in the cabildo." He also declared that "during a visit to the town, the governor of Texas, García Larios, attempted to remove Rodríguez from his position as councilor due to the aforementioned reasons, but this was prevented by the efforts of the missionary fathers." He clarified that he had heard this from others, and did not witness it himself.

The second witness, José el Canario,[22] married to Polonia Granados, expressed himself in similar terms, reiterating at the end of his declaration that it was publicly known that the missionaries supported Antonio Rodríguez Mederos.

The most important witness was Juan Curbelo, who answered all of the questions and affirmed that "as a result of Rodríguez's statements, the cabildo and the CONQUISTADORS, by whom I mean the Canarian colonists, lost their case against the missions."

The other witnesses—Juan Quiñones, Matías Montesdeoca, Miguel de Castro, and José Antonio Rodríguez—also answered affirmatively to all of the questions, while another witness, Marcelino Martínez, added to the fourth question that "Antonio Rodríguez asked for 100 pesos from the candidates for mayor, and returned them only when Carvajal had to go to Mexico and did not stand for election."

While the declaration of Marcelino Martínez was important, the most crucial testimony during the court proceedings was from José Leal, who had been the president of the cabildo and mayor on the day the accusation against Antonio Rodríguez was presented.

In his declaration he states that "the case against Antonio Rodríguez presented to Governor Pedro del Barrio by the cabildo was inspired solely by the hatred and ill will felt toward Antonio Rodríguez Mederos. While it is true that I initially made a declaration against him, today I must unburden my conscience as if I were before God, and I regret my words and declare that I signed them under duress." He went on to propose a number of witnesses who would declare in favor of Antonio Rodríguez.

The judge, Pedro del Barrio, accepted the declarations, including that of José Leal, but he considered the witness statements to be sufficient and felt that there was no need for the witnesses proposed by José Leal. On November 24, 1749, he issued a decree ordering the accused, Antonio Rodríguez Mederos, to defend himself in the proceedings and bring the trial to a lawful conclusion.

The accused man was notified of this decree in prison, where he had been in isolation for four months and one day, unable to participate in the evidence gathered against him. For this reason, he declared in a statement that "I will neither answer nor name an attorney because I wish to appeal to His Excellency the Viceroy." His unfamiliarity with legal terms due to his isolation led him to express himself in this way, although what he really wanted, as we shall see, was the recusal of the judge.

Later that day the judge decreed that "in the light of the most unreasonable response from the accused, Antonio Rodríguez, he is required to name an attorney and present evidence, since this is the process established by the king's justice for concluding the trial, after which the losing party may appeal to a higher authority."

In this unusual decree, the judge exhaustively explained the procedure to the accused party, who had apparently refused to participate in the proceedings, rather than declaring him to be in contempt of the court. In a fit of didactic passion, he continued, explaining that "if the accused does not appear in the proceedings, the case will not pass to a higher authority, and instead this judge will pronounce a sentence based on the available evidence, which can then be appealed. And the decision on whether the accused will be sent to the superior judge as a free man depends on the outcome of these proceedings." This decree was sent to Antonio Rodríguez on the same day.

Rodríguez's advisors, the missionaries and the captain of the presidio, hastily sent him a document through his wife; he signed the document and submitted to the proceedings, calling for what he should have requested in response to the first decree: the recusal of the instructing judge.

The document was presented before the court on October 5 and demanded "the recusal of the judge and governor and captain general of the province of Texas and New Philippines." It also complained of his imprisonment and lack of communication and offered to provide bail if necessary, although it noted that this should really be paid by his opponents due to the extreme poverty in which he now found himself, after months in custody.

In a desperate attempt to remove the governor from the case so that it would instead be judged by the viceroy of New Spain—who resided in Mexico City where the missionaries and military officers had more influence—the document proposed that "the proceedings should be closed and a copy sent to the viceroy, until such time as he names a replacement judge or transfers the proceedings to a new governor." This was a veiled threat to the judge, who could be replaced not only as judge but also as governor. The statement continues: "Only to this person named by the viceroy will I explain the reasoning behind my request for recusal and why I have not defended myself in these proceedings." It concludes, "In view of the foregoing, I assume that the judge will recuse himself, with the understanding that my actions are without enmity."

The document was admitted to the proceedings, but on October 9 Mederos was sent another decree which did not address the topic of recusal but demanded that he name an attorney to defend him. He replied, "I have not named an attorney out of ignorance of the charges against me and the identities of my accusers. Now that I have been informed, tomorrow, October 10, 1749, at ten o'clock I will send a written response in my defense."

This change of attitude is surprising. Leaving the important issue of judicial recusal unresolved, he decided to take part in the proceedings and to prepare his defense in just one day.

And indeed, on the promised day and time, he presented an extensive document. He began by styling himself as "Councilor and one of the founders of Villa de San Fernando in the province of Texas and the New Philippines," and set forth the following points:

1. "Notification was given this month of October in a dispatch sent to the court proceedings that I required bail in order to address the judicial recusal. However, not only was I incapable of paying the bail, but I was also unable to name an attorney, for the reasons that I will give to the viceroy or to the new governor." He continued, "I do not understand your partial

prohibition of my proposal, and I therefore reiterate my call for Your Honor to recuse yourself from this special case."

2. Once again he insists that the proceedings be closed and bail be granted "and with these actions demonstrate that Your Honor is not guided by partiality but rather by the cause of justice. In this way I may resort to this form of natural law, and may appeal before His Excellency's higher court, since the instance of appeal was instituted in order to prevent the brutal and irreparable oppression that will result from each and every one of the charges presented against me by my opponents."

By virtue of this appeal, "In order to save my honor, I hereby request that I remain in possession of all of the privileges invested in me as member of the cabildo; to the contrary, it will appear from this day on that the success of my opponents is guaranteed, since without wishing to mock the law, Your Honor has omitted ALL EVIDENCE IN MY FAVOR."

If there had been any doubt that the missionaries were writing the documents for the defense of Antonio Rodríguez Mederos, this text dispelled it. It is inconceivable that an illiterate colonist would make this argument based on natural law, with the structure, framework, and legal understanding that this document demonstrates.

It was admitted to the proceedings. It would be logical to assume that its reasoning would finally resolve the issue of the recusal. But once again the judge showed his partiality when, five days later, he admitted a document from the cabildo clearly showing that they knew of Rodríguez's statement. It declares that:

1. All of the accusations have been proven by the testimonial evidence provided by the cabildo.

2. The presence of Rodríguez, even imprisoned, disturbs the community and the cabildo with his lies and dirty tricks.

3. The judge should decree his exile from the town in order to restore the peace.
4. Your Honor decree his exile before you depart on your royal visit to the presidio of La Bahía del Espíritu Santo, since we fear that he will flee to the missions.

In light of the proceedings thus far, and considering the rebellious attitude shown by Antonio Rodríguez, who was refusing to participate despite the judge's warnings and detailed explanation of the legal process, on October 15, 1749, the judge issued a ruling which admitted the prior text from the cabildo to the records. He also announced that "following witness ratification, the court records will be brought forth and a sentence will be issued. The parties will be notified of the ruling in person or through their attorney. The ruling may be appealed before the viceroy, who will be sent a copy of the court records, and an additional copy will be stored in this courthouse for safekeeping."

This latest decree shows us how careful the judge was being in leaving a copy of the records, since he was well aware of the huge influence of the true enemies of the cabildo, for whom it would be easy to make the records disappear during the journey to Mexico for an appeal to the viceroy.

To finalize the proceedings, the judge ordered the ratification of the witnesses. This was carried out between October 16 and 21, after which the records were sealed for sentencing.

Meanwhile Antonio Rodríguez remained under arrest. His situation had improved, since he had been moved from the Royal Houses to his own home and was guarded by a corporal and four soldiers. He had been in prison since July 22 and, faced with the imminent ruling of the court case without the judge's recusal or the admission of his appeal to the viceroy without a prior judgment, he decided to escape from his house, just as the cabildo had warned. The judge had clearly demonstrated that he was in favor of the cabildo, and so the prisoner sent Captain Urrutia to the missionaries with a desperate plea.

"I am sent by Councilor Antonio Rodríguez," the captain said to Father Benito, "to ask if you will give him refuge in the mission, and protect him with your ecclesiastical immunity. He feels that this is the only way to defend himself in these proceedings, and that by living in the mission you will be better able to counsel him in writing documents for his defense."

"Captain, you may tell Rodríguez that not only can he count on our ecclesiastical protection but also, more importantly, that we will continue to defend him in the proceedings, although we cannot do so officially. The documents we prepare will be signed in his name, until we can find him a good attorney, an honest and trustworthy man, who can sign the documents that we draft."

Even before Urrutia returned with the missionaries' answer, Antonio Rodríguez was certain that they would give him refuge in the San Antonio mission, and he began to plan his escape. He needed to wait until his good friend, Corporal Juan de los Reyes, was on guard duty at his house.

Juan de los Reyes understood the circumstances of the personal battle waged by Arocha and Álvarez, rather than the cabildo, against Rodríguez, and he also recognized the good work Rodríguez had done for the town during his time as councilor. He agreed to let him escape on the condition that he himself accompany him and receive protection from the missionaries.

The escape was planned for November 4, 1749, at five o'clock in the morning, while Juan de los Reyes's soldiers slept deeply after a large supper prepared by Antonio Rodríguez's wife, having been abundantly supplied with wine.

At a signal from Juan Reyes, the two men mounted horses that had been prepared earlier, and fled to the San Antonio mission.

The next morning the news spread like wildfire through the small town. Francisco de Arocha and Vicente Álvarez were furious with the governor, since they had warned him of exactly this risk in the last document they presented to the court.

The arrival of Rodríguez and his companion at six o'clock in the morning caused quite a stir at the mission. The friars were getting ready to oversee the work of their Indian laborers in the fields. Only the father superior, Friar Benito Fernández, showed no surprise, since he had known that the escape would happen that day and had been watching for their arrival from the bell tower of the mission since three o'clock in the morning. The two men embraced and were embraced in turn by the friars. Antonio Rodríguez swiftly passed into the father superior's office, where they spent the next three hours calmly discussing the situation and drawing up a plan for his defense in the proceedings to come.

"We should await further developments," said Friar Benito. "There is no doubt that your escape will cause uproar, and we should wait for the reactions of the cabildo on the one hand, and the governor and judge on the other. If he was in favor of the cabildo before, he will now be even more strongly on their side. In this case, the viceroy would surely be more in favor of the judge and the cabildo, since your escape will presuppose an admission of guilt. For the moment, we should send a letter to our superior in Mexico so that he can communicate this development to the viceroy before the news reaches him through other means. In your defense, we must claim the unjust persecution by both the cabildo and the governor and judge himself. At the same time, we will consider how best to prepare your defense, and once we see how they react, we will work from there."

Meanwhile Arocha and Álvarez were informed of the escape at seven o'clock in the morning, when fresh soldiers arrived to relieve the guards. They called an emergency meeting of the cabildo and agreed to visit the governor in his house immediately.

Pedro del Barrio, visibly worried by the news that had already reached him before the members of the cabildo arrived, received them at once.

"We warned you, Don Pedro, in our last motion presented to the court, that if Antonio Rodríguez were not carefully watched, he would flee to his protectors, the missionaries, and this is exactly what happened last night!" began Francisco de Arocha.

But the governor had already thought of a graceful solution to this unpleasant situation. "Of course I knew this, and it is just what I was hoping for," he said. "By protecting him, the missions have directly challenged the judicial authority, and as I am at this time both judge and governor of the province, they have challenged the viceroy himself. Their request that I should recuse myself as judge and appeal to the viceroy will now never succeed, since he would logically support his representative, myself, the judge of this case and the governor of this territory. Rodríguez's flight and the missions' protection makes them both guilty. But to do things correctly, gentlemen, first we should make an official record of Antonio Rodríguez's escape and the ecclesiastical protection that the missionaries have granted him."

None of the councilors had expected such a logical solution from the governor. They immediately filed a report in the court records which stated: "On November 4, at five o'clock in the morning, Antonio Rodríguez Mederos tricked his guards and escaped from his house, where he was being held under arrest by order of the governor and judge of these proceedings." This report was signed by the judge himself.

They then went to Antonio Rodríguez's house and opened another report, which read that "when questioned, one of the guards stated that Antonio Rodríguez escaped during the night. When asked who the head of the guards was at that time, he replied that it was Corporal Juan de los Reyes, who had also fled with the prisoner, and that both men had taken refuge in the San Antonio mission. In light of this, the guard on the house was lifted." Based on the contents of these reports, the cabildo, as the accusing party, was asked if they wished to appeal to the viceroy, to which they replied, "We cannot appear before the viceroy as we have already spent too much money on court cases since our constitution. We therefore submit to the sovereignty of His Excellency Pedro del Barrio to determine the great damage that Antonio Rodríguez Mederos has caused to this town."

On August 31, 1750, two copies of the proceedings, totaling twenty-four pages, were signed and certified; one was sent to the royal presidio of Los Adaes, where the judge, Pedro del Barrio, was in residence, while the other was delivered to the cabildo, in the name of José Padrón, town magistrate. This was nine months after Antonio Rodríguez Mederos had escaped.

IV. Illegal Intervention in the Proceedings by the Prosecutor of the Hearing in Mexico

AUGUST 1802

From the day after Rodríguez's escape to the San Antonio mission, he met regularly with the father superior of the missions to plan his defense together.

One morning early in December 1749, Friar Benito called Antonio Rodríguez into his office and said, "I have been thinking that it would be very useful to have a prosecutor intercede in the case, by providing a report in your favor. I have listened carefully to you during the last month you have spent under our protection in the mission, and I have drafted a report that could be presented in the proceedings by a prosecutor."

Antonio Rodríguez took the report, and after reading it slowly, said, "Father, I think this is a magnificent idea, but unfortunately I do not know any prosecutors. And certainly none that I could ask to present a report that you have written."

"Do not worry about that; our order has already spoken to a prosecutor who would be willing to intercede by signing the document that we send him. He understands the grave injustice that has been committed against you and against our order over the years since the cabildo was formed."

So it was that on January 5, 1750, the prosecutor Antonio de Andreu submitted a report to the proceedings, even though the court records had been closed for sentencing since October 21, 1749. It was presented as a report for the viceroy and did not take into account any of the evidence previously presented during the trial. It began by falsely stating the offices held by Rodríguez, calling him councilor of the province of Texas, rather than of the San Fernando cabildo. It also discussed the validity of the ten witness statements against the accused, and declared: "Firstly, Antonio Rodríguez Mederos requests that his personal rights be restored, since he has been deprived of his office and honors." This was based on an interview with Captain Toribio de Urrutia, who said that "the aforementioned councilor, Antonio Rodríguez Mederos, was shackled and imprisoned in the royal houses, in a room with no roof and guarded by eight soldiers who were expressly ordered to prevent him from speaking to anyone."

The second section, based on half-truths provided by the captain of the presidio and the missionary fathers, attacks the governor, alleging that "after five years of peace and harmony, since the arrival of Governor Pedro del Barrio, who was also the judge in these proceedings, there have been endless lawsuits." It continues, "Since his arrival he has done nothing but stir up trouble and commit injustices against the missionary fathers, the captain of the presidio and the people." Among the most serious accusations against Governor del Barrio is the allegation that "he charges a fee of eleven pesos to register a brand for horses, cattle, or mules, six pesos to authenticate them, six pesos to confirm registration fees and eleven pesos for those who are not registered. All of this money is shared with the solicitor."

After accusing the governor of fraudulent business practices and allowing gambling, it alleges that, "according to our information, the governor has forced both soldiers and officers to appeal to the viceroy on his behalf in order to keep their positions."[23] It then recounts how the councilor Antonio Rodríguez Mederos had been imprisoned and removed from office for declaring himself in favor of the father superior of the missions in a petition that also involved the governor, thus making it impossible "to reach a solution."[24]

Another section of the document insisted that Antonio was also persecuted by the cabildo for "telling the other members of the cabildo that the 11,000 pesos granted by the viceroy for the church were spent on other matters."

It ended by emphasizing to the viceroy that there were insufficient motives for Antonio Rodríguez's removal and humiliation, and therefore requested that "the solicitor and secretary of the cabildo, Francisco de Arocha, be expelled from the town for sedition and disturbance of the peace." It also requested that "Antonio Rodríguez be freed at once and cleared of all costs, that he be restored to his office as member of the cabildo, and that he be granted the right, if he sees fit, to sue for damages."

This was a petition that had nothing to do with the proceedings thus far, and the enormous influence of the missionaries behind the prosecutor can be clearly seen in the request that "the governor be required to protect the missions, and in particular the missionary fathers, against the constant attacks by infidels and apostates, and that the two disputes be resolved between the governor and the captain of the presidio, who has always been of such great help to the colonists and the missions."

In light of this document, which falsified events and ignored all of the evidence presented by the cabildo during the trial, the case was ruled in favor of Antonio Rodríguez based exclusively on the reports submitted by the missionaries and the captain of the presidio. The military judge, the marquis of Altamira, signed a missive which interfered with the proceedings by ordering that "the captain of the royal presidio of Sacramento, José de Ecay y Musquis, recommended as judge in the proceedings concerning the new missions of San Javier, must free Antonio Rodríguez Mederos and restore him to his position as councilor of Villa de San Fernando following the recommendations of the prosecutor to His Excellency the viceroy."

Not satisfied with this, the missionaries appealed to the military judge, the marquis of Altamira, to send letters to the governor to the effect that "he should work more closely with the captain of the presidio, Tomás de Urrutia" and that "Ecay y Musquis, the judge appointed to the proceedings, should investigate the claims made by the prosecutor against the governor, Pedro del Barrio, after concluding the case of the cabildo and Antonio Rodríguez." This letter was dated January 30, 1750.

Faced with this arbitrary judgment, the cabildo reacted by granting broad powers to another Canary Islander, José Curbelo,[25] which allowed him to represent the cabildo "wherever necessary and before any court, to defend the rights of the cabildo established by the Canary Islanders who founded Villa de San Fernando in the province of Texas or New Philippines."

Curbelo traveled to Mexico City, and named Francisco Abaurrea Ataiza, a resident of the city, as representative of the cabildo. Abaurrea immediately appeared before the court in Mexico "to declare that in this government there are legal proceedings against Antonio Rodríguez Mederos for corruption, for which he was suspended from his office as town councilor. As authorized representative in this case, I hereby request the court files." This appearance occurred on November 6, 1750.

CHAPTER 6

Parallel Maneuvers by the Cabildo and the Missions outside the Proceedings

I. The Cabildo's Actions

OCTOBER 1802

Francisco de Arocha had received news from Mexico City through his man there, the cabildo's Basque representative, Francisco Abaurrea Ataiza, to the effect that the rumors in the viceroy's palace led him to predict that the sentence would be in favor of Antonio Rodríguez. This would imply his immediate reincorporation into the cabildo of San Antonio as councilor. On hearing this news, Francisco de Arocha immediately called the cabildo together for an emergency session to name new magistrates. This way, if the judge supported Rodríguez, it would be impossible for him to take up his position as it would already be filled.

Arocha read the minutes from the previous meeting and then, as requested by the president of the cabildo, Juan José Padrón,[26] he addressed the following words to his colleagues: "Gentlemen, we have called this emergency session because the town cannot continue without filling the office of magistrate. This position has been vacant since July 22, 1749, due to the imprisonment of the previous incumbent, Antonio Rodríguez Mederos, as decreed by the lawsuit that this cabildo filed against him. I believe that this vacancy should be filled as soon as possible, in order for the cabildo to function properly."

The motion was proposed by the councilor Antonio de los Santos, as noted in the minutes, "because the previous councilor to hold this office fled from justice, and there was no competent person to take his place."

José Padrón and Ignacio Lorenzo de Armas were nominated as first magistrates. José Antonio Rodríguez and José Pérez Casanova were nominated as second magistrates. José Padrón was unanimously elected first magistrate, and José Antonio Rodríguez was chosen as second magistrate. According to the minutes, "both men were sworn in by shaking hands with the councilor, who gave them their official seals."

As soon as they had been sworn in, they sent a certified copy by special post to Joaquín de Osoria y Vostera, captain of the presidio of Espiritu Santo and deputy general of the Province of Texas, so that he could approve the election. The election was confirmed by the captain on November 28, 1750.

II. Actions Taken by the Soldiers and Priests

As we have seen, according to the prosecutor's account, the disagreements between the missions and the governor arose "because Antonio Rodríguez was persecuted and imprisoned for testifying in favor of the father superior of the missionaries on a matter in which the governor was an interested party who instigated his troops to write to the viceroy asking that he remain in office."

All of this began long before the report from the prosecutor; more specifically it arose from a document written on September 1, 1749, which reveals the true nature of the affair.

In this document, the officers of the presidio of San Antonio de Béjar—Lieutenants Juan Galván Álvarez and Manuel Carvajal, Sergeant Juan Cortinas, and Corporals José Miguel Sosa and Francisco Flores Carvajal—state that "the reverend fathers of the missions, and in particular Father Mariano de los Dolores, defamed the good conduct and talents of the Governor, since they were enraged after he refused to bestow water and lands to the San Javier mission. For this reason, and for all of the merits of his character, we hereby request that Antonio del Barrio retain his post as governor."[27]

A month later another request was sent, this one from the presidio of los Adaes. As a consequence, on November 6 the marquis of Altamira sent a letter to the viceroy, advising him that he had received the referenced texts "which demonstrate that a clear difference exists between the governor of the province of Texas, the captain of the San Antonio presidio, and the apostolic father of the College of the Cross of Onesetano with respect to the new missions that they wish to establish along the San Javier River."

As we have seen, the differences between the democratically elected cabildo of Villa de San Antonio and the captain of the presidio began the moment the cabildo was formed. The conflict was continuous and only intensified over the years. During the proceedings initiated by the cabildo against the councilor Antonio Rodríguez, at the instructions of the missionaries, Captain Toribio de Urrutia stood against the cabildo, and without even being part of the proceedings he sent a document opposing the cabildo and in favor of Antonio Rodríguez Mederos. Without measuring his words, and pressured by the skillful missionaries, he used very harsh terms to accuse his immediate superior, the general and instructing judge of the proceedings, Pedro del Barrio. The governor in question made very good use of this document against him, and at the instigation of Francisco de Arocha, Del Barrio informed Captain Urrutia in the dispatches of November 3, 1750 that he had been removed from his office as chief justice of Villa de San Fernando de Béjar. Pedro del Barrio was simply complying with the agreement signed by the cabildo on January 1, 1750, which stated that Villa de San Fernando would choose their own high magistrates.

Captain Urrutia immediately wrote a letter to the cabildo of Villa de San Antonio, insisting that he would remain in the office of chief justice of the cabildo of San Fernando, which he was occupying in the absence of Antonio Rodríguez. He stressed that he only held the office temporarily until Rodríguez returned to his post since, according to his sources, the sentence would be made in his favor.

The cabildo received Captain Urrutia's letter and notified him in turn that his removal was not, in fact, new, and that they had not informed him earlier in order to avoid precisely this situation. In removing him from office they were merely complying with a dispatch from the viceroy of New Spain, Pedro Cebrián y Augustín, Count of Fuenclara, signed in Mexico City on February 13, 1744, which read: "The captain of San Antonio de Béjar, Toribio de Urrutia, is hereby notified that, on pain of removal from his office and severe punishment, he is to refrain from harassing or disturbing the poor Canarian colonists, either in person or in writing. He is to respect their civilian offices and positions, and as a soldier he must respect the exceptions and privileges that have been granted to them."

Apart from expressly recognizing the privileges given to the Canary Islanders, this letter is important because it makes a perfect distinction between the civil administration of the cabildo and the military administration which only had authority over the soldiers in the fort. It continued: "The captain shall not interfere with the administration of justice among these colonists and other residents of Villa de San Fernando, since this responsibility has already been entrusted to the magistrates and the other figures empowered by the cabildo. Nor shall said captain exceed his authority by exercising jurisdiction over a cause other than those of his officers and soldiers of the Indians of the missions."

If there was any room left for doubt, the cabildo extinguished it in the final paragraph of their answer to Pedro de Urrutia, "In this way we will continue to be supported by this higher order, invested with the jurisdiction of higher justice, as stated in a superior order."

This official letter was dated September 17, 1750. The captain received a letter with the same date from the viceroy, sent at the instigation of the governor and the attorney for the Canary Islanders in

Mexico City, Mr. Abaurrea, ordering him to cooperate more with Del Barrio.

Captain Urrutia, having lost the office of chief justice of Villa de San Antonio, saw from this letter that he was seriously endangering his post as captain of the presidio, and decided to answer the viceroy in the most respectful terms in order to preserve his position. “As I am humbly devoted to executing the duties of my office,” he wrote, “it is my only desire, and also my unquestioning obedience to Your Excellency’s order, to continue cooperating harmoniously with the governor as I have been instructed, without offering the slightest opposition or disobeying Your Excellency’s higher mandate.”

CHAPTER 7

The Controversial Reinstatement of Antonio Rodríguez Mederos in the Cabildo

I. The Cabildo Does Not Accept the Reinstatement of the Councilor

OCTOBER 1802

While the different parties continued to take action outside the proceedings, at the viceregal palace in Mexico City a warrant was signed on June 17, 1750, by Joaquín de Ecay y Musquis, lieutenant of the presidio of Santa Rosa and commander of the detachment stationed on the Santander River. This document notified the cabildo of Villa de San Fernando that, by an order of Viceroy Francisco de Güemes y Horcasitas dated November 3 of that year, they were commanded "to free Antonio Rodríguez Mederos, reinstate him to his office, and restore his honor. As holder of the appropriate authority and the only person in a position to solve the issue with exact justice, I hereby request this of the cabildo in the name of the viceroy. Additionally, I require that the records of the proceedings in the town archives be delivered to me."

The importance of this intervention by the viceroy's envoy, and his delivery of these demands for reinstatement, show us the degree of influence that the missions held with the viceroy in Mexico City. While the cabildo's meddling had only managed to draw attention to the captain of the presidio and bring about his removal as chief justice of the town and a reprimand from the governor, the missionaries' actions caused Antonio Rodríguez to win the lawsuit, without even presenting evidence during the proceedings.

These demands were presented to the cabildo on June 18. The cabildo's response made no mention, however, of the reinstatement of Antonio Rodríguez; it noted that there were two demands and therefore decided to answer the first before proceeding to the second. In their answer to the warrant, the cabildo said that "although it was agreed during the proceedings that a certified copy of the court records would be sent to the town archives, after seven months this has still not arrived, and we hereby request that the relevant authorities be ordered to send it."

Surprised by the cabildo's answer, Ecay sent a message to the presidio of Los Adaes, who replied that "we could not send the records because we did not receive them."

Nevertheless Ecay decided to enforce his orders at least partially and instructed Antonio Rodríguez to leave his sanctuary in the San Antonio mission as a free man. He also ordered that Rodríguez be returned to his office and his honor with no impairment and stressed that he could sue for compensation for any damages and injuries by filing charges with the new judge, Ecay y Musquis. At the same time he required the cabildo "to hold a regular meeting on June 19."

On receiving this notification from Judge Ecay, and before the next meeting of the cabildo, Arocha and Álvarez decided it would be completely illegal to reinstate Antonio Rodríguez as councilor without a prior decree from the viceroy on the defendant's release. The author of the warrant was demanding his freedom and yet said nothing more than that he should be returned to his office, etc. The two friends therefore agreed on the following reply to Judge Ecay: "If this decree to reinstate Antonio Rodríguez Mederos as councilor is the only decree in existence, then we cannot possibly permit him to return to his office until His Excellency the Viceroy of New Spain has determined the question of his release. The legal case against him remains open, and the instructing judge decreed his imprisonment.

This is an attempt to reinstate the accused party with no prior ruling on the proceedings in question."

With this response, the cabildo of San Antonio de Béjar, the only one in the entire history of North America composed entirely of Canary Islanders, sets an example in matters of law and justice. First of all, a sentence must be passed on the open case. Before Rodríguez could be returned to his position on the cabildo, the question of his guilt or innocence with respect to the charges against him, and his subsequent release, must be determined. This legal subtlety expressed by the cabildo only becomes clear after a careful reading of the warrant. It only states that "he be reinstated to his office and restored to his honor." But before doing so the cabildo quite rightly reminded the judge that the accused man had been imprisoned and had escaped, and that he could not be reinstated without some kind of ruling on the charges and a sentencing. If he so desired, let him appeal to the King, and let the case be decided by that appeal, but not by a judicial order which circumvented the proceedings before a sentence had even been passed.

This was the cabildo's first response to the warrant sent by the viceroy. After studying the matter in more depth over the following days, however, on August 25 the cabildo decided to make an additional statement of opposition to the proposed course of action, since it had bypassed all of the established procedural rules in the following three ways:

1. Because the defendant had not appeared during the legal proceedings, either in person or represented by an attorney.

2. He escaped from house arrest, which he had been granted in deference to his office as councilor, and took refuge in the San Antonio mission, where he was under ecclesiastical protection.

3. He sent a list of accusations against the cabildo directly to the viceroy, a complete violation of the process, since an appeal to

> the viceroy should only occur after a sentence has been issued in the first instance by the judge who is hearing the case.

The cabildo concluded by requesting a certified copy of the viceroy's orders to add to the court records.

Ecay, exasperated by the cabildo's procrastination, sent a decree on August 26 ordering them "to deliver the court records as instructed within four hours, since the sixty-six-day delay in complying with the warrant is on account of this cabildo."

Faced with this assertive demand, the cabildo immediately decided to submit the records which were, after all, in their possession.

The delivery of the records, together with the cabildo's firm refusal to reinstate Rodríguez to his office on solid legal grounds, caused Ecay to adopt a more balanced position. He accepted that the warrant had been partially complied with after the cabildo sent the records but did not reinstate Antonio Rodríguez, "since he took refuge in the San Antonio mission." He then ordered that, without violating ecclesiastical immunity, the accused be notified that he was required to name an attorney to represent him.

The notification was sent the same day, August 27, and Rodríguez appointed as his attorney, Cristóbal de los Santos Coy,[28] who immediately accepted and was granted "fourteen nights to formulate a statement for the defense."

II. A New Twist in the Proceedings, Counterarguments, and Sentencing

NOVEMBER 1802

Cristóbal de los Santos Coy drafted his counterargument within the established time limit. If there remained any doubt that the defense was being written by the missionaries, this document provided overwhelming evidence, since it is absolutely inconceivable that a simple schoolteacher could have prepared a document with such expert structure and deep understanding of law.

The contents were as follows:

> I, Cristóbal de los Santos Coy, resident of this town and attorney for the defense in this case, having received a copy of the court records, hereby affirm in the defense of the accused party:
>
> That my client, Antonio Rodríguez Mederos, founder of this town and councilor since its founding, was ousted from his office for no apparent reason, and was notified that he should cease to attend the sessions of the cabildo. A month and a half after he had been removed from office, when the governor of the Province of Texas discovered that my client had appealed to the viceroy against this injustice, he instigated charges against the defendant. This was easily accomplished, since his compatriots, Vicente Álvarez Travieso, chief bookkeeper of the cabildo, and Francisco José Arocha, solicitor and secretary, sworn enemies of Rodríguez, obtained sufficient votes in the cabildo for charges to be filed against my client. These charges were then rebutted by the first mayor of the town, José Leal, who confessed that, "the list of charges was not drafted by the cabildo, but only signed by its members, including myself. When I realized that the charges were fictitious and that I was party to a crime, I declared the truth."
>
> The wrongful charges against my client were made falsely in the name of all of the residents, because the cabildo has never forgiven him for testifying against them before the viceroy in Mexico City during an unjust case brought against the reverend missionary fathers. Ever since the cabildo lost that case, they have called my client a traitor and have used every possible means to drive him from the town.
>
> In his role as councilor of the cabildo, on numerous occasions Antonio Rodríguez requested an audit of the 11,000 pesos that your

lordship the viceroy sent for the construction of the town church. Travieso received these funds on behalf of the cabildo, and they have never been clearly accounted for, hence the repeated requests for closer scrutiny. Furthermore, Antonio Rodríguez stated on record that he had proof that Álvarez Travieso had disposed of large sums of this money before construction on the church had even begun, and for this reason the viceroy called for a judicial audit of this town. My client explained all of this in writing to the governor, who did not admit it as evidence, even though he had admitted the alleged charges presented by the cabildo against my client. This clearly demonstrates the alliance between the governor and his compatriot Álvarez Travieso against my client.

Based on these unfounded charges, the instructing judge of the case, coincidentally the very same governor, Antonio del Barrio, decreed violent imprisonment against my client, in order to condemn him as swiftly as possible. The foregoing circumstances are all against divine and natural law. If the governor decreed violent imprisonment for Rodríguez, and the reverend fathers protected him, then why not decree the imprisonment of the reverend fathers as well?

The testimonial evidence presented by the cabildo is also invalid, because although all of the witnesses had certainly heard of the charges against the defendant, none of them had actually witnessed anything.

With respect to the ninth accusation, which alleges that Rodríguez disgraced Canary Islanders everywhere during his trips to Mexico and as a result of the debts he has incurred, it is important to distinguish between incurring a debt and incurring a bad debt. The mere fact that a person owes money does not mean that he is an idle vagabond, since this would imply that he was not working to repay his debts.

At this time my client does not owe more than 500 pesos, since he has already paid 500 for nine loans through his work over a year and two months. He is clearly neither idle nor a vagabond, because through his careful management in the cabildo, forty houses have been built in this town. The stones for these houses were carried by his men and his carts, and Rodríguez himself participated in the construction, often moving soil alongside the other workers, with no regard for his dignity as councilor.

He worked in the same way on the construction of the church, and also on the cultivation of sugarcane and corn. It is true that Governor Francisco de Larios attempted to oust my client as councilor during his visit to the town, but he did not do so after a warning from the reverend fathers before the court. These are righteous, God-fearing, religious men, who illuminate our vanities, our ignorance and our errors, and have no need for aid or arguments to convince all people that they carry the weight of reason. Nothing has been proven against my client thus far, and it is absolutely inconceivable that his accusers, the cabildo and the Canarian community they claim to represent, had sent a report directly to the viceroy regarding Antonio Rodríguez's reputation, life, and habits, and proposing him as captain of the new presidio that is to be established in San Javier. Álvarez Travieso presented this document personally in Mexico, and claimed that if Rodríguez was named captain of San Javier, the Canarian colonists would have a market for the sale of their corn, vegetables, cheeses, and other goods.

They have refused to allow my client to appeal to His Excellency the Viceroy, alleging that as it was not an appeal of a sentence or a judicial ruling, it was therefore out of order. They demanded that he name an attorney to represent him in court so that the case could proceed, or a defense attorney would be officially named for him, without taking into account that his appeal was made solely to remedy the errors committed in the court by the judge's personal involvement in the case. Because of the personal enmity with which the judge-governor proceeded against my client, he could not hope to receive a fair hearing. My client therefore neither appeared in court, nor named a defense attorney, and although he understood that an appeal is usually against a previous ruling, he decided to appeal to the viceroy to protect himself from an unjust sentence.

With respect to the cabildo's arguments against my client which state that: "Antonio Rodríguez unsettled the Canarian community by warning that the cabildo had voided a dispatch in which His Excellency the Viceroy ordered that the lands and water belonging to the Canary Islanders were to be shared with the other residents."[29] This is a baseless accusation, since it occurred when my client was held in solitary confinement in prison. The fact of the matter is that when the other residents received no reply from the viceroy to their initial petition, they reiterated their request, asking once again when the lands and water would be distributed between them. When the cabildo of Villa San Antonio, composed entirely of Canary Islanders, learned about this second petition, they ordered the immediate arrest of the attorney representing the other residents. When the viceroy learned of this, he ordered that land and water be distributed among the other residents, but this still has not occurred due to opposition from the cabildo, thus causing great harm to these poor people. As time passed and this was not implemented, the tension between the Canarian community and the cabildo on one side, and the other residents on the other, grew and intensified, since the Canary Islanders not only had land and water, but also ruled the entire town through the cabildo in accordance with their own interests. The other residents therefore petitioned the viceroy once again, not only for land and water, but also for the right to participate in the cabildo and the governing of the town.

The statement ends by requesting:

1. That the demands laid out in this document be granted, namely, that Antonio Rodríguez be reinstated to his office as

councilor, since none of the charges against him have been proved.

2. His Excellency's orders should have been carried out, but were not because Francisco de Arocha and Vicente Álvarez Travieso were afraid to reinstate him in the cabildo lest my client discover their wrongdoing and abuse. For this reason they have refused to answer Your Excellency's warrant to reinstate him. My client appointed me to defend him in this case because of my confidence that the current judge will be removed from the case. For this reason, I hereby request that Your Excellency grant a writ of inhibition against the judge, as the law sets forth in such cases.

   Such a writ is a legal recourse of natural law used in courts to prevent an interested party from taking sides for unjust revenge. If this inhibition is accepted, then my client is willing to submit to the sentence dictated by the chief justice of the town, Captain Urrutia, who was unfairly removed from office by the cabildo.

   I apologize in advance for any legal or formal errors in this document; this is because I am not an attorney by training, and there are no attorneys throughout the region.

   On this day, October 3, 1750, the court documents are hereby submitted to the higher jurisdiction of His Excellency the Viceroy of New Spain, Francisco de Güemes y Horcasitas.

The viceroy immediately dictated an order directing Judge Ecay y Musquis to set bail for Antonio Rodríguez so that he may be freed. On October 12 Antonio Rodríguez presented a document which explained that "I am unable to pay bail as I have been persecuted for the last two years and have been forced to take refuge in the San Antonio mission, but I can name residents of the town who will act as my guarantors." The viceroy accepted, and on October 30 the following people appeared in the proceedings:

Toribio de Urrutia, captain of the royal San Antonio presidio

Diego Román, other resident

José Leal, Canary Islander

Martín Flores, other resident

Manuel Niz, town councilor and father-in-law of Antonio Rodríguez Mederos

Juan José Montesdeoca, other resident

Matías de Zerola, other resident

Juan Leal, Canary Islander

Juan Paulín Márquez, other resident

Ignacio Zepeda, other resident

Domingo Flores, other resident

Francisco de Estrada, other resident

The men declared for the record that they "are directly, jointly and individually responsible for the personal safety of Antonio Rodríguez Mederos, for whom they offer themselves as security in the manner set forth by law in the paragraph addressing types of guarantees, and that they agree to renounce any and all laws which might be in their favor."

On receiving the presentation of bail by such wealthy townspeople, Ecay y Musquis decreed the release of Antonio Rodríguez Mederos on October 30, 1750.

The cabildo, in turn, refused to receive the notification of the defendant's freedom until November 16, and four days later they finally sent the court records to Mexico.

The viceroy, Güemes y Horcasitas, eventually ruled in favor of Antonio Rodríguez due to the lack of evidence and decreed his reinstatement and reincorporation to his office as councilor of Villa de San Fernando de Béjar.

And so ended the cruelest persecution between Canary Islanders that has ever been seen in the history of North America.

CHAPTER 8

Consequences of the Lawsuit Pursued by the Cabildo of Villa de San Fernando de Béjar against Its Councilor, Antonio Rodríguez Mederos

I. The Removal of Judge Ecay y Musquis

NOVEMBER 1802

Petition by the Cabildo of Villa de San Fernando to the Viceroy of New Spain

In a meeting of the cabildo on October 22, 1750, a request was drawn up for the removal of Ecay y Musquis, the new judge named by the viceroy on the case of the cabildo versus Antonio Rodríguez. They sustained that "the aforementioned judge overstepped his authority by sending a report to the viceroy which included all manner of lies, and thus led to the release of Antonio Rodríguez Mederos. This cabildo believes that the judge violated His Excellency's mandate by making biased claims, which is evidence that he did not comply with His Excellency's orders due to UNDUE INFLUENCE and special interests." This decision was made by the councilors José Padrón, Vicente Álvarez Travieso, Martín Lorenzo, and José Arocha, solicitor and secretary of the cabildo. The cabildo achieved absolutely nothing with this complaint, since Ecay y Musquis continued in his post and Antonio Rodríguez continued as town councilor.

The Resignation of the Solicitor and Secretary of the Cabildo, Francisco de Arocha

Francisco de Arocha continued as solicitor for the town and secretary of the cabildo for some six more years, until in a truly moving letter, reflecting his depression and perhaps his remorse for having dragged his family to such a far off land, he wrote:

> To the illustrious cabildo, source of justice and law in Villa de San Fernando. I, Francisco de Arocha, resident and solicitor of this town, hereby present the following appeal to the cabildo in the manner established by law. I have served His Majesty THE KING, our Lord, and the people of this town for twenty-six years in the position of official solicitor, which has permitted me to support my large family. However, my mind is tormented: my duties weigh heavily upon me and I feel the close approach of death. For this reason, I have on several occasions presented my resignation, which thus far has not been accepted. As a Christian, my only desire is to die at peace and with a calm mind, and I therefore have no choice but to beg you, in the name of justice, to allow me to freely and honorably resign from this office of solicitor and secretary of the cabildo. I resign in the form and manner that the law requires, so that another may take my place, or so that the cabildo may petition the governor to request that the viceroy name an honorable person to occupy the position.
>
> In the few hours of life that remain to me, my only desire is to be free of this office, and in this way to obtain some peace of mind. As my request is entirely in agreement with the principles of Christianity, equality and justice, I therefore appeal to your sensitivity and compassion. I beseech you to inform me of your decision immediately upon receiving this document.
>
> San Fernando de Béjar, January 13, 1757

In the face of this dramatic petition, his resignation was accepted immediately.

CHAPTER 9

Other Interesting Matters in the History of the Canary Islanders in Texas

I. Lawsuit Filed by Francisco José de Arocha and José Curbelo against the Governor of the Province of Texas and New Philippines, Francisco de Larios

These proceedings really began with an accusation from the captain of the presidio of Our Lady of Pilar and Los Adaes, on June 4, 1746. As was habitual in those days, two Canary Islanders appeared as co-litigants: one of them, of course, was Francisco de Arocha, the solicitor and secretary of the cabildo of Villa de San Fernando, and the other was the councilor José Curbelo. Of the many allegations contained in the accusation, most of which were military in nature and have no bearing on our history of the Canary Islanders, I will mention only those few that did directly affect the Canarian colonists, and which led to their appearance in the lawsuit.

The third charge reads:

> In violation of the ordinances, he employs soldiers to farm the land and care for cattle and mules, and sends them long distances to sell goods exclusively for his personal benefit.
>
> He also uses families brought from the Canary Islands and relatives of members of the presidio for his personal service without paying them. He makes money from the products grown by the soldiers, selling them to the few towns in the area and to other military detachments so that the poor Canarian families cannot compete with their own products, since the governor's prices are always lower as he has free labor and uses military carts for transport.

> He did not purchase the Canary Islanders' harvests, and as a result when he ordered goods with no prior arrangement, there was not enough, since they had only produced enough for their own use. Under the pretext that he needed food for his troops, he imported it from other places, buying the harvests of the French colonists from villages along the border with Louisiana. The Canarian families were thus forced to leave the area since the soldiers could not buy their harvests: only the governor had money to purchase goods and therefore dominated the markets. So in the end, these Canarian families were unable to settle here, to found cities capable of defending themselves, to gain the respect of the neighboring French colonies and savage tribes, and to aid our military in containing them.

In reply to this document, the military judge, the marquis of Altamira, wrote a memorandum on July 23, 1746, recommending that "in view of the impossibility of investigating the facts of the matter, the merchant Juan Antonio Bustillos shall prepare a detailed and precise report. He is the person best able to do so, since he was captain of the presidio of la Bahia for eleven years and was later governor of the Province of Texas and New Philippines."

The accused governor answered through his attorney, Diego Giraud: "The Canarian families are exaggerating, since they do not live in Los Adaes, but instead live 300 leagues away in Villa de San Fernando. No colonies have been established in this region as it is most remote and has no natural advantages. Furthermore, the payment of soldier's salaries in kind and not in money is an accepted practice based on the regulations for interior regions dated April 20, 1729, and approved by his majesty. To conclude, there is absolutely no evidence of illegality with respect to the governor's actions."

Legally, this attitude was quite correct. It was clear that under these circumstances the Canary Islanders were in the governor's hands. Faced with these reasonable arguments from the defense, he was absolved of all charges, and the sentence was issued on January 10, 1747.

Entry from the Journal of María Curbelo Perdomo

FEBRUARY 20, 1803

I feel very ill. I can no longer write. Today, at eighty-six years of age, I said my last farewell to my son, Cristóbal. I finally understand that the secret hope instilled in us by our parents—to return to the Canary Islands—has been dashed forever. I will never go back, and I pray that someday someone will take this journal there.

PART TWO

CHAPTER 1

I. María Jesús Curbelo

JANUARY 1844

I am María Jesús Curbelo Delgado,[30] great-great-granddaughter of Juan Curbelo and Gracia Umpiérrez, colonists who founded San Antonio, Texas, the first capital of the province of Texas or New Philippines. My ancestors traveled from the Canary Islands in the year 1730.

I have inherited a diary written between 1800 and 1803 by my aunt María, known as Aunt Canary, who was the last member of the original group of families who arrived from the Canary Islands. When I began to read it, I was moved by the vision she had of the future development of these lands; lands that will someday be lost to us due to the nefarious policies of our mother country. Despite repeated warnings from the cabildo of San Antonio, our rulers have failed to take measures against the invasion, which was peaceful at first, but later violent, of colonists from the northern American states.

After reading the diary, I feel compelled by an unstoppable desire to continue her narrative, by adding the events that have occurred in San Antonio since the death of my great-great-aunt María, especially since I have been a protagonist in some of these occurrences. I, María Jesús Curbelo Delgado, daughter of José Curbelo Amador and Josefa Sauceda, am the first descendant of the Canarian founders of Villa de San Antonio to marry one of the North American colonists. I married John W. Smith, one of those ranchers from the north who peacefully invaded San Antonio from the state of Louisiana. I am also the first Canary Islander to marry a Methodist, and to suffer the scorn and hatred of all of the Spaniards, who consider us traitors to our religion, our ancestors, and to our country.

Today, in my advanced years, I look back on my life and evaluate the decision I took so long ago (and I believe that readers of this diary can imagine what it cost me to do so). I truly believe that despite the persecution that my children and I were subjected to over the years, and which we still suffer now, my choice was correct, especially considering the number of Spaniards who subsequently followed the same path.

One of the motives that pushed me into making this important decision was the attitude of the Catholic missionaries toward my Canarian ancestors.

Paradoxically, it was among the Methodist colonists from the north that I found the neighborly love, charity, and community spirit, for Catholics and Methodists alike, that the Catholics preached about but did not practice in their daily life. The doctrine from Rome was the official faith, and they persecuted the Methodists. The Methodists held secret meetings in the barns of their ranches, while others kept watch for the possible arrival of soldiers sent by the powerful Catholic Church.

I attended many of these meetings, during which they spoke of the struggle against alcohol and the sins of the flesh, and the debauched customs of those who claimed to be Catholics. According to one preacher, the Catholics persecuted them because in their inner conscience they felt guilty that the Methodists were more faithfully obedient to the doctrine of Christ than they, who claimed to be the champions of the True Faith. I also remember how they even spoke of joining the northern states, and how they sent spies who compiled exhaustive military and religious reports to prepare the way for the invasion of Texas and union with the Yankees. This eventually occurred, as I will narrate in this diary using detailed reports that I found among the papers of my deceased husband.

Yes, in this respect I am similar to my aunt María, who found herself in a privileged position for narrating the events that occurred in her time, since she was the sister-in-law of two permanent fixtures on the cabildo, Francisco Arocha and Vicente Álvarez Travieso, married respectively to her sisters Juana and María. Furthermore, her second marriage was to Cristóbal de los Santos Coy, who was the attorney for the defense of one of the other great protagonists in the history of the cabildo of San Antonio, a councilor in charge of construction works who built all of the irrigation canals and aqueducts for the town and the missions.

My husband, John W. Smith, known as "el Colorado" for the color of his hair, came from Louisiana and knew the territory of Texas like the back of his hand, which made him one of the best caravan guides in the region. He was the first Anglo-Saxon mayor of San Antonio. His first term of office was from September 19, 1837, to March 9, 1838, after the occupation of Texas by the Anglo-Saxons.

The councilors who accompanied him in office were Manuel Martínez, Francisco Bustillo, Ramón Treviño, Pedro Flores Morales, Gabriel Arriola, Rafael Herrera, Francisco Grau, and Francisco A. Ruiz, all men of Spanish descent.

His second term as mayor of the town of San Antonio was from January 8, 1840 to January 9, 1841. During this period, all of the councilors were Americans, marking the definitive end of its domination by Spaniards. The councilors who accompanied him were Cornelio Van Ness, George Blow, and John McMullen. Finally, my husband was, until his death, representative for Texas in the Congress of the Republic in Washington-on-the-Brazos.

II. A Nation Awakens

While all this was occurring in the Viceroyalty of New Spain, the north was being colonized by companies. In the colony of Virginia, the Quakers and the Germans established themselves rapidly. In 1621 the Dutch West India Company obtained the rights to what would become the colony of New Amsterdam, later New York.

This company promised to grant lands there to anyone who brought fifty workers with them.

In 1732 a new colony was founded in the south by the English philanthropist and general James Edward Oglethorpe. It was located in Georgia.

All of the settlements were eventually converted into English colonies, and by 1750 they were highly autonomous.

The Indians called these Englishmen from the north "Yankees," possibly a mispronunciation of the French word for English, "Anglais."

To the east of Texas was the border with Louisiana, where the French would in 1713 found New Orleans in honor of the duke of that name.

The complex European political chessboard of that era impacted the New World. France and Spain were united by family alliances, and in 1762 Louis XV decided to rid himself of the distant and uncomfortable colony of Louisiana by giving it to his cousin Carlos III as compensation for his losses in the Treaty of Fontainebleu.

During that time Texas and Louisiana experienced a period of great prosperity, since both belonged to Spain and therefore had no border between them.

Louisiana was returned to France in 1800, and on December 20, 1803, it was ceded to the United States for $15 million, one of the best real estate deals in history.

In 1776 news reached the cabildo of San Antonio of the declaration of independence by the northern colonies, as the Anglo-Saxon settlements outside their borders were known, which had been on the path to independence from England since 1774.

A crucial event occurred when the continental congress, created by the colonists, founded the continental army on June 14, 1775, and named George Washington its commander in chief the following day.

This uprising of the English colonies in North America was supported by France and Spain, united once more by a family pact. While this was taking place in North America, and as Louisiana was given back to the French and then to the United States, the Canary Islanders saw how, little by little, Baptist, Presbyterian, and Methodist colonists began crossing the borders from the north and east, and settling with neither authorization nor license.

III. The Foreigners

MARCH 1844

The rulers of New Spain were always worried about foreigners. When Juan Leal Goraz took office as the first president of the cabildo of San Antonio, he received a royal missive from His Majesty Philip V dated June 19, 1730, forwarded by Juan de Acuña, marquis of Casafuerte and viceroy of New Spain, which read:

> Inasmuch as I have made repeated resolutions to end illicit trade, I hereby inform my viceroy of New Spain, and the presidents, tribunals, governors, etc. of those domains, that under no circumstances whatsoever shall they permit even the slightest illicit trade in those provinces. They shall pay particular attention to the ports and borders where illicit clothing is brought inland, and they are charged with the strict enforcement of this most serious matter. The punishment for foreign offenders is set forth in Law 7, Book 9, Title 27, which imposes the penalty of death and seizure of goods for those who commit this offense.

By 1757 the news sent regularly from the cabildo of San Antonio to the viceroy of Mexico had begun to mention fears of a possible peaceful invasion by colonists from this northern area of Texas. While Juan Curbelo was president of the cabildo of San Antonio, he received a royal missive forwarded by Viceroy Agustín de Ahumada,[31] which stated:

> News has reached our lord, the king (God save him), that undeterred by the strict prohibitions contained within the laws of these

> kingdoms, numerous foreigners have entered this part of America from Europe to trade and settle in our territories, with no letters of naturalization or other required licenses. Repeated mandates and orders have been sent to successive viceroys (my predecessors), charging us with the most exact vigilance. We are to impede their entrance, and since tolerating these persons can cause great harm, our ultimate goal must be the complete eradication of all foreign individuals from Spanish domains who are found to be trading or living in this kingdom. In pursuance of the most effective fulfillment of the aforementioned Royal Orders in the strictest possible manner, I hereby direct the governor of the Province of Texas to make a public proclamation of this resolution, to the effect that within one month all foreigners inhabiting the territory and holding valid passports must leave. They shall present themselves at the naval offices in the town of Jalapa, and shall appear before representatives of the fleet and the respective judges, together with two or three members of this cabildo, so that they may examine and record the foreigners in their districts and jurisdictions. These individuals should also be warned that they will be required to present the licenses they used to enter this kingdom, and that if their papers are found to be falsified, they will be punished to the full extent of the law.

Despite the King's concerns over the peaceful invasion of the province of Texas by foreigners from the north, his only actions were to send royal orders full of good intentions, rather than soldiers to enforce these royal orders and guard the borders more effectively. So the unauthorized colonists continued to settle in Texas with complete impunity.

While Miguel Cortan was president of the cabildo (a man from the peninsula, not a Canarian colonist, but married to María Polonia Álvarez and forced on the cabildo by his powerful father-in-law, Vicente Álvarez Travieso, to govern on his behalf), on October 19, 1767, he received a royal missive that clearly shows the royal preoccupation not only with the invasion of foreign colonists but also with the fact that clerics from other religions were accompanying these foreigners and plotting against the Canarian settlers and Spanish rule. I will take the trouble to transcribe the entire missive here, since its contents are most interesting.

> THE KING
>
> In consideration of the grave difficulties experienced by the American kingdoms upon the settlement of religious foreigners with no bonds of loyalty to the Nation, and aflame with passions that are at variance with my domains in the Indies, for which reason the laws of those lands expressly prohibit them.
>
> On consultation with my Extraordinary Council on September 29, I have resolved that from this day forth no permits will be granted to foreign clergymen or religious men of any school or status, and that all clergymen and religious figures who live in those domains will be removed from America. To this effect, the strictest orders are hereby issued to the viceroys, audiences, governors, archbishops, bishops, ecclesiastical cabildos, and religious superiors, in which they are commanded to send these men to Spain. They shall accept complete responsibility for any failure to do so, or for any perceived lenience when dealing with this severe problem, and my Council of the Indies and its attorneys will ensure the scrupulous enforcement of these orders... and will know if they have been complied with. Furthermore, a list shall be sent, without delay, of foreign clergymen and religious figures, which shall contain their names, status, residencies, provinces, and the convent where they took holy orders. This list shall also include foreigners who have arrived from Spain or from other kingdoms, and those individuals who were ordained and processed there. This document is written by the hand of my secretary, the undersigned, as is my will. San Lorenzo, October seventeen, seventeen sixty-seven.

✧ ✧ ✧

After the third family pact was signed between France and Spain, and branches of the Bourbons of Italy were later added, England quickly understood that while the alliance did not specifically name an enemy, it could be clearly seen that this was an alliance of Catholic countries against Protestant ones, and was aimed at them. With no warning beyond an ultimatum, England attacked Spain's overseas territories, and captured Cuba and Manila. In the face of this, on March 23, 1762, the marquis of Cruillas[32] sent a message to the cabildo of San Antonio, of which Juan José Flores was president, announcing that "the situation of our court, and the grave news that has recently arrived which indicates that our forces will join the current war between France and England in favor of the former. To this effect we should stand prepared against any invasion, insult, or expedition proffered by the latter."

Two days later, on March 25, he broadened these instructions, reiterating that the presidios on the border be fully manned and equipped with firearms, swords, and lances in order to drive back an invasion by the English, adding that "the peaceful Indians should be observed and interrogated when any movements of their people or of foreign nations are detected, or if they are about to enter our kingdom."

On June 25, 1762, the cabildo of San Antonio received their instructions on how to participate in the war against England. It was declared that "since the opening of hostilities, it should be understood that we are in a state of war against the British nation, in support of the French armies fighting with the tenacity and strength appropriate to the honor of His Catholic Majesty in all the domains of the universe."

It was also ordered that wherever Englishmen were found, they should be attacked as sworn enemies of the faith, the state, and the crown.

IV. Problems in Spain with the Church

JUNE 1844

Meanwhile on the peninsula, events were unfolding rapidly. On Palm Sunday, 1766, riots broke out against the minister of war and finance, the marquis of Esquilache, with people taking to the streets and shouting, "Long live the king; death to Esquilache," after the king replaced Miguel de Muzquiz with Esquilache.

The most important repercussions, however, for the Canarian colony in San Antonio, were felt when the Society of Jesus was expelled from Spanish territories. It will never be known what truly motivated the king to take this decision. It is believed that it stemmed both from the participation of the Jesuits in organizing the riots, and from their fierce resistance to the royal solution in the case of the Colonia del Sacramento, which indicated their clear desire for independence in their missions in Paraguay.

On November 10, 1767, the cabildo received a royal decree, which stated:

> Let it be known that in the kingdoms of the Indies, article nine of the royal pragmatic sanction must be observed and implemented with the full force of the law. This article declares that all members of the Society of Jesus are to be exiled from my kingdoms, and their earthly goods and possessions seized. The return of any individual from this group to these domains is strictly prohibited, and the legal authorities are empowered to take the severest action required. Article ten of said pragmatic sanction sets forth that even in possession of a dispensation from the pope, no member of the society, either priest or lay member, may remain, nor may they move into another order in furtherance of returning to my kingdoms.

The atmosphere in Spain was exceptionally tense after the expulsion of the Jesuits. Many priests began openly preaching against the king and the politicians, which I believe makes the royal decree of May 23, 1768, especially interesting:

> Having denounced to our council the book *Incommoda probabilismi*, written by Friar Luis Vicente Mas de Cafavalle, of the Order of Preachers, first professor of Santo Tomás at the University of Valencia, printed in that city with the proper licenses, and rejecting the doctrines of REGICIDE and TYRANNICIDE, among others, the king ordered the confiscation of the original and a printed example, in order to determine whether its writing and sale were appropriate. It was then examined with great care and due diligence, and it was concluded that it had been printed with the appropriate legal licenses and formalities; and in uncovering this error in the records, made during the fifteenth session of the General Council of Constance in the year 1415, he has shown himself to be a worthy member of the illustrious Order of Preachers. In his intelligence, he considered the findings of many attorneys on the subject, provided in the council records from the eleventh of this month, and it is hereby declared that we will stamp out the roots and seeds of the pernicious doctrine of REGICIDE and TYRANNICIDE, which has been printed by many authors and can be read in many books, since it is destructive to the state and the public good. We are thus called upon to order: That the aforementioned work be sold and distributed: That Graduates, Professors, and Teachers of the universities and schools of these kingdoms swear, upon entering their posts, that they will observe the teaching of the doctrine contained in the referenced section fifteen of the Council of Constance: And that as a consequence, they will neither believe nor teach, even in the most hypothetical sense, the doctrine of REGICIDE and TYRANNICIDE against the legitimate powers. March 13, 1778.

This royal decree worried the Canary Islanders, since its contents were a clear indication of the troubled state of affairs in our homeland, and we were further surprised that same year, when it was made known that:

> On this day, July 14, the council herein announces by royal decree: The good example of the secular and regular clergy transcends the entire body of subjects in a nation as religious as Spain. To love and respect the members of the royal family and the government is an obligation dictated by the fundamental laws of the State, and taught by the divine word to the people. All priests must consider this to be a most solemn point of moral behavior, and they should instill these principles into the people, not only through their sermons, spiritual exercises, and devotions, but also, and more importantly, by abstaining, at all times and in all conversations, from declamations and rumors injurious to members of the government which might contribute to the propagation of hatred toward them. We hereby beseech and command our kingdom's priests to capture and deliver to us any friar, cleric or hermit, or any other religious figure, who might make declarations of this nature (that is, against the king, the royal family, the State, or the Government).

The same decree states that His Majesty the King, "having taken all prudent and effective measures dictated by the love of peace conducive to ending the war between France and England, has seen that the latter country delays out of bad faith, and refuses, in the most improper terms, to accept the just proposals put forward by His Majesty. The king has thus determined to declare war on Great Britain, and forthwith all subjects of these kingdoms should be on guard against the English and should endeavor to harm them by arming ships as privateers, with the security that His Majesty grants them entire enjoyment of the booty seized from the subjects of England."

As I have mentioned, these developments greatly disturbed the Canarian colonists. We had struggled considerably against the missions, and their representatives were our enemies since they had plotted against our interests as citizens on many occasions. However, when the Society of Jesus was declared enemy of the king, together with its priests who spoke ill of the king, the royal family, and the government, we were compelled to consider the other religions that we knew were followed by the people settling here from the English colonies to the north. Many of we Canary Islanders already spoke their language, and as farmers we often traded with the foreigners, who were initially accepted with some precautions but were later welcomed more fully, together with their customs and religion.

Meanwhile, the Spanish government worried more about protecting the galleons that traveled back to the peninsula laden with gold and silver than about defending the lands they had conquered. Thus, toward the end of 1779, the cabildo of San Antonio received a royal order dated July 15 of that year, which declared: "The officers and sailors of privateer crews who have received injuries in combat and are unable to continue service will be attended to and provided for in accordance with the proposals to this end made to me by the commanders of the respective departments, and in line with their position in the Naval Accounting Office if they are registered, or their rank on the privateer vessel if they are not; pensions shall also be granted to widows of those who have died in combat."

This royal directive clearly shows how the territories were governed from the court—the cabildo of San Antonio had little need to commission privateers since it was not a seaport, and the aid that we needed was for the land border. Upon receipt of this directive, the cabildo of San Antonio agreed to propose a similar disposition to the viceroy but on land, to encourage colonists to come and populate these regions, together with a promise of land and water for farming, as had been done in 1731 for our Canarian ancestors.

This request from the cabildo of San Antonio received an answer.

The decree on privateers, which was much discussed here in San Antonio, did not seem to be an isolated incident, judging by a document that came into my hands. It was a secret report, presented in 1783 by the Count of Aranda, minister to Carlos III, which discussed

REAL CEDULA
DE S. M.
EN QUE SE INSERTA
LA REAL ORDENANZA
DE CORSO
CON LAS DECLARACIONES
convenientes para su observancia
en los dominios de Indias.

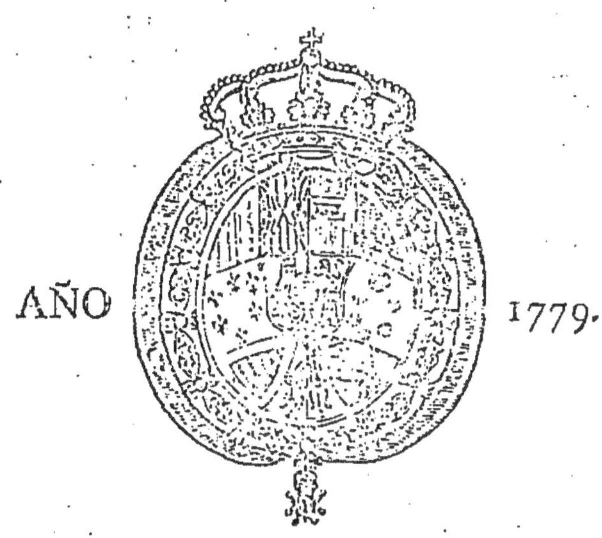

AÑO 1779.

EN MADRID:

EN LA IMPRENTA DE PEDRO MARIN.

N.º 61

NOS EL PRESIDENTE REGENTE, y Oydores de la Audiencia Real y Chacillería de esta Nueva España en la que actualmente reside el Superior Gobierno de élla:

POR QUANTO POR EL CORREO Mensal que ha llegado hoy á esta Capital se ha recibido la Real Orden del tenor siguiente.

„ Despues de haber empleado el Rey todos los prudentes y „ eficaces medios, que le dictan siempre el amor á la paz, y el bien „ de la humanidad, para terminar la guerra entre la Francia y la „ Inglaterra, ha visto que esta Potencia dilata de mala fé, y aun „ reusa en términos impropios acetar las justas proposiciones que „ S. M. la ha hecho en calidad de poderoso mediador; y como „ los fines de la Corte de Londres se dirigen á ganar tiempo, y „ á procurar Indemnizarse de la pérdida de sus Colonias sobre „ los Dominios Españoles de Indias, segun los insultos, y pre-pa-

bernadores y Justicias de su distrito los exemplares acostumbrados. Dado en México á doce de Agosto de mil setecientos setenta y nueve.

D. Francisco Romá y Rosell.

Antonio de Villaurrutia y Salcedo.

Diego Antonio Fernandez de Madrid.

D. Francisco Xavier de Gamboa.

Francisco Gomez de Algarin.

Miguel Calixto de Acedo.

Balthasar Ladron de Guebara.

Por mandado de S. A. la Rl. Aud. Gobernadora

DON CARLOS POR LA GRACIA DE DIOS,

REY DE CASTILLA, DE LEON, DE ARAGON, DE LAS DOS SICILIAS, DE JERUSALÉN, DE NAVARRA, DE Granada, de Toledo, de Valencia, de Galicia, de Mallorca, de Sevilla, de Cerdeña, de Cordova, de Córcega, de Murcia, de Jaén, de los Algarves, de Algecira, de Gibraltar, de las Islas de Canarias, de las Indias Orientales, y Occidentales, Islas, y Tierra firme del Mar Occeano, Archiduque de Austria, Duque de Borgoña, de Brabante, y Milán, Conde de Abspurg, Flandes, Tiról, y Barcelona, Señor de Vizcaya, y de Molina, &c.

POR quanto concedo permiso á vecino de para armar en guerra su
de porte de toneladas poco mas ó menos con cañones y nombrad
correspondientes, y hasta el número de hombres de tripulacion, á fin de que pueda salir á hacer el corso contra los vasallos del Rey de pedreros, y las demas armas y municiones
Inglaterra, y con vandera española correr los mares de América sin pasar á los de Europa y apresar todas las embarcaciones propias de los enemigos
de mi Corona. Por tanto ordeno que los Virreyes, Gobernadores, Intendentes ó Ministros encargados de este asunto en mis dominios de Indias despues
de recibidas á su satisfaccion las fianzas que presentare el citado armadór en seguridad de su buena conducta, de que se abstendrá de hacer extorsion á las embarcaciones de las naciones amigas ó neutrales, á menos que las halle navegando sobre costas de mis dominios, ó dadas fondos en calas, ensenadas ú otros parages
sospechosos contra lo convenido en los tratados, y de que conducirá las presas que hiciere á puertos de mis dominios de Indias sin disponer de ellas tratandolas
como á tales, hasta que examinadas se resuelva su legitimidad, le permitan armarla y tripularla con el número de gente que juzgue conveniente, entregandole la lista
certificada de ella, y praéticando en todo lo que tengo dispuesto en mi Ordenanza de corso de primero de Julio de mil setecientos setenta y nueve, Real Ce-
dula de quince del mismo y últimas Reales ordenes.

Y mando á los Oficiales generales ó particulares, Comandantes de mis esquadras y baxeles, á los Virreyes, Capitanes ó Comandantes Generales de reynos
y provincias, á los Gobernadores, Corregidores y Justicias de los pueblos de las costas de mar de mis expresados dominios, á los Intendentes, Oficiales Reales y
Jueces de arribadas en ellos establecidos, y á todos los demas vasallos mios á quienes pertenece ó pertenecer pueda, no le pongan embarazo, causen molestia ó
detencion, antes le auxilien y faciliten lo que hubiere menester para su armamento, navegacion y corso; y á los vasallos y subditos de los Reyes, Principes y
Republicas mis amigas ó aliadas; á los Comandantes, Gobernadores ó Cabos de sus provincias, plazas, esquadras y baxeles requiero que asimismo no le impi-
dan su libre navegacion, entrada, salida ó detencion en los puertos, á los quales por necesidad ó inevitable accidente se conduxere, permitiendole que en ellos
se bastimente y provea de todo lo que necesitare: á cuyo fin he mandado despachar este Pasaporte refrendado de mi Secretario de Estado y del Despacho Universal de Indias. Dado [illegible]

Yo El Rey

[illegible]

the independence of the English colonies after the Treaty of Paris had been signed in 1783. It considered how we, the Canary Islanders of Texas, as the report called us, had been sending petitions directly to the ministers in Spain, because ever since the founding of our city, the complaints that we had naively sent first to the governors of the province, and later to the viceroys, had come to nothing, because these officials were often the cause of the complaints to begin with. In this document, the Count of Aranda recommends to Carlos III that "you rid yourself of the possessions on the American continent, and conserve only the islands of Cuba and Puerto Rico, due to the immense difficulty of maintaining such vast territories. This is evident from the abuses suffered by the poor inhabitants at the hands of their governors; the distance from the highest authority causes years to pass before complaints from the people can be brought to justice, and during this time the residents are subjected to the whims of local authorities (we know of many such cases from the Canary Islanders of Texas); it is most difficult to know the truth from so far away, and finally, the viceroys and captains general, as Spaniards, always obtain favorable rulings from Spain. These circumstances cannot but make the inhabitants of the Americas discontent, and force them to work toward independence as soon as the opportunity arises.

"The independence of the English colonies offers freedom of conscience and the opportunity to establish new settlements over vast territories, which is exactly what made those men become colonists. They seized Florida, and later took over our territories in the province of Texas which were closest to the border; territories that we could not hope to defend due to their distance from the Spanish heartland."

The Count of Aranda continues, reasoning that "man is the same everywhere, and the difference in climate does not change the nature of our feelings; he who sees the opportunity to gain power and to grow, will take advantage of it. How can we expect the Americans to respect the Kingdom of New Spain, when they have the opportunity to take advantage of this rich and beautiful country? Nothing, sir, can prevent the growth of the Anglo-American colonies."

His report ends with the observation that "this federal republic still in its infancy is nothing more than a pygmy. But the day will come when it will be a giant, even a colossus, on the continent. The opportunities for the population to grow in such an immense territory will attract men here from all over the world. In a few short years we will see, to our regret, the tyrannical existence of this colossus."

A similar, even more dismal, opinion was offered by another Spanish ambassador, esteemed by the North American authorities.

Today, after reading Aranda's memorandum, I am better able to understand the attitude of the authorities in Spain to the problems created by the northern American states, and this report by the Spanish ambassador to the American authorities, Luis de Onís, clarifies their position even more. He wrote:

> Every day the ambitious ideas of this Republic (U.S.A.) are developed further. This government has proposed for itself nothing less than setting the extent of its boundaries at the mouth of the North River, or the Río Bravo, and following its course all the way to the Pacific, thus including the provinces of Texas, New Santander, Coahuila, New Mexico, and part of the provinces of New Vizcaya and Sonora. While this undertaking might seem like a delusion to all sensible people, I can assure you that the project exists, and that maps of these provinces have already been drawn up by order of the government, and even include the island of Cuba as a natural part of the Republic.

CHAPTER 2

I. The Irrigation System in San Antonio

SEPTEMBER 1844

Notwithstanding the conflicts between the cabildo and the missions located along the San Antonio River, it is an unquestionable fact that both parties took advantage of Antonio Rodríguez's knowledge of the construction of irrigation canals and channels gained while working with his father on the Tenoya water board back on Gran Canaria. It is also evident that the system he designed for distributing water from the canals and channels also used methods that he had learned on Gran Canaria.

The San Pedro canal, built for the exclusive use of the Canarian settlers by the cabildo of San Antonio, and under the direction of Antonio Rodríguez Mederos, continues to supply water to the surrounding lands even today. It was also known as the "mother canal."

The oldest direct reference to a rotation in the use of the San Pedro canal appears in a document from 1750, which discusses the development of irrigation from the San Javier River, where it was thought that there was not enough water to serve both agricultural and domestic needs. The argument against this was based on the experience of the San Pedro canal with which the Canary Islanders watered their lands, since they could water an equal area with a smaller volume of water. The document reads: "The short gully from which the islanders have dug a canal with a lesser volume is sufficient for fifteen participants, without including five other days that are ceded to the landowners in the town."[33]

Here is the first appearance of a reference to fifteen participants, corresponding to the first fifteen Canarian colonists, who were able to complement their basic water allotment by renting extra hours to the cabildo.[34]

All authors on the subject seem to agree that the oldest reference to the word *dula*[35] is in a document from 1791, where the inspector Pedro Nizas reported on the irrigation potential of the bay of Goliad on the San Antonio River, explaining that "certain places are not unfavorable, where with one canal we could create four *dulas* from the river, on account of its gentle current."[36]

The first sales of land that I have found which mention water rights as units of time associated to the plots, and undoubtedly referring to hours in the water rotation, include the sale by the captain of the San Antonio presidio, Toribio de Urrutia, to Antonio Rodríguez Mederos, resident, Canarian founder, and town councilor of "a stone house, destroyed by two floods, a shed for fodder. The lot where the house is located is twenty yards wide and is adjacent to two lots of land in the south of the town, with water for twenty-four hours every twenty days. This land was acquired under the conditions of colonization by Juan Leal Álvarez, who transferred it to me with the rights acquired as first colonist for 333 pesos." This document is dated Saturday, April 12, 1749.[37]

There is another sale by Antonio Rodríguez Mederos to Miguel de Castro of "two lots in the pasture to the south of the town and one day of water every twenty days; this is the same land that I purchased from Captain Toribio de Urrutia, which he acquired from Juan Leal Álvarez." This document is dated April 28, 1749.[38]

Subsequent to these sales, I have found transfers of land together with rights to hours of water during the division of the estate of the deceased Canarian founder Vicente Álvarez Travieso. On June 12, 1787, his ranch and mules were divided between his children—Tomás, Catalina, Rita, and Juana—and each was granted "two hours and forty minutes of water on the day corresponding to them."[39]

It can be clearly seen that the water distribution system in San Antonio was copied from the Canary Islands and, more specifically,

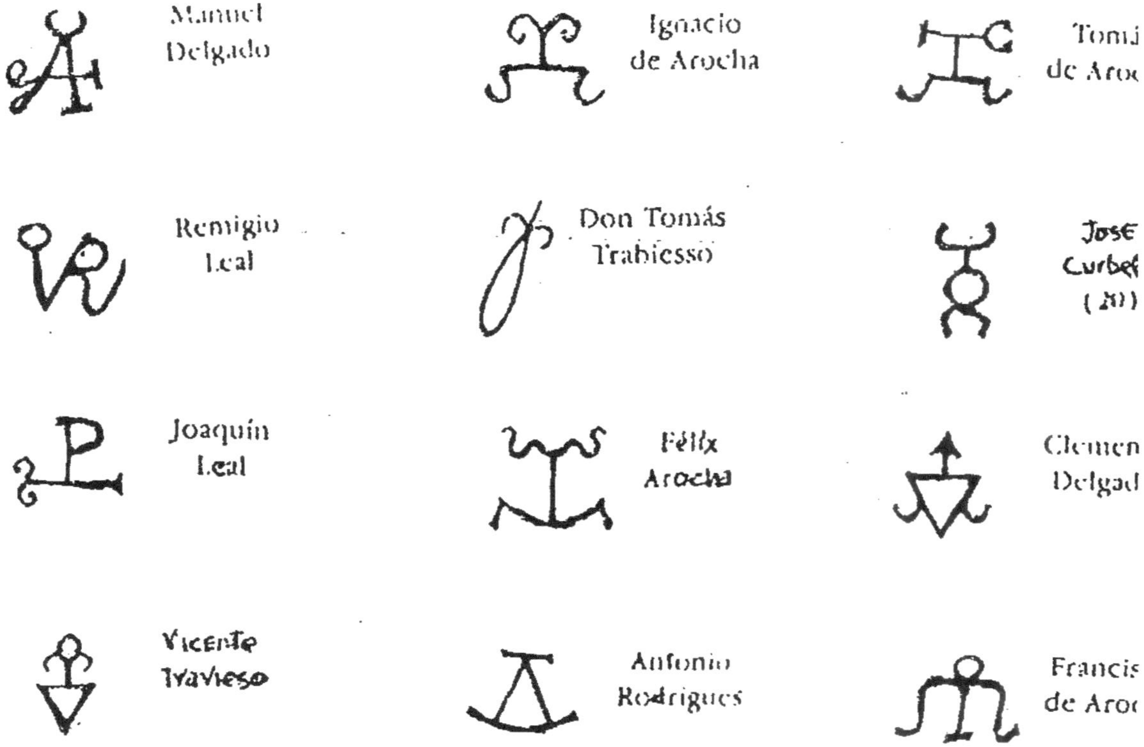

Manuel Delgado

Ignacio de Arocha

Tomá de Aroc

Remigio Leal

Don Tomás Trabiesso

Jose Curbel (20)

Joaquín Leal

Félix Arocha

Clemen Delgad

Vicente Travieso

Antonio Rodrigues

Francis de Aroc

Hierros de las ganaderías de los descendientes de colonos canarios en 1816, en San Antonio de Texas.

from Gran Canaria. This is evident first because the town's irrigation systems were built by Antonio Rodríguez Mederos, from Gran Canaria and the only expert for miles around, and second because the water shifts were for twenty-four hours every twenty days. This twenty-day rotation, or *dula*, is identical to the system used by the Tenoya water board in Gran Canaria where Antonio Rodríguez Mederos[40] had worked.

II. Canarian Estates

The Canary Islanders who owned the most important ranches were the Arocha and Delgado families, with the San Rafael de Patoguiya ranch; the Álvarez Travieso family, with the San Vicente mule ranch; and the Granados family.

My aunt María has already written of how the cabildo struggled against the religious and military powers right from the start, in a battle to gain recognition of their authority from the missionaries and the soldiers. In this vein, I have found an interesting report opposing the Canary Islanders, written by the viceroy of New Spain, Pedro Cebrián y Agustín, count of Fuenclara.

The report is dated April 17, 1745, and states: "The fourteen Canarian families have sued not only the reverend fathers of the five missions, but also the Indians who reside in the missions, the captain of the presidio, and the forty-nine other families settled there; it seems that they wish to be alone, in sole possession of the region. Perhaps they do not find enough space in this area, in this vast, entire province."

III. The Virgin of Guadalupe

Since this town was founded, we have worshipped the Virgin of Candelaria and her Most Holy Son Jesus Christ, a custom brought by our parents from the Canary Islands. Although many of us were born on the islands, we left them at a very young age, and the only Canarian customs we remembered were those that our parents taught us, and this tradition was sacred. For this reason, there was uproar in the Canarian community over the royal decree from His Majesty Fernando VI, which reached the cabildo in January 1751, while the president of the cabildo was José Padrón, and the viceroy of New Spain was Güemes y Horcasitas. In it the king explained that "the Abbot and the Council of the Holy Church of Our Lady of Guadalupe, outside Mexico City, and the Council of Justice of this city, have described, in letters dated March 18, 1756, the growing extent of the worship of that miraculous image and universal patron, held as such in all of the northern Indies. By virtue of the insufficiency of alms collected to sustain the costs of the church and its studies, I have been urged to order that all the inhabitants of his kingdoms in the northern Indies who enjoy the benign and general protection of this miraculous image, as is public and well known, leave mandatory pious legacies to the Sanctuary of the image of Our Lady of Guadalupe. The amount shall be at the discretion of the testator, and may not be considered a fee or a tax, nor as payment of damages, but rather as a spiritual benefit."

IV. Creation of the Lottery in the Viceroyalty

MARCH 1848

When we arrived in 1731, one of the worst afflictions of this viceroyalty was gambling. It was pervasive not only in the army, but also among the civilian population. Even before we settled in these lands, vigorous measures had been put in place by the then-viceroy, the marquis of Casafuerte, prohibiting sergeant majors from working for gambling houses and serving at the tables.

There was even a "Treatise on Gaming," written by Friar Francisco de Alcover, which described all of the games in existence at that time, and the tricks used through words, signs, or facial expressions, since professional gamblers from the north often surprised wealthy, inexperienced players. In all military bases and, according to the men, in the brothels, they also played cards.

When Miguel Cartari was mayor, he received a royal decree from the viceroy, Carlos Francisco de Croix, dated February 13, 1778, which read: "In response to the proposals made by the Cabildo of San Antonio, and attesting to the vice of strong games and gambling, and after promulgating numerous laws and statutes prohibiting these excesses, His Majesty hereby abolishes all special jurisdictions and immunity with respect to this illegal behavior for the military, the navy, and the Royal House, and even for the grandees of Spain." Thus it was declared that all holders of special legal privileges would be subject to ordinary justice without exception, even if they were members of the military, and that the ordinary magistrates could proceed against the transgressors; for this reason, "The only way to ensure full compliance with this law, and to root out this abominable vice, the origin of so many ruinous and deplorable occurrences in these American domains, is if the judges have methods other than declaring ineffectually against the military privileges that the majority of the inhabitants of these lands enjoy."

Despite the royal opposition to gambling, the royal treasury, always short on funds, convinced the king to establish the General Royal Lottery of New Spain, and the Particular Royal Lottery, by royal decree on September 19, 1770. Both were governed by the same regulations. A planned fund of one million pesos would be obtained through the sale of 50,000 tickets at twenty pesos per ticket, and 14 percent would be deducted to cover costs. The 867,000 pesos that remained would be divided into 5,000 prizes of different values.

The court always ruled in ignorance of the realities of the province of Texas and New Philippines. As I have already mentioned, we were witness to the growing invasion of settlers, and our concerned cabildo repeatedly asked the governor, and even the viceroy of New Spain, for reinforcements on the border, either in the form of more colonists or armed garrisons. In 1770, however, the mayor of San Antonio, Francisco Flores de Abrego, received the royal decree by Carlos IV, covering the "Royal Ordinance on Privateers" with the

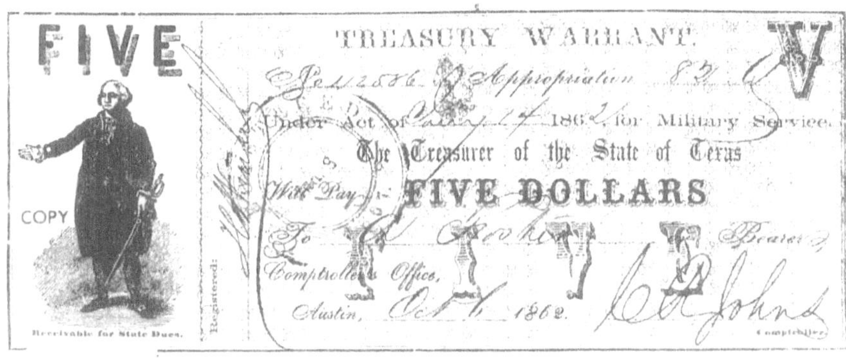
FIVE
COPY
Receivable for State Dues.
TREASURY WARRANT.
V
Under Act of
for Military Service.
The Treasurer of the State of Texas
Will Pay
FIVE DOLLARS
To
Bearer
Comptroller's Office,
Austin,
Registered:
Comptroller

TWELVE MONTHS AFTER A DEFINITIVE TREATY OF PEACE BETWEEN THE CONFEDERATE STATES & THE UNITED STATES
100
THE STATE OF LOUISIANA
WILL PAY TO BEARER
ONE HUNDRED DOLLARS
TREASURERS OFFICE
SHREVEPORT
COPY

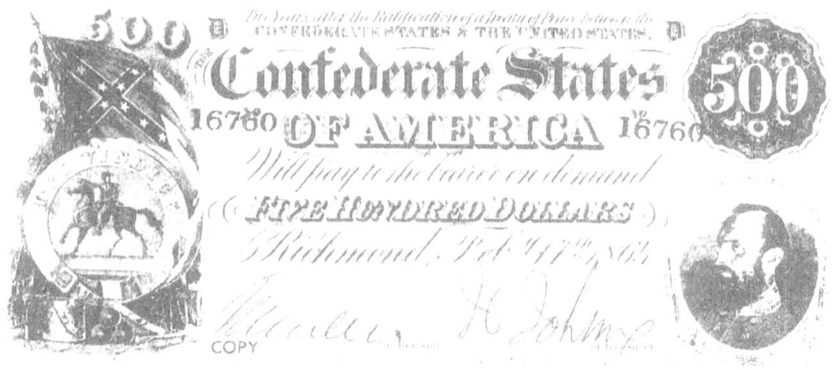
500
CONFEDERATE STATES & THE UNITED STATES.
The Confederate States
16760
OF AMERICA
16760
500
Will pay to the bearer on demand
FIVE HUNDRED DOLLARS
Richmond,
COPY

appropriate declarations for its observance in the domains of the Indies, which proves my point perfectly.

V. Money and Banking in San Antonio

The descendants of the Canary Islanders, together with other colonists who had arrived later, agreed that we would retreat to our ranches and live simply on what we could produce, since this was enough for our survival, and we would only go into the town to buy what was absolutely necessary. However, as we only bought essential items in the town, this created huge problems for the governor and the viceroy because money became scarce. The only money in circulation came from the salaries of the soldiers and the civil servants who lived in the town, and from the payments made by the state to merchants for provisions.

These payments arrived in San Antonio twice a month but were never enough. The economic chaos was so great that when the soldiers or their families went to buy goods, the merchants often had no coins to give them as change and were forced to offer them credit or to take goods in exchange, which led to protests not only by the merchants but also by the soldiers and civil servants. This crisis coincided with the settlement in the town of merchants arriving from Europe and led to an urgent meeting of the cabildo in 1817, presided over by Francisco Flores. It was resolved to send a report to the governor in order to manifest the need to put an end to this grave situation, and to allow the emission of money in San Antonio. As a result the colonel and governor of Texas, Manuel Prado, issued an ordinance authorizing the local jeweler, Manuel Barrera, a Spaniard born in Coahuila in 1770, "to emit 500 pesos in *jolas* with a value of 1/2 a real each, by virtue of the scarcity of change, which is making trade slow and inefficient. These *jolas* will circulate in the town and will activate trade."

This official communication was dated March 20, 1817. On December 6, 1818, the next governor and commander of the province,

Antonio Martínez, issued a decree granting the monopoly on issuing coins in the town to José Antonio de la Garza, born in San Antonio on May 30, 1776, in the Garza family house on the corner of the canal and Veramen Street. According to this decree, de la Garza was to issue 500 pesos in *jolas*, valued at half a real.

Standing as witnesses for José Antonio de la Garza were José María Zambrano and the youngest councilor on the cabildo, Felipe Enrique Neri, Baron of Bastrop,[41] together with the solicitor Manuel Iturri Castillo, who acted as guarantor. The word *jolas*, used for the first coins issued in San Antonio, is derived from *joya*, or jewel, which was what the natives called precious stones. The coins issued by José Antonio de la Garza had his initials and the year they were issued on one side, and a star on the other. This symbol would later be adopted for the flag of the Republic of Texas, called the Lone Star State.

Although the first official bank was established in San Antonio in 1822 under the name Texas National Bank, in reality the first bank not only in San Antonio but in the southwestern United States belonged to José Antonio de la Garza, since his coins were circulating right up to 1822. After his death, the private bank of the Garza family was run by his son, Leonardo.

CHAPTER 3

I. Indian Attacks

JUNE 1849

Besides the problems with the missionaries, we were always afraid of attacks by the Apache Indians.

Even during our journey from Veracruz to San Antonio, we were attacked while crossing the Río Grande at midnight. We did not suffer any human casualties, but we lost horses and supplies. We were defended by an escort that rode to our aid from the San Antonio presidio, but these soldiers carried off fifty horses and mules, some yoked together and others unsaddled.

The second attack occurred between the Río Frío and the Río Hondo, but as we had been warned that we were already in Apache territory, we managed to drive them away, killing one Indian.

But the matter did not end there; after we founded the city the attacks were continuous.

Despite this, it was only officially decided to use the army to challenge the Apaches in 1739, eight years after the founding of the cabildo, and only after repeated petitions to the governor. Many prisoners were taken when the army attacked, and these were sold as slaves despite the missionaries' vociferous protests.

The Apaches attacked over and over again, and on one occasion killed nine peasants. In June 1745, fifty Apaches banded together and attacked the San Antonio fort and the town itself.

Breaking with their usual customs, they attacked at night, but despite the element of surprise, our defenses held and they were forced to flee.

Thanks to the endeavors of the Franciscan father Santa Ana, who was in Mission Concepción in 1749, we were able to make peace with the Apaches.

Their chief, "Red Hair," adorned with paint and feathers, danced with Father Santa Ana, holding him by the hand, around a great stone in the center of the city square.

This peace lasted for many years, despite sporadic attacks.

In 1779 ten Apaches attacked the governor's palace in an attempt to kill him, but they were driven off by the guards.

Two members of my family died at the hands of the wild Indians: José Antonio, son of my brother José, and Rafaela Serra.

José Antonio, as lieutenant, was governor of the province of Texas and lived in San Fernando, along with five other citizens, of whom he was the only Canary Islander. He was murdered by Lipan Indians.[42]

One of José Antonio's sons, Juan José, was an expert on the struggle against the savages during the worst period of attacks on the Canarian colonists. He had a deep understanding of the customs of the Comanche, Lipan, and Talmacano Indians.[43]

The Indians who inhabited these lands, and who were distinguished for their bravery, were the Comanches and the Apaches.

The Comanches were always the unquestioned victors over the other tribes, except for the Guasas, a tribe of giants who were capable of catching a running horse and knocking it down. In 1751 San Antonio was attacked by Comanche Indians, and many missionaries were killed.

II. The Zebulon Montgomery Pike Expedition

MAY 1858

After the sale of Louisiana to the northern states in 1803, politicians in both Spain and the viceroyalty, and as a result, the cabildo of San Antonio and the town in general, realized that the doors to the northeast of the viceroyalty had been opened to the northern states. With this acquisition of Louisiana, the northern states unilaterally established a de facto border much farther to the west, along the Río Nueces, to the west of the San Antonio River and near the Río Grande to the north. At a stroke they took possession of a large part of the province of Texas, with no resistance whatsoever from Spain.

Although the province still belonged to Mexico, northern colonists settled there without authorization, and Spain had no control over this due to a grave lack of guards on the border.

On taking office on March 4, 1829, President Andrew Jackson stated that "Texas must be ours... peaceably if we can, forcibly if we must."

The strategy of the United States was, on the one hand, to continue sending unauthorized settlers, and on the other, to foment Texan independence by promising them aid.

But there was more—much more. The president sent a series of spies who studied the region exhaustively. The most important spy, due to the huge impact his reports had, was Zebulon Pike.

Zebulon Montgomery Pike, an ambitious young man, was born in New Jersey in 1779. He was a protégé of the commander-in-chief of the U.S. Navy, James Wilkinson, who gave him the difficult task of exploring the provinces of Louisiana and Texas with a group of men. Their objective was to make an exhaustive report on the province, to be used in a future invasion attempt. In 1806 the Pike expedition headed to Texas, where Pike was taken prisoner by the governor of Coahuila and Texas, Antonio Cordero, and the governor of Nuevo León, the Canary Islander from Tenerife, Simón de Herrera y Leyva.

Among my deceased husband's documents I have found part of Pike's diary, and I will now copy the most important parts as a legacy for the future, and for the history of the Canary Islanders in Texas. From these notes, we can see how a Canary Islander, Simón de Herrera y Leyva, also participated actively against the invasion of spies from the northern states.

Pike's diary begins by recounting the events that befell him on June 7:

SUNDAY, JUNE 7TH. Came on fifteen miles to the [Medina] Mariano River—the border between Texas and Coquilla—a pretty little stream, [on which was a] rancho. Thence in the afternoon to San Antonio. We halted at San José mission, received in a friendly manner by the priest of the mission and others.

We were met out of San Antonio about three miles by Governors Cordero and Herrera in a coach. We repaired to their quarters, where we were received like their children. Cordero informed me that he had discretionary orders as to the mode of my going out of the country; that he therefore wished me to choose my time, mode, etc.; that any sum of money I might want was at my service. In the evening his levee was attended by a crowd of officers and priests, among whom were Father MacGuire and Dr. Zerbien. After supper we went to the public square, where the two governors joined in a dance with people who in the daytime would approach them with reverence and awe.

We were here introduced to the sister of Lieutenant Malgares's wife, who was one of the finest women we saw. She was married to a Captain Joaquín Ugarte, to whom we had letters of introduction.

MONDAY, JUNE 8TH. Remained at San Antonio.

TUESDAY, JUNE 9TH. A large party dined at Governor Cordero's, who gave as his toast: "The President of the United States—Vive la." I returned the compliment by toasting "His Catholic Majesty." These toasts were followed by one to "General Wilkinson." One of the company then gave a toast to "these gentlemen, their safe and happy arrival in their own country, their honorable reception, and the continuation of the good understanding which exists between the two countries."

WEDNESDAY, JUNE 10TH. Another large party at the governor's. He toasted "my companion, Herrera."

THURSDAY, JUNE 11TH. Preparing to march tomorrow. This evening we had a conversation with the two governors, wherein they exhibited tremendous knowledge of our political and executive system.

FRIDAY, JUNE 12TH. One of the captains from the kingdom of Nuevo León having died, we were invited to attend the burial and accompanied the two governors in their coach, where we had an opportunity to view the solemnity of the interment and the ritual of the Spanish church, attended by the military honors which were conferred on the deceased by his late brethren in arms.

Governor Cordero gave the information of my intended expedition to the commandant-general as early as July, the same month that I took my departure. His information was received via Natchez.

SATURDAY, JUNE 13TH. This morning 200 dragoons were marched to the coast, to look for the English, and this evening Colonel Cordero was to have marched to join them.

The information contained in Pike's diary is most important, as is the exhaustive report he delivered to Gen. James Wilkinson, on April 17, 1808. I hereby transcribe this report in its entirety, to give future readers an idea of our social and religious life in San Antonio during this period.

We marched at seven o'clock, Governor Cordero taking us in his coach about two leagues, accompanied by Father MacGuire and Dr. Zerbien. It would not be improper to mention something about Father MacGuire and Dr. Zerbien, who certainly treated us with all imaginable attention while at San Antonio.

Father MacGuire was an Irish priest, who formerly resided on the coast above Orleans and was known for his hospitable and social qualities. On the cession of Louisiana, he followed the standard of "the king, his master, who never suffers an old servant to be neglected."

He received at Cuba an establishment as chaplain to the mint of Mexico, whence the instability of human affairs carried him to San Antonio. He was a man of chaste classical taste, observation, and research.

Dr. Zerbien formerly resided at Natchez, but due to financial problems immigrated to the Spanish territories. Being a young man of a handsome person and an insinuating address, he had obtained the goodwill of Governor Cordero, who had conferred on him an appointment in the king's hospital, and many other advantages by which he might have made a fortune; but he had recently committed some very great indiscretions, by which he had nearly lost the favor of Colonel Cordero, though while we were there he was treated with attention.

We said friendly goodbyes to all of our friends in San Antonio. I will here attempt to portray a faint resemblance of the characters of the two governors whom we found at San Antonio; but to whose superexcellent qualities it would require the pen of a master to do justice.

Antonio Cordero is about five feet, ten inches in height, fifty years of age, with fair complexion and blue eyes; he wore his hair turned back, and in every part of his deportment was legibly written "the soldier." He yet possessed an excellent constitution, and a body which appeared to be neither impaired by the fatigues of the various campaigns he had made.

He was one of the select officers who had been chosen by the court of Madrid to be sent to America to discipline and organize the Spanish provincials, and had been employed in all the various kingdoms and provinces of New Spain.

Through the parts which we explored he was universally beloved and respected; and when I pronounce him by far the most popular man in the internal provinces, I risk nothing by the assertion. He spoke Latin and French well, was generous, gallant, brave, and sincerely attached to his king and country. Those numerous qualifications advanced him to the rank of colonel of cavalry, and governor of the provinces of Coahuila and Texas.

His usual residence was Montelovez, which he had embellished a great deal, but since our taking possession of Louisiana he had removed to San Antonio, in order to be nearer the frontier, to be able to apply the remedy to any evil which might arise from the collision of our lines.

Simon de Herrera is about five feet, eleven inches high, has a sparkling black eye, dark complexion and hair. He was born in the Canary Islands, served in the infantry in France, Spain, and Flanders, and speaks the French language well, with a little English. He is engaging in his conversation with his equals; polite and obliging to his inferiors, and in all his actions one of the most gallant and accomplished men I ever knew. He possesses a great knowledge of mankind from his experience in various countries and societies, and knows how to employ the genius of each of his subordinates to advantage.

He had been in the United States during the presidency of General Washington, and had been introduced to that hero, of whom he spoke in terms of exalted veneration.

He is now lieutenant-colonel of infantry, and governor of the kingdom of Nuevo León. His seat of government is Mont El Rey; and probably, if ever a chief is adored by his people, it is Herrera. When his time expired last, he immediately repaired to Mexico, attended by 300 of the most respectable people of his government, who carried with them the sighs, tears, and prayers of thousands that he might be continued in that government.

The viceroy thought proper to accord to their wishes pro tempore, and the king has since confirmed his nomination.

When I saw him he had been about one year absent, during which time the citizens of rank in Mont El Rey had not suffered a marriage or baptism to take place in any of their families, until their common father could be there, to consent and give joy to the occasion by his presence.

What greater proof could be given of their esteem and love? In drawing a parallel between these two friends, I should say that Cordero was the man of greatest reading, and that Herrera possessed the greatest knowledge of the world. Cordero has lived all his life a bachelor. Herrera married an English lady in early youth, at Cadiz; one who by her suavity of manners makes herself as much beloved and esteemed by the ladies as her noble husband is by the men. By her he has several children, one now an officer in the service of his royal master.

The two friends agree perfectly in one point—their hatred to tyranny of every kind; and in a secret determination never to see that flourishing part of the New World subject to any other European lord. But should Bonaparte seize on European Spain, I risk nothing in asserting that those two gentlemen would be the first to throw off the yoke, draw their swords, and assert the independence of their country.

Before I close this subject, it may not be improper to state that it is thanks to Governor Herrera's prudence that we are not now engaged in a war with Spain. This will be explained by the following anecdote, which he related in the presence of his friend Cordero, and which was confirmed by him.

When the difficulties commenced on the Sabine, the commandant-general and the viceroy consulted each other and mutually determined to maintain inviolate what they deemed the dominions of their master. The viceroy therefore ordered Herrera to join Cordero with 1,300 men, and both the viceroy and General Salcedo ordered Cordero to attack our troops should they pass the Hondo River. These orders were positively reiterated to Herrera, the actual commanding officer of the Spanish army on the frontiers.

III. Population and Main Settlements: San Antonio

San Antonio, the capital of the province, lies in lat. 29° 50′ N. and long. 101° W. and is situated on the headwaters of the river of that name; it contains perhaps 2,000 souls, most of whom reside in miserable mud-wall houses, covered with thatched grass roofs. The town is laid out on a grand plan. To the east of it, on the other side of the river, is the station of the troops.

About two, three, and four miles from San Antonio are three missions, formerly flourishing and prosperous. Those buildings, for solidity, accommodation, and even majesty, were surpassed by few that I saw in New Spain. The resident priest treated us with the greatest hospitality, and was respected and beloved by all who knew him. He made a singular observation relative to the aborigines who had formerly formed the population of those establishments under charge of the monks. I asked him what had become of the natives. He replied that it appeared to him that they could not exist under the shadow of the whites, as the nations who formed those missions had been nurtured, taken all the care of that it was possible, and put on the same footing as the Spaniards; yet, notwithstanding, they had dwindled away until the other two missions had become entirely depopulated, and the one where he resided had not then more than sufficient to perform his household labor.

Nacogdoches is merely a station for troops and contains nearly 500 souls. It is situated on a small stream of the Toyac River. The population of Texas may be estimated at 7,000. These are principally Spanish, Creoles, some French, some Americans, and a few civilized Indians and half-breeds.

TRADE AND COMMERCE. This province trades with Mexico by Mont El Rey and Montelovez for merchandise, and with New Orleans by Natchitoches; but the latter trade, being contraband, is liable to great danger and risks. They give in return specie, horses, and mules.

AGRICULTURE. The American emigrants are introducing some little spirit of agriculture near Nacogdoches and the Trinity; but the oppressions and suspicions they labor under prevent their proceeding with that spirit which is necessary to give success to the establishment of a new country.

ABORIGINES. The Tancards are a nation of Indians who rove on the banks of Red River and are 600 men strong. They follow the buffalo and wild horses and carry on a trade with the Spaniards.

They are armed with the bow, arrow, and lance. They are erratic and confined to no particular district. They are a tall, handsome people; in conversation they have a peculiar clucking, express more by signs than any savages I ever visited, and in fact language appears to have made less progress. They complained much of their situation and the treatment of the Spaniards; are extremely poor, and, except the Apaches, are the most independent Indians we encountered in the Spanish territories. They possess large droves of horses.

There are a number of other nations now nearly extinct, some of which are mentioned by Dr. Sibley in a report he made to the government of the United States on these subjects.

A few, and very few indeed, of those nations have been converted by the missions, and these are not in that state of vassalage in which the Indians farther to the south are held.

GOVERNMENT AND LAWS. Perfectly military, except as to the ecclesiastical jurisdiction.

MORALS AND MANNERS. Being on the frontier, where buffalo and wild horses abound, and not engaged in any war with savages who are powerful, they have adopted a mode of living by following those animals, which has been productive of a more wandering disposition around the capital (San Antonio) than in any other of the provinces. Cordero, restricting by edicts the buffalo hunts to certain seasons, and obliging every man of family to cultivate so many acres of land, has in some degree checked the spirit of hunting or wandering life which had been hitherto so very prevalent, and has endeavored to introduce, by his example and precepts, a general urbanity and suavity of manners which rendered San Antonio one of the most agreeable places that we met with in the provinces.

MILITARY FORCE. There were in Texas at the time I came through 988 men, from the actual returns of the troops which I have seen, 500 of whom were from St. Ander and Nuevo León, under command of Governor Herrera. The disposition of those troops is as follows: 388 at San Antonio, 400 at the cantonment of [Blank] on the Trinity, 100 at the [crossing of the] Trinity, and 100 at Nacogdoches. The militia, a rabble made somewhat respectable by a few American riflemen who are incorporated amongst them, are about 300 men, including bow and arrow men.

RELIGION. Catholic, but much relaxed.

HISTORY. To me unknown, except what can be extracted from various authors on that subject.

GENERAL REMARKS ON NEW SPAIN

To become acquainted with all of the civil and political institutes of a country requires a perfect knowledge of the language, a free ingress to the archives, and a residence of some years; even then we can scarcely distinguish between the statute laws and common law, derived from custom, morals, and habits. Under those circumstances, it cannot be expected that I shall be able to say much on the subject, as I possessed none of the above advantages.

I will, however, offer a few observations. To a stranger it is impossible to define the limits of the military and ecclesiastical jurisdictions; in every affair which relates to the citizens, and in fact with the soldiery, the force of superstition is such that I am doubtful whether they would generally obey one of their officers in a direct violation of the injunction of their religious professions. The audiences of Mexico and Guadalajara were formed, no doubt, as a check on the immense power of the viceroy. The number of members composing each is to me unknown, but they are formed of the viceroy as president, with two votes, generals, and bishops. To their jurisdictions the appeals from the judgment of the intendants and all subordinate officers may be made in civil cases; but the military and ecclesiastical decisions are distinct. Notwithstanding all this semblance of justice, should an individual dare to make the appeal and not succeed in establishing the justice of his claim to redress, he is certainly ruined.

The captain-generalcy of the internal provinces appeared to me to be much more despotic, for the laws or regulations were issued in the form of an order merely, without any kind of a preamble whatsoever, except sometimes he would say, "By order of the king."

MORALS AND MANNERS. For hospitality, generosity, and sobriety the people of New Spain exceed any nation perhaps on the globe; but in national energy, patriotism, enterprise of character, or independence of soul, they are perhaps the most deficient. Their women have black eyes and hair, fine teeth, and are generally brunettes.

I met but one exception to this rule, at Chihuahua—a fair lady, who, by way of distinction, was called "the girl with light hair."

They are all inclining a little to embonpoint; but none or few are elegant figures. Their dress generally is short jackets and petticoats and high-heeled shoes, without any head-dress. Over the whole dress they have a silk wrapper, which they always wear and, when in the presence of men, affect to bring over their faces, but from under which you frequently see peeping a large sparkling black eye. As we approached the Atlantic and our frontiers, we saw several ladies who wore the gowns of our countrywomen, which they conceived to be much more elegant than their ancient costume. The lower class of the men are generally dressed in broad-brimmed hats, short coats, large waistcoats, and small clothes always open at the knees (owing, as I suppose, to the greater freedom it gives to the limbs on horseback), a kind of leather boot or wrapper bound round the leg somewhat in the manner of our frontier-men's leggings, and gartered on. The boot is of a soft, pliable leather, but not colored. In the eastern provinces the dragoons wear, over this wrapper or boot, a sort of jack-boot made of sole-leather, to which are fastened, by a rivet, the spurs. They are always ready to mount their horses, on which the inhabitants of the internal provinces spend nearly half the day. This description will apply generally to the dress of all the men of the provinces for the lower class; but in their cities, among the more fashionable, they dress after the European or United States modes.

Both men and women have remarkably fine hair, and pride themselves in the display of it. Their amusements are music, singing, dancing, and gambling.

The latter is strictly prohibited, but the prohibition is not much attended to. Dancing is usually between one man and two women. The dancers exhibit the motions of the soul by gestures of the body, snapping the fingers, and sometimes meeting in a stretched embrace. The fandango is danced to various figures and numbers.

The minuet is still danced by the superior class only. The music made use of is the guitar, violin, and singers.

Their games are cards, billiards, horse-racing, and cock-fighting, the first and last of which are carried to the most extravagant lengths, losing and winning immense sums. The present commandant-general is very severe with his officers in these respects, frequently sending them to some frontier post in confinement for months, for no other fault than having lost large sums at play.

At every town of consequence is a public walk, where the ladies and gentlemen meet and sing songs, which are always on the subject of love or the social board. The females have fine voices, and sing in French, Italian, and Spanish, the whole company joining in the chorus. In their homes the ladies play the guitar and generally accompany it with their voices. They either sit down on the carpet cross-legged, or loll on a sofa. To sit upright in a chair appeared to put them to great inconvenience; although the better class would sometimes do it on our first introduction, they soon took the liberty of following their old habits. In their eating and drinking they are remarkably temperate. Early in the morning you receive a dish of chocolate and a cake; at twelve you dine on several dishes of meat, fowls, and fish, after which you have a variety of confections, and indeed an elegant dessert; then drink a few glasses of wine, sing a few songs, and retire to take the siesta, or afternoon's nap, which is taken by rich and poor. About two o'clock the windows and doors are all closed, the streets deserted, and the stillness of midnight reigns throughout. About four o'clock they rise, wash and dress, and prepare for the dissipation of the night. About eleven o'clock some refreshments are offered, but few take any, except a little wine and water and candied sugar.

The government has multiplied the difficulties of Europeans intermarrying with the Creoles or Mestizos to such a degree that it is difficult for such a marriage to take place. An officer wishing to marry a lady not from Europe is obliged to acquire certificates of the purity of her descent 200 years back, and transmit it to the court, when the license will be returned; but should she be the daughter of a man of the rank of captain or upward this nicety vanishes, as rank purifies the blood of the descendants.

The general subjects of conversations among the men are women, money, and horses, which appear to be the only objects, in their estimation, worthy of consideration. The most important goal was to obtain money and many horses. The men only regard women as objects of gratification to the sensual passions, and do not otherwise communicate with them. The beggars of the City of Mexico are estimated at 60,000 souls; what must be the number through the whole kingdom. And to what reason can it be owing that, in a country superior to any in the world for riches in gold and silver, producing all of the necessaries of life and most of its luxuries, there should be such a vast proportion of the inhabitants in want of bread or clothing? It can only be accounted for by the tyranny of the government and the luxuries of the rich.

TRADE AND COMMERCE. The trade and commerce of New Spain are carried on with Europe and the United States by the port of Vera Cruz solely, and with the East Indies and South America generally by Acapulco; and, even at these ports, under such restriction as to productions, manufactures, and time, as to render it of little consequence to the general prosperity of the country. Were all the numerous bays and harbors of the gulfs of Mexico and California opened to the trade of the world, and a general license given to the cultivation of all the productions of which the country is capable, with freedom of exportation and importation, with proper duties on foreign goods, the country would immediately become rich and powerful, and a proper stimulus would be held out to the poor to labor. The country abounds in iron ore, yet all the iron and steel, and articles of manufactures, are obliged to be brought from Europe, the manufacturing or working of iron being strictly prohibited.

The works of the Mexicans, in gold, silver, and painting, show them naturally to have a genius which, with cultivation and improvement, might rival the greatest masters of either ancient or modern times. Their dispositions and habits are peculiarly calculated for sedentary employments, and I have no doubt, if proper establishments were made, they would soon rival, if not surpass, the most extensive woolen, cotton, or silk manufactures of Europe. Their climate is proper to raise the finest cotton in the world, and their sheep possessing all the fineness of wool for which they are so celebrated in Spain. The following statements I have had from so respectable a source, and they are so confirmed by my own observations, that I think much reliance may be placed on their correctness. The mint coins, per annum, at least, $50,000,000 in silver and $14,000,000 in gold, the one-fifth of which (the duty) is equal to $12,800,000.

The duties on foreign goods and the amount paid by the purchasers of monopolies may be estimated at $4,000,000; which, with the duty on gold and silver, makes the annual revenue $16,800,000. The civil list of the kingdom is $580,000, the military $7,189,200; these together amount to $7,760,200, which, deducted from the gross revenue of $16,700,000, leaves a clear revenue for the king from his Mexican dominions of $9,030,800.

The money paid for the support of the clergy is not included in this estimate, as they receive their revenue through its own proper channel. The best paid officers under the government cost the king nothing in a direct line, yet the oppressive manner in which they pay themselves and impoverish the people would render it better policy to abolish their impositions and pay them out of the public treasury by a direct salary. The European troops are some of the choicest regiments from Spain; consequently, we may put them on the supposition that they are well disciplined, and officered by men of honor and science.

The regular troops of the kingdom who are in the viceroyalty, acting from the stimulant of ambition and envy, are supposed to be equal to their brethren from Europe. The militia, with the regular officers, are likewise good troops, but are not held in so high estimation as the other corps. Those three corps, forming a body of 23,288 men, may be called the regular force of the kingdom, as the militia of 139,500 would, in my estimation, be of no more consequence against the regular troops of any civilized power than the ancient aborigines of the country were against the army of Cortes.

The appearance of the Spanish troops is certainly, at a distance, very military; their lances are fixed to the side of the saddle under the left thigh. On the right the carabine is slung in a case to the front of the saddle, or pommel, crosswise, the breech to the right hand; and on each side of the saddle, behind the rider, is a pistol; below the breech of the carabine is slung the shield.

They have in general the arms of Spain with Carlos IV, with gilt on the outside, with various other devices, which add much to the elegance of their appearance on horseback. These shields are only calculated to be of service against savages who have no fire-arms. The dragoons of the viceroyalty do not make use of the lance or shield, but are armed, equipped, and clothed after the modern manner.

Their dress is a short blue coat, with red cape and cuffs, without facings, leather or blue cotton velvet small-clothes and waistcoat, the small-clothes always open at the knees.

Their horses are small and slender-limbed, but very active and capable of enduring great fatigue, with a high projecting pommel. They are probably the most expert horsemen in the world.

At each post is a store, called the king's, where it was the original intention of the government that the soldiers should be supplied with provisions, clothing, arms, etc., at a cheap rate; but it being a post generally given to some young officer to make his fortune, they are subject to great impositions. When a dragoon joins the service he receives from the king five horses and two mules, and this number he is always obliged to keep good from his own pocket; but when he is discharged, the horses and mules receive the discharge mark and become his private property. They engage for five or ten years. A private dragoon considers himself upon an equality with most of the citizens and infinitely superior to the lower class, and not unfrequently you see men of considerable fortune marrying the daughters of sergeants and corporals.

Corporal punishment is contrary to the Spanish ordinances. They punish by imprisonment, putting in the stocks, and death. As a remarkable instance of the discipline and regularity of conduct of those provincial troops, although marching with them and doing duty as it were for nearly four months, I never saw a man receive a blow or put under confinement for one hour. How impossible would it be to regulate the turbulent dispositions of the Americans with such treatment!

The discipline of their troops is very different from ours. As to tactics or military maneuvers, I never saw a corps of troops exercising as dragoons, but frequently marching by platoons, sections, etc. On a march a detachment of cavalry generally encamp in a circle. They relieve their guards at night; as soon as they halt the new guard is formed on foot with their carabines, and then marched before the commandant's tent, where the commanding officer of the guard invokes the holy virgin three times. Their sentinels are singing half the time, and it is no uncommon thing for them to quit their post to come to the fire, go for water, etc.—in fact, after the officer is in bed, frequently the whole guard comes in; yet I never knew any man punished for those breaches of military duty.

Their mode of attack is by squadrons, on the different flanks of their enemies, but without regularity or concert, shouting, hallooing, and firing their carabines; after which, if they think themselves equal to the enemy, they charge with a pistol and then a lance. From my observation on their discipline I have no hesitation in declaring that I would not be afraid to march over a plain with 500 infantry and a proportionate allowance of horse artillery of the United States army, in the presence of 5,000 of these dragoons. Yet I do not presume to say that an army with that inferiority of numbers would do to oppose them. The conclusion must not be drawn that I consider they are more deficient in physical firmness. It arises solely from the want of discipline and confidence in each other.

The traveling food of the dragoons in New Mexico consists of a very excellent species of wheat biscuit, and shaved meat well dried, with a vast quantity of red pepper, which they then pour on their broken biscuit, when the latter becomes soft and excellent eating.

Farther south they use large quantities of parched corn-meal and sugar, as practiced by our hunters; in short, they eat very well.

From the physical as well as moral properties of the inhabitants of New Spain, I do believe they are capable of being made the best troops in the world, possessing sobriety, enterprise, great physical force, docility, and a conception equally quick and penetrating.

The mode of promotion in the internal provinces is singular, but probably productive of good effects. Should a vacancy of first lieutenant offer in a company, the captain commanding nominates, with the senior second lieutenant, two other lieutenants. The general selects two for a nomination to the court. As the letters of nomination are always kept a secret, it is impossible for the young officers to say who is to blame if they are disappointed.

The king of Spain's ordinances for the government of his army are generally founded on justice and a high sense of honor. They provide that no old soldier shall ever be discharged the service, unless for infamous crimes. When a man has served with reputation for fifteen years and continues, his pay is augmented; twenty years, he receives another augmentation; twenty-seven years, he receives the brevet rank and pay of an ensign. Those circumstances are a great stimulant, although not one in a thousand arrives at the third period, when they are permitted to retire from the service with full pay and emoluments. All sons of captains, or of grades superior, are entitled to enter the king's schools as cadets, at the age of twelve years.

The property of any officer or soldier who is killed on the field of battle, is not liable to be taken for debt, and is secured, as well as the king's pension, to the relatives of the deceased.

There is another principle defined by the ordinances, which has often been the cause of disputes in the service of the United States. The commandant of a post receives no orders from a general for he is responsible to the king alone for his post. That principle, according to my ideas, is very injurious to the country which adopts it. The principle is also subversive of the very root of military subordination and discipline, where an inferior should in all cases obey a superior.

RELIGION. It forms a subject with which I am very imperfectly acquainted; but, having made some inquiries and observations on the religion of the country, I will freely communicate them, fearful at the same time that I lay myself open to severe criticism. The kingdom of New Spain is divided into four archbishoprics, viz.: Mexico, Guadalaxara, Durango, and San Luis Potosí. Under these again are the sub-bishoprics—deacons, curates, etc., all of whom are subject and accountable to their immediate chief for the districts committed to their charge, and the whole are again subject to the ordinances of the high court of inquisition held at the capital of Mexico, whence are fulminated the edicts of their censure against the heresies and impious doctrines of modern philosophy, both as to politics and religion. I am credibly informed that the influence of that tribunal is greater in his Catholic majesty's Mexican dominions than in any Catholic country in Europe or perhaps in the world. A few years since they condemned a man to the flames, for asserting and maintaining some doctrine which they deemed heretical; and a Jew who was imprudent enough to take the image of Christ on a cross, and put it under the sill of his door. They likewise examine and condemn to the flames all books of a modern sentiment, either as to religion or politics, and excommunicate anyone in whose hands they may be found.

I recollect to have seen a decree of theirs published in the Mexican gazettes, condemning a number of books, "as heretical and contrary to the sacred principles of the holy Catholic church, and the peace and durability of the government of his Catholic majesty." Amongst these were mentioned:

Helvetius on Man, J. J. Rousseau's works, Voltaire's, Mirabeau's, and a number of others.

The salaries of the archbishops are superior to those of any officers in the kingdom; the bishop of Mexico's being estimated at $150,000 per annum, when the viceroy's is $80,000. Those incomes are raised entirely from the people, who pay no tax to the king, but give one-tenth of their yearly income to the clergy, besides the fees of confessions, bulls, burials, baptisms, marriages, and a thousand impositions which the corruption of priestcraft has introduced, and which have been kept up by their superstition and ignorance. Notwithstanding all this, the inferior clergy, who do all the slavery of the office, are liberal and well-informed men. They are generally Creoles by birth, and always kept in subordinate grades, without the least shadow of a probability of rising to the superior dignities of the church.

POLITICS. It has often been a subject of discussion with politicians, in what manner a mother country should treat her distant and powerful colonies, in order to retain them longest in their subjection; for the history of all nations and all ages has proved that no community of people separated from another by an immense ocean will remain long subject to the mother country. But there is a line of conduct which certainly must retard it in a great measure.

The two great examples of English and Spanish America are before our eyes. England gave us liberty to pursue the dictates of our own judgment with respect to trade, education, and manners, by which means we increased in power, learning, and wealth, with a rapidity unknown in the annals of the world, and at the first attempt to infringe the rights which we had hitherto enjoyed, asserted that claim which nature and the locality of our situation gave us a right to demand and a power to defend. Spain pursued a different line of conduct toward her Mexican dominions, which might be termed a conquered kingdom, rather than the settlement of a savage country, and has so carefully secluded all light from bursting in on their ignorance, that they have vegetated like the acorns in the forest. The approximation of the United States, with the gigantic strides of French ambition, have begun to arouse their dormant qualities, and to call into action the powers of their minds on the subject of their political situation. An instance of their disposition for independence has been exhibited in their feeble attempts at a revolution on the 15th of January, 1624, under the viceroyalty of Diego Carrello Galves; the insurrection on the 8th of June, 1692; and more recently, in 1797, under the Count de Galves, when they proclaimed him king of Mexico in the streets of the capital, and 130,000 souls were heard proclaiming: "long live Galves, king of Mexico."

It was then only for him to have willed it, and the kingdom of Mexico was lost to Charles IV forever. But preferring his loyalty to his ambition, he rode out attended by his guards to the mob, with sword in hand, crying out "Long live his Catholic majesty, Charles IV" and threatening to put to instant death with his own hand any persons who refused immediately to retire to their houses. This dispersed the people. In another quarter of the kingdom an immense number had also collected and proclaimed him king. He sent 10,000 men against them, dispersed them, and had four beheaded.

Those firm measures saved the country at that period, and for them he received the greatest honors from the court of Spain; but was poisoned a short time after, fulfilling the maxim that "it is dangerous to serve a jealous tyrant." For such always conceive that the same power which stilled the ocean's rage can by its will raise the storm into all of the majesty of overwhelming fury.

England would naturally have been the power they would have looked up to, in order to form an alliance to secure their independence; but the insatiable avarice and hauteur exhibited by the English in their late descents at La Plate, with the disgrace of their arms, has turned their views from that nation. They therefore have turned their eyes toward the United States, who has within her power ample resources of arms, ammunition, and even men, to assist in securing their independence, and who in that event would secure to herself the almost exclusive trade of the richest country in the world for centuries, and [the opportunity] to be her carriers as long as the two nations exist.

Twenty thousand auxiliaries from the United States under good officers, joined to the independents of the country, are at any time sufficient to create and effect the revolution.

These troops can be raised and officered in the United States, but paid and supplied at the expense of Mexico. It would be requisite that not only the general commanding, but that every officer, down to the youngest ensign, should be impressed with the necessity of supporting a strict discipline, to prevent marauding, which should in some instances be punished with death, in order to convince the citizens that we come as their friends and protectors, not as their plunderers and tyrants.

Washington, April 12, 1808.
Signed, Z. M. Pike.
Cap. 1st. US Infantry Regiment.

CHAPTER 4

Consequences of the Pike Expedition

MAY 1865

The intentions of Pike and his expedition resulted in an ongoing correspondence between General Wilkinson and Nemesio Salcedo, governor of the interior provinces of the Viceroyalty of New Spain, that began with a letter dated October 10, 1808:

> Headquarters of the United States Army
>
> Sir:
>
> The long and unexpected detention of the military group commanded by Lieutenant Pike within Your Excellency's jurisdiction, without knowing what may happen (or so the lieutenant informs me), has induced the President of the United States to ask me to investigate this detention and to request his freedom with a passport of safe-conduct to the left bank of the Sabine River.
>
> Your Excellency has surely seen in Lieutenant Pike's instructions that his orders prohibited his reconnaissance beyond the waters of the Red River, and I can assure you that it was only his ignorance of the geography of the country that caused him to enter Spanish territory. I hereby give you my word of honor as a man and as a soldier that Lieutenant Pike had no other intentions, and that his arrival in San Antonio was as much of a surprise for me as I am sure it was for you. Rather like the crew of a battered ship who suddenly arrive at a familiar place, these unfortunate wanderers, after much suffering, have asked for mercy (under the laws that so determine

it) from Your Excellency. I am most surprised by the continued detention of the sergeants after the liberation of the lieutenant, in particular considering that at this time we western nations should be strengthening our bonds of friendship.

Captain Hughes, one of my aides-de-camp, who has the honor of delivering this letter to Your Excellency, is a man of honor and a trusted officer, and can take charge of Lieutenant Pike's sergeants; under the custody of your security guards he will bring them back to their country.

I have the honor of remaining at your disposition, with my highest consideration,

JA. WILKINSON

James Wilkinson to Daniel Hughes

Carlisle Headquarters, October 13, 1808

You should proceed with speed down the Ohio and Mississippi Rivers to Fort Adams. Upon arrival, you are to present the letters you carry to Colonel Cushing and the chief of the district, and you will receive four hundred dollars from the latter for your expenses. The colonel will give you a boat and crew for descending the Red River to Natchitoches, and will give you the instructions he considers opportune. I will also give you an order for Lieutenant-Colonel Freeman for three horses, for your comfort.

Once you have prepared your equipment you should begin your journey to the capital of the interior provinces of Mexico. Upon your arrival, present this letter to the captain general and ask him for the liberation of Lieutenant Pike's sergeants and men. If you are successful, you should request a passport and an escort to the Spanish border, in order to return to Natchitoches without delay.

> Inform me by post when you arrive and, after resting, return to headquarters by the easiest and most economical route.
>
> If, despite using all of the necessary arguments, you are still not permitted to enter Spanish territory, you should write to the captain general and let him decide what is to be done. If the captain general refuses to surrender the men, then your mission has reached its end, but if he proposes to send them, you should await their arrival and then lead them to Fort Adams.
>
> In the course of this mission you are advised to be as economical as possible and to avoid expenses, and in your relations with the Spanish officers you should observe impeccable conduct.
>
> I remain at your disposal, sincerely
>
> JA. WILKINSON
>
> Please consider the above as my only instructions.

This invasion was not sent out in peace, since it was comprised of members of the United States army, as Wilkinson himself recognizes in his abovementioned letters to Captain Hughes. If any doubt remains, it can be dispelled completely by this letter that Jefferson, the president of the United States himself, sent to Claiborne on October 29, 1808, stating the following:

> We shall be well satisfied to see Cuba & Mexico remain in their present dependence; but very unwilling to see them in that of either France or England, politically or commercially. These are sentiments which I would wish you to express to any proper characters of either of these two countries, and particularly that we have nothing more at heart than their friendship.

The detention and subsequent liberation of Pike's spying expedition generated a series of reports and much correspondence, which I will endeavor to reproduce in their entirety, given how important they are.

Report to Pedro Cevallos, November 24, 1808

My dear Sir:

In his letter 887 dated July 22, the Marquis of Casa Irujo informed you of the contents of a letter that he had received from the general commander of the Interior Provinces, advising him that in the area of San Antonio de Béjar, Texas, they had arrested an expedition of American explorers commanded by Lieutenant Pike and a Dr. Robinson. The letter also mentioned that said members of the expedition were taken to Chihuahua, the capital of the interior provinces, where they were released shortly afterward, and taken back to the United States. These men were obliged to leave behind their documents, and the general commander has written to the American General Wilkinson complaining of the offense committed against His Majesty and His territories by these explorers.

Although we have received no word on the subject here from the general commander of the exterior provinces, in Irujo's letter His Excellency recommended that: "Salcedo should be reprimanded for liberating the intruders and must be informed that should these circumstances repeat themselves then their liberty must not be guaranteed without a formal petition from the American government and a formal promise that they will be punished upon their return to their country, to His Majesty's satisfaction."

This was communicated to Salcedo on September 28.

The State Department received this letter 17 from Salcedo on May 9, in which he reports the arrest of the North American expedition in the same terms mentioned in Trujo's letter: "the pretext given by the explorers was that they had become lost while attempting to explore the borders and territories of the upper part of Louisiana; liberty was granted to the members of the expedition, who were taken to the United States along with a formal complaint from Salcedo to the American General Wilkinson."

Salcedo also included copies of the letters and documents taken from Lieutenant Pike and held in the headquarters, and I have included the index herein.

It is easily deduced from these journals that although they are written with great artifice, the real objective was not only to reconnoiter upper Louisiana, but also the interior provinces, as well as to convince various Indian nations living within His Majesty's territory to do what the Americans considered pertinent.

The reason Salcedo freed the members of the expedition is that when he received orders from Your Excellency's Ministry and the Ministry of War to detain the expedition, he was told to act with moderation, in the same way as when he detained the previous expedition with Mayor Freeman.

However, although it can be appreciated that Salcedo's actions impeded the success of two American expeditions, for which he certainly deserved His Majesty's gratitude, he was mistaken in setting this latest expedition free, since the contents of the letters gave him more than enough reason to detain them. The moderation that His Majesty wished to employ during these incidents with the American commanders is strange, since they had been clearly warned of the need to respect the regulations for foreigners wishing to cross His Majesty's borders.

Salcedo was also mistaken in moving them to Chihuahua, since during the journey they were able to familiarize themselves with the territories they crossed. However, it must be said that he did so because he had no guarantee that they would arrive safely by other means, or that they would be safe staying in San Antonio de Béjar.

Salcedo mentions that he lent Pike 1,000 *duros* for expenses during the return journey which, along with the other expenses incurred by the expedition, should be requested from the American government. In practice this will go nowhere, since the American government will never confirm that the expedition was authorized.

The aforementioned sums of money could legally be demanded from Pike, and if he is unable to pay them we can turn to the members of the expedition.

At this point, it appears that: I. Salcedo should be thanked for detaining the expedition, and informed that he erred in setting them free, especially since there was proof of their crimes contained within the letters and papers confiscated. II. Foronda highlighted to the American government how well the explorers were treated, but at the same time underscored that if this happens again we will take very different measures. III. Your Excellency also emphasized the issue with the Secretary for International Affairs of the American government. IV. The aforementioned papers make it appear that General Wilkinson was working against us even though he appeared to have good relations with Spain; as Your Excellency knows, Wilkinson's attitudes toward us are being investigated thoroughly. It will be clear to Your Excellency that if by some accident it were established in the Ministry that Wilkinson was paid by Spain several years ago, and received the money years ago, we should investigate the matter with the utmost delicacy.

My dear Sir:

Your Excellency's rapid decision with respect to Lieutenant Pike's incursion into the interior provinces with a group of explorers is being implemented through the Secretary for Foreign Affairs of the United States, the commander-in-chief of the interior provinces, etc.

Included is a copy of the documents already sent to His Majesty by Salcedo, which explain everything related to this expedition, together with a translation of said documents. There are also complaints regarding the chaotic disorder in which the Marquis of Irujo has left the archives, which reflects the enormous amount of work that the Secretary of the Consular Corps, Carlos Mulvery, has on his hands at this moment. Also included are the written requests to Pike for the return of the thousand *duros* lent to him by Salcedo, in an act of excessive generosity.

It would be most interesting for His Majesty to study in depth the letters from Foronda and the response from Madison, which are attached.

In Madison's response to Foronda, Your Excellency will note the promptness with which the American government agreed to repay the thousand *duros* advanced by Salcedo—a clear sign that the government was well aware of the expedition. This government gives two excuses for Pike's actions: the first is the pretext that they were lost, which was also alleged by Pike when he was arrested, and the second is the claim by the Americans that the limits of Louisiana should extend to the northern Río Grande. This is a ridiculous excuse, and even if it were true, his incursion into these territories would have been enough to justify his arrest by His Majesty's forces.

In his letter 29, Foronda complains that the Marquis of Casa Irujo did not want to send the letters related to the Pike affair. Irujo's justification is his wish not to jeopardize his properties in the event that said letters were found on the boat by the English.

There is also another letter from Foronda, number 39, which deals in part with this topic, although it is mainly concerned with the response from Madison to the protest for damages from the Miranda Expedition and, as it rightly mentions, the topic is mainly covered in this letter.

My dear Sir:

One of the decisions taken by Your Excellency with respect to the incursion of Pike and his expedition of explorers into the interior provinces was the order that a note be delivered to the hand of the

Secretary for Foreign Affairs of the United States, dated November 27, a summary of which is attached.

In response, the Americans notify Your Excellency that they were not aware of this expedition and therefore know nothing, and can only imagine that its goal must have been scientific or commercial. If by any chance the members of the expedition were hostile, there is no doubt that the American government would have taken the appropriate measures to punish them. Finally, rest assured that Your Excellency's note will be conveyed to their government.

At the same time, the secretary adds that while his government tirelessly demonstrates its ties of friendship with the Spanish government, the commanders of the Spanish colonies do not cease to upset the Americans. As evidence of this he mentions that the free navigation of the Mobile River is not permitted to American citizens, not even to the naval garrisons of the American army who wish to travel up the river to reach their headquarters. This is the first time that an American authority has officially complained about this situation.

My dear Sir:

The preceding extract contains everything that has occurred with respect to the Pike Expedition in Texas.

In the light of its contents, His Majesty ordered that instructions be sent to the commander-in-chief of the interior provinces and the Secretary of Foreign Affairs of the United States.

The communication sent to the commander-in-chief noted that His Majesty had not approved the liberation of the expedition members, in particular since no formal and official petition from the United States had been received. The commander-in-chief replied that in the event of another incursion, he would act in accordance with His Majesty's wishes.

He says that he used the same moderation that was used with Major Freeman's expedition along the waters of the Colorado River, and that although he sent Pike's men back to the United States, he still has seven soldiers and an interpreter imprisoned, and will take no decisions with respect to their fates until His Majesty conveys his wishes. He also informs that these expeditions have run up costs of over 21,655 pesos, which should clearly be demanded from the American government. To this end, he sent the bill to the Secretary of Foreign Affairs, but the American government has not yet responded, thus the abovementioned eight people should be held until an answer is forthcoming.

His Majesty should know that a member of this expedition, a man named Julián Mike, has murdered one of his companions, another American named Soldier Millar Done.

The commander-in-chief has sent the testimony and the sentence from the trial, so that His Majesty may determine his will. At this point it is important to decide whether the Council of the Indies should send on the documentation, so that you may advise on the best possible course of action: either the commander-in-chief could pass sentence in Chihuahua, or the criminal could be brought before the American government.

Pedro Cevallos to the Council of the Indies
Aranjuez, November 24, 1808

My dear Sir:

In November last year, my ministry was informed though letters from the United States, from the commander-in-chief of the interior provinces of New Spain, of the arrest of an expedition of American explorers who had left Louisiana to cross the provinces, under the command of Captain Montgomery Pike. Both the discovery of suspicious orders and letters in their possession written by persons employed by the American government, and the fact that the explorers were taken to Chihuahua and later freed by the provincial government, thus allowing them to return to the United States with loans of money, were all communicated to me in detail.

At the same time, His Majesty approved the interruption of said expedition in accordance with the instructions the governor had previously received. However, His Majesty also reproached the person who set them free before the North American government had actually requested it. His Majesty ordered me to write to the commander-in-chief appearing in copy number 2 and number 3, in order to inform the North American court of this matter and to show them the excessive benevolence with which these men who violated our territorial borders were treated.

On learning that the king did not entirely approve of his benevolence, the commander-in-chief of the interior provinces wrote to this ministry in January of this year informing that it was still possible to carry out His Majesty's will in part; he then proceeded to detail the crime that one member of the expedition had committed against another, which was still awaiting trial. A reply was sent to this letter ordering him to free the few men from the expedition still in custody, except for Sergeant Mike, which is most contradictory since we would then have liberated all of the members except the leader; furthermore, we had already guaranteed the American government that we would return all of the men.

Finally, with respect to Sergeant Mike, responsible for the murder of the soldier Millar Done in His Majesty's domains, the Supreme Council of the Indies should review the accompanying copy of the trial records and the letter dated last May 1, and should communicate its opinion to His Majesty.

God save His Excellency

(Unsigned)

(Pedro Cevallos) to Valentín de Oronda.
Aranjuez, November 24, 1808

To the Secretary of Foreign Affairs of the United States of America.

With respect to the contents of letters 106 and 107 from Your Excellency regarding the demand made to the United States government for the amount of 21,655 pesos, representing the cost of the Pike Expedition to the Royal Treasury, the Supreme Council of Spain and the Indies has instructed me to inform you that several members of the expedition are still being held in the interior provinces, a measure which would be unnecessary if the American government were to show any interest in our claim. The council has therefore instructed me to send an order to the captain general of the interior provinces requesting that the detained individuals be released, with the exception of a certain Mike, a sergeant who says he serves the United States, since he has murdered another American soldier named Millar Done in His Majesty's domains, and his case is being heard by the courts of justice.

Nevertheless, you must understand that our benevolence in freeing both groups of men presupposes that this action will not repeat itself, and if this does occur then we will respond with the full force of the law, as His Majesty informed you in his letter of November 25, 1807.

(Unsigned)

Zebulon Montgomery Pike's expedition was the most important one organized by the government of the northern American states, since it was composed of professional soldiers with a clear intention to invade the province of Texas. The town of San Antonio, and therefore the province of Texas, had always been coveted by the northern states.

CHAPTER 5

I. Moses Austin

MARCH 1870

We descendants of the Canary Islanders, and the Spaniards in general, are increasingly worried about the influx of clandestine colonists who are settling in these vast territories of the province of Texas. They take over lands on the very outskirts of San Antonio, two or three days away on horseback, and we only learn of their existence when they come into the city for provisions and materials to work their fields.

The first colonist who officially appeared in the town with the express permission of the governor to settle here not only with his family, but also with as many American colonists as he wished, was a Yankee from Connecticut named Moses Austin.

The political atmosphere in the city was increasingly tense; the mayor, José Angel Navarro, who had traveled the whole viceroyalty from San Antonio to Mexico City, had already talked to several councilors about the negative feelings toward Spain that he had encountered during his latest visit to the capital, both in Mexico City itself and in all of the other towns he had passed through. The mood is quite general, from Río Bravo to Mexico, but it is far more acute here in San Antonio, not just among the Spaniards but also among the numerous Yankee colonists who are attempting to convince us to unite with them and begin a fight for the independence of the province of Texas.

So as I mentioned, on January 17, 1821, Moses Austin received official authorization to bring 300 families of Yankee colonists to settle on the outskirts of San Antonio.

He had only brought a handful of colonists when, on February 24, Mexico declared its independence from Spain. Moses Austin, who had traveled to Missouri to search for new settlers for Texas, died suddenly on June 10, 1821.

II. Mexican Independence

In 1821 there were rumors of an imminent Mexican declaration of independence. In the town, or more specifically in the San Antonio town council, we received the declaration of independence on October 1 of that year, which read:

DECLARATION OF THE INDEPENDENCE OF THE MEXICAN EMPIRE

> The Mexican Nation, which for three hundred years had neither had its own will, nor free use of its voice, leaves today the oppression in which it has lived.
>
> The heroic efforts of its sons have been crowned today, and consummated in an eternal and memorable enterprise, which a spirit superior to all admiration and praise, out of love and for the glory of its Country started in Iguala, continued, and brought to fruition, overcoming almost insurmountable obstacles.
>
> Restored then this part of the North to the exercise of all the rights given by the Author of Nature and recognized as unalienable and sacred by the civilized nations of the Earth, in liberty to constitute itself in the manner which best suits its happiness and through representatives who can manifest its will and plans, it begins to make use of such precious gifts and solemnly declares by means of the Supreme Junta of the Empire that it is a Sovereign nation and independent of old Spain with which henceforth it will maintain no other union besides a close friendship in the terms prescribed by the treaties; that it will establish friendly relationships with other powers, executing regarding them whatever declarations the other sovereign nations can execute; that it will constitute itself in accordance to the bases which in the Plan of Iguala and

the Treaty of Cordoba the First Chief of the Imperial Army of the Three Guarantees wisely established and which it will uphold at all costs and with all sacrifice of the means and lives of its members (if necessary); this solemn declaration, is made in the capital of the Empire on the twenty-eighth of September of the year one thousand eight hundred and twenty-one, first of Mexican Independence.

The descendants of the primitive Canarian colonists, founders of San Antonio, have always considered ourselves to be Spaniards, despite having been born in these lands. We have not been like so many other descendants of immigrants who were born here and therefore consider themselves to be more "American," as they call themselves. This declaration of independence broke our hearts. As many of us commented, it felt as though something had broken inside us. I, in particular, felt an emotion that I simply could not explain. Something between fear and uncertainty. Everything had suddenly come crashing down, but we still had to carry on as normal.

The only thing I can remember that I am actually able to put into words is that I felt, more deeply than ever, the tremendous desire that our ancestors had instilled in us to return to our Canary Islands. It had always seemed an almost impossible desire, but the full awareness of that impossibility dawned clearly on me that fateful day. Upon hearing the public reading of the declaration, I felt as though an axe had cut my umbilical cord.

In that same month of October, the first attempt at a violent invasion from North America began. An individual named Norton, a self-proclaimed general, landed in the Bay of the Holy Spirit. He was defeated and taken prisoner along with fifty of his men, who claimed to be merchants.

By this time Moses Austin, that first colonist I spoke of earlier, had died, and the new government of Mexico did not recognize the authorization to bring colonists here which had been granted by the Spanish authorities. His son, Stephen Austin, traveled to

Mexico City, and after two years of bureaucratic struggles with the Iturbide government, he managed to get the permit validated and continued his father's work, bringing around 700 families to the area.

Colonists continued to arrive, uncontrolled by the distant Mexican government, which made the same mistake as the Spanish government in abandoning their vigilance of the long border between Texas and the northern American states. From the information I have been able to gather from the San Antonio town council, in 1829 there were twenty thousand North Americans and only five thousand Spaniards in Texas.

Of course, all of these colonists arrived in Texas and found themselves to be in a majority, one which had long wished to declare independence from Mexico and create an independent state. It was therefore in this vein that the colonists Dunn Hunter and Hayden Edwards attempted to make an independent republic in Texas named Fredonia. They joined forces with the Cherokee Indians. When the Mexican government heard, they sent a squadron under the command of Mateo Ahumada, who defeated and dispersed them, executing Hunter and the Cherokee chief, Fields.

The revolt was put down, but the Mexican authorities began to distrust the American colonists from the north. Stephen Austin was in agreement with Hunter and Hayden, but tried to convince them not to begin their rebellion since it was not the right moment. When this attempt failed, as he had warned them it would, Austin saw that he was in danger of losing his good name and standing with the Mexican government as a settler from the north, and was obliged to write a manifesto setting forth how ill-founded it was to propose independence for Texas. Austin's report stated:

> The region of Texas was a distinct and separate province in the time of Spanish rule, and as such it participated in the war for independence; it was represented in the founding congress and provisionally

joined with Coahuila by the law of May 7, 1824, to form the State of Coahuila and Texas. It is exclusively agricultural, and its inhabitants work the land and possess the virtues of industry, firmness of character, fixed customs, a burning love of freedom, and the swift and rational administration of justice, which generally animate this most interesting of classes among all of the enlightened countries. They have conquered these lands by force of arms, battling constantly against the barbarian Indians, and with their plows they have put an end to the desert; they are by habit pioneers.

The most important goods produced in Texas are cotton, maize, beans, indigo, tobacco, vegetables, lard, cheese, butter, and all kinds of livestock known in the Republic. Its rivers and streams provide abundant opportunities for establishing mills and for manufacturing. The climate is hot in summer, cold in winter, and unhealthy on the rivers near the coast of the Gulf of Mexico, which run from the Sabinas River to the Nueces; there are ports for medium sized ships, and abundant timber for their construction.

All those who have knowledge of trade in Texas cannot but be aware of the Mexican markets, which are the best in the world for Texan products; deseeded cotton is worth seven to eight pesos per arroba[44] in Mexico, Puebla, San Luis, etc., while in the United States and in Europe it is worth from two to four pesos.

Corn in the ports of Matamoros, Tampico, Veracruz, and Campeche is worth between four and six pesos per fanega, while in Texas it is worth from six reales to one peso, and nearly the same in New Orleans; pork lard is worth one to two reales per pound in the Mexican ports, while in New Orleans and other parts in the north it is worth half a real more, and the same proportion can be seen with all of the products from Texas.

The export of goods to foreign countries can evidently be carried out under the Mexican flag just as easily as with that of any other nation; Texas will receive foreign goods in exchange for its products, while its fellow Mexican citizens receive gold and silver.

The laborers from Texas believe that in agricultural production they can compete with the landowners and farmers from the southern part of the Republic, along the coast of the Gulf of Mexico. This is due not only to the Texans' customs and their practical knowledge of agriculture, but also, at least for many years, to the natural fertility of the fields, the gentleness of the climate, and the proximity to the markets; as a consequence they are able to sell their products in the gulf ports at lower prices than those of equal quality from estates in other regions.

This competition will always be beneficial to the nation, since it rapidly foments the progress, true growth, and independence of the Republic by increasing industrial and agricultural production everywhere, particularly products for export abroad.

Today the Republic's exports have been reduced to gold and silver and little more; as a result, the Mexicans are other nations' miners. If this state of affairs were to change, they would pay for imports with agricultural products such as sugar, cotton, indigo, cacao, etc. Add the mines to our flourishing agriculture, and in a few years Mexico will be an interesting tableau of wealth and prosperity, as yet unknown in the world.

Trade from the Texas ports with the interior of the Republic by land offers nearly the same advantages as coastal trade, since the land is flat and well-suited for roads and highways to Monclova and the other towns of Coahuila, the northern pass into the state of Chihuahua, and to New Mexico. It is worthy of note that nearly two million pesos of merchandise enter New Mexico and Chihuahua from Missouri, crossing nearly four hundred leagues of desert. This trade with Missouri is entirely unnatural considering the geographical situation of the country; it is evident that they are drawn by the ports of Texas. It would not be difficult to open roads from Texas to the State of Chihuahua and New Mexico; it would be less than half the distance that goods currently travel from Missouri, and it would pass entirely through Mexican territory in the interior of Texas, which can be populated to provide abundant resources to facilitate transportation. The labor of opening these roads is certainly of the utmost importance, since it would alter the route of trade that currently comes from Missouri, located in a foreign country, to the Mexican ports of Texas. This would cause the earnings from freight and transport costs to pass from the Missouri shipping companies to Mexican citizens; it would increase the income from maritime customs; it would provide goods to the inhabitants of the interior at lower prices than goods from Missouri due to the decrease in distance and shipping costs; it would attract inhabitants to the unpopulated lands of the interior, who would settle along or near the trade route and would pacify the barbarous Indians who are currently marauding the borders of Chihuahua, all at no cost to the government; it would form a new and very strong chain for strengthening the union of Texas with the more remote interior states. These trade routes have been one of Austin's favored projects, and he has worked enthusiastically for the advancement of his adopted nation. However, it is a huge undertaking which progresses slowly, and thus requires the protection of the General Government and the State, and the concession of certain special privileges and advantages.

The federal system is based on individual and general happiness, and the different parts of a society so constituted are cemented to form a national union by their mutual interests and particular coexistence, in harmony with a common goal. When applying these principles to Texas, it is evident that instead of disgust at being a state of the Mexican Federation, and at the common interest as part of the national interest, the financial and other interests of Texas will further strengthen its union with the Mexican republic, and should be better promoted as part of the national interest, as in any other nation.

In 1822 the provinces of Texas, Coahuila, Nuevo León, and Tamaulipas decided to meet in Monterrey, with the intention of separating from Mexico and forming a federation with that country. At the same time, the governor of Texas, who was not invited to the meeting, recruited volunteers in San Antonio who, together with the friendly Indian tribes, were in favor of the central Mexican government. No descendants of the Canary Islanders joined the expedition. We "Canary Islanders" held a meeting, and the general feeling was that despite being born in these lands, we considered ourselves to be first and foremost Canary Islanders, and therefore Spaniards, and that fighting in favor of the central Mexican government was not our problem. It would have been a very different matter to fight for Spain.

Applications for grants of land in Texas continued to be submitted. Diego Barry, Tadeo Ortiz, and Felipe O'Reilly asked for 6,000 square leagues of land to be populated by 10,000 Irish and Canarian catholic families to offset the arrival of the Anglo-Saxons, but this was never granted to them.

III. Disillusionment among the "Canary Islanders"

Due to their proximity to the capital, the southern regions have always been much more heavily populated. We Canary Islanders (as we still proudly call ourselves) have always felt incredibly sad at how alone we are in these lands, neglected and abandoned, and subject to all manner of danger, including attacks from wild Indians. We have never been understood, even when these territories belonged to Spain, and over the years we have received a series of absurd orders, as I have already mentioned in this diary. I will never forget the dismay felt in the colony when we requested more soldiers or more Canarian colonists from Madrid to populate the area, only to discover that in Madrid they were more concerned with defending their European politics in their wars against England, or passing royal decrees naming us privateers so that we would fight against the English by sea, even though our town was in the interior of the province. We are now independent from Spain, but are even less understood by Mexico, which governs us from the capital where they have no understanding of reality here in Texas.

For this reason we have begun to ask ourselves if it would not be better to do as the American colonists say, and make war on Mexico in order to gain independence.

IV. Massive Settlement of Anglo-Saxon Priests, Professionals, and Merchants in the Province of Texas

A constant stream of foreigners continues to arrive in San Antonio with the express permission of the Mexican government, which, like the Spanish government before it, does not understand that the many legally settled foreigners also bring with them a huge number of illegal settlers: and the Mexican government does nothing to rectify this situation. It is clear that at this rate the territories will pass swiftly into the hands of the Yankees.

The governor of the state of Coahuila and Texas, José María Viescas, is granting the highest number of authorizations for foreigners to settle in these lands, either as liberal professionals, colonists, or industrialists.

Decrees 63 and 66 arrived at the San Antonio town council on September 23 and 29, 1828, and on the basis of the first decree the governor announced:

> Without increasing the twenty-three years of privileges conceded by article 1.0 of Decree 46 to citizens JUAN WOODBURY and JUAN CAMERON for the exploitation of iron and coal mines, said privileges are hereby extended for one year more, the term set forth in article 3.0 of the aforementioned decree, for the introduction and installment of machines and the construction of offices for the use of the metal industry.
>
> As constitutional governor of the state, I hereby order full compliance with this decree, and command that it be printed, published, and circulated.

Through this decree, Governor Viescas granted a twenty-three-year monopoly on this huge business enterprise to foreign citizens, although clearly logic dictates that the descendants of the Canarian founders should have been given priority; we are the founding community of the first democratic town council, and the ruling majority in the town during all of the important moments of its development into the city of Villa de San Antonio, the first capital of the state of Texas. Slowly but surely Viescas is installing foreigners into every profession. Although these appointments were unjust, the all-powerful governor totally disregarded the complaints of the descendants of the Canarian founders, and began making a series of appointments that were not only unjust but also illegal. The second decree, number 66, received on September 29, 1829, "grants special dispensation to Eleuterio María de la Garza from the number of training hours required by law, so that he may become an attorney." This appointment had been requested by descendants of Canary Islanders, with accredited legal practices, and been refused.

The oldest Canary Islanders told us youngsters that the Mexicans had never forgiven us for founding San Antonio instead of them, and for ruling the municipal government from 1731 to 1821, the year of Mexico's independence from Spain.

Governor Viesca's insensibility reached such heights that he not only granted concessions and illegally recognized degrees but, even more seriously, granted citizenship to foreigners. For example, Decree 75, dated February 8, 1828, states that "Santiago Power is hereby declared to be a citizen of the State, and this government thus orders the issuance of the documents corresponding to this honor."

As I described earlier, the Yankees have huge commercial influence, with the establishment of concessions to foreigners as colonists or industrialists, but their settlement has also brought us their social and religious customs and their language, which is so different from our own. Although at first we did not welcome them, little by little they have taken root among us and have become friends with our children, as we began to realize that they are not as wicked as the missionaries had warned us.

The number of Catholic priests in these lands is dwindling fast, and this means that we have more contact with the American priests than with the Catholics.

Aware of our lack of priests, Governor Viesca himself sent a decree to the San Antonio town council which read as follows:

> Decree 77. The Constitutional Congress of the free, independent, and sovereign state of Coahuila and Texas hereby decrees the following: In accordance with the religious authorities of the state, the government herein requests from the bishops of the Federation the clergymen required for the parishes of the new population of the department of Béjar.

The governor continued to grant concessions to foreigners rather than to Canary Islanders, which is why Decree 78 of February 13, 1829, granted Juan Lucio Woodbury two more years to the term set out in article 8 of the Colonization Law of March 24, 1825, for executing the contract made with the state government on November 14, 1826.

Alarmed at the reports sent by the San Antonio town council concerning the arrival of so many Anglo-American colonists, the Mexican congress commissioned Gen. Manual Mier y Terán to lead an expedition to the province of Texas in order to report directly on what exactly was happening there.

On February 4, 1828, the general and Lt. José María Sánchez met with my husband John W. Smith, Austin, and other Anglo-Americans, asking them to account for the illegal arrival of so many colonists. Despite the firm denial of both these men, Lieutenant Sánchez later wrote the following in his diary:

> The North Americans have taken possession of most of eastern Texas, and have done so without the knowledge of the authorities.

They immigrate incessantly with no interference whatsoever, and take possession of any land which appeals to them, without asking for permission: they simply dismount and build a house. And so it is that the majority of this department's inhabitants are North Americans, with the Mexican population [here he includes us, although we have always considered ourselves Canary Islanders first] reduced to San Antonio and Nacogdoches, two miserable towns that have no more than three thousand inhabitants between them.

The state government, located in el Saltillo, should be ensuring the preservation of by far its most interesting and valuable department by taking extreme measures to keep foreign hands from stealing it. However, it has not the slightest awareness of either the territory itself or of what is occurring here. This can be seen from the reports of the government's concessions of land to *empresarios*[45] from foreign colonies, and on verifying these reports against the map we have found that it has granted concession upon concession...

The Supreme Government of the Federation has sent repeated, emphatic reports of the imminent danger that this exceptionally interesting department will be captured by the ambitious North Americans. Secret agents are tricking the bureaucrats into believing that the risks do not exist and that these reports are exaggerations produced by men of cowardly spirits. So the authorities slacken their watch, and the enemies from the north seize every opportunity to advance, little by little, toward their true objective, which is well known to all.

V. The Anglo-Saxon School System

As can be seen in the aforementioned decrees, in order to disguise the truth and to avoid scandals in the Spanish colony, the Yankees asking for concessions gave themselves Spanish names, by mutual consent with the governor, although they could not conceal the Anglo-Saxon roots of their surnames.

The Anglo-Saxon influence is rapidly increasing, and the indifference and corruption of the Mexican government is astonishing; the awarding of citizenship, the granting of colonies, and the bestowal of liberal professions all have their price, established, unofficially of course, by Governor José María Viesca. For this reason, the Anglo-Saxon influence today, in 1828, is now unstoppable.

Through Decree 92, from May 14, 1829, it was agreed to establish a school based on the Lancaster System of mutual instruction.

We Canary Islanders were totally ignorant of this system and gathered in the town hall to demand explanations.

Professor Baker received us, and explained that the system was invented in England by the Quaker preacher Mr. Lancaster, and arose from the English government's unconcern with primary schooling. Here in Texas, in this enormous territory neglected first by the Spanish government and now by the Mexican government following independence from Spain, the same problem is occurring as in England, and this is why he had proposed to the state governor that this system be implemented in Texas. He explained that the system was quite simple: the students were divided into classes, separating reading and writing on the one hand, and Professor Akerman's sciences and arts on the other. He assured us that all of the classes would be taught under the beliefs of the Catholic religion. The most advanced student in the class would, following the precise indications of the teacher, instruct the other students. Mr. Baker insisted that the school would employ strict discipline with all of the students, who would only progress to the following grade once they had learned everything from the grade they were in. Rebels would be sent to special tutors, who would stimulate them with daily exercises, although he did not explain how this would work.

When we left the meeting, we all understood exactly where this was leading. Although their influence on the community was already increasing, by taking over the education of our children it was inevitable that they would grow up to be Yankees themselves. And this is exactly what happened.

The corruption and immorality of the governor reached such heights that he used Decree 96 of July 6, 1829, to annul Degree 26 and grant his own son, Juan Antonio Viesca, a contract "to establish in the state a machine to extract water from the depths of the earth, and to make it flow along the surface." While this in itself was immoral, he went still further in the third article of the decree, stating that "for the span of eight years from the passing of this law, it is strictly forbidden for any other person to establish machines of this type, without previous agreement with the recipient of this decree."

CHAPTER 6

I. Announcement of the Spanish Invasion of Mexico

On July 20, 1829, amid the injustice, the corruption, and the atrocities committed by the Mexican government against the descendants of the Canarian founders of San Antonio, simply for their allegiance with Spain, the colony was finally given a glimmer of hope. On returning from a business trip to Mexico City, my brother José Antonio brought news of a proclamation by the general of the vanguard of the Spanish Army, Isidoro Barradas, which stated the following:

> Inhabitants of New Spain:
>
> His Excellency the Captain General of the Island of Cuba addresses you in the name of the King, Our Lord, and proclaims: "I stand before you on your beaches together with the first division of the royal army, which will occupy this kingdom in furtherance of the establishment of order and good government fitting for the best of the Mexican Kings. I come neither to avenge insults nor satisfy base passions for that which has occurred in this kingdom; all this will be forgotten, as is the Royal Will of your noble and ever-lasting sovereign. The bayonets I bring will not be used against you, but will be driven into the breasts of those who wish for the disturbances to continue, and who persist in disregarding the will and mercy of our generous monarch. As a faithful executor of the Royal Will, I offer you my word of honor that this will be accomplished rapidly, and that in the calm that follows you may then compare and judge the difference between three hundred years of happiness and the seven years of atrocious disorder that you have suffered. Thanks to DIVINE providence, you will shortly be liberated from this terrible curse."

Mexicans, the time has come for a rebirth of peace and the former abundance; leave behind the iniquitous band of anarchy that has destroyed this beautiful kingdom, enriching only the upstart adventurers from the North and the leaders who tyrannize you. Remain calmly in your homes, dedicate yourself to your work, and both you and your properties will be respected as sacred.

The division that I have the honor to lead is a model of discipline and obedience. The soldiers are your brothers: we are united in our religion, our language, our customs, and our traditions, and the same blood flows in our veins. If any individual from this division forgets his duties, and commits acts which are in violation of my will, I assure you that I will punish him with the full force of our ordinances and laws.

In all parts of these lands so favored by nature's bounty, the grim effects can be seen of the remarkable disorder that the wickedness of some and the imprudence of others have instilled into every part of the social structure. Classes and hierarchies are confused, ministers at the altar are vilified and disrespected, the sacred worship of the Savior of mankind is forgotten or even mocked, secret societies are authorized and protected, and in shadowy secret meetings crimes are planned and daggers are sharpened; the roads, towns, and cities are plagued by outlaws from the North and the unruly and wild masses, who are brought daily into the streets by your senseless governors to push through their shortsighted plans; you have become accustomed to pillaging, murder, and all manner of scandals. What remains of that peaceful country, model of Christianity and worthy imitator of European Spain in the practice of every virtue?

Mexicans, in the Royal name of His Majesty Fernando VII and in fulfillment of his royal wishes, I hereby offer you the opportunity to cast a thick veil over everything that has occurred in the past eight years, and I promise you that no person will be hurt or persecuted in any way, no matter their political opinions and behavior during that disgraceful time. This is the express will of His Majesty, who from his royal throne has looked with compassion upon the misfortunes and unhappiness of his beloved children in New Spain.

Havana, June 17, 1829.

Signed, Francisco Dionisia Vives

This proclamation was like a bright a ray of light shining on the colony of Canarian descendants. Because we are located on the border with Louisiana where the Yankees cross illegally from the north, we are treated as Mexicans by the Yankees, and the government to which we have belonged for eight years persecutes us as Spaniards.

This new development filled us with the hope that Spain would return to govern these territories, although without repeating the same errors that it made for the last three centuries, despite the constant warnings from the San Antonio town council that more colonists were needed and greater vigilance required on the northern and western borders with Louisiana.

On September 10 the Mexican government issued Decree 105, which read, "In light of the news of a possible Spanish invasion, all single Spaniards and widows without children remaining in these lands are forthwith obliged to make a mandatory loan of one third part of their capital; those married Spaniards without children and widows with a single child, one fifth, and those with more than one child, one eighth."

Thus the capital of the Spaniards living in Mexico was to be confiscated and added to the state's income, under the pretext that they would join the invasion or that they lived in Spanish domains.

During the time the government considered itself to be at war due to the threat of an imminent invasion, they deducted 15 percent from the salaries of public employees. In this way the government was able to arm all of the state's local militia, which was forced to submit to military regulations.

This decree greatly affected the Canary Islanders since we had all be born here and did not wish to be taxed as Spaniards. Thanks to the efforts of the mayor Manuel Arciniega, this decree was not applied to the descendants of the Canary Islanders despite, I repeat, our clear sympathies with the Spanish cause.

News reached us in San Antonio that the Spanish expedition had landed, and taken control of Tampico and Pueblo Viejo. In the face of this attack, the Mexican minister of war, Felipe de la Garza, proposed that the president of the Republic pass a law offering the members of the Spanish expedition a monetary reward to lay down their arms and swear never to serve in the Spanish army again.

News arrived that the Spaniards had left a garrison in Cabo Rojo which had been surprised by the distinguished patriot Captain Olarte de Tuxpen, who had captured their provisions of vast stores of hardtack and ground coffee, as well as weapons and ammunition.

The Dutch chargé d'affaires announced in writing on April 12, 1828, that the Spanish government had purchased ten thousand rifles, which he believed were to be sent to Havana in order to outfit the expedition. In another note he announced that the purchase had been increased to 82,000 rifles.

A June 10 memo by a foreign correspondent draws the attention of the government to the rumors that Madrid, excited by the clamors of the Spanish émigrés, is redoubling its efforts to send a formidable expedition against the Republic, in the light of which he makes several observations on how important it is that Colombia and Mexico unite to attack Cuba together.

On August 30 the chargé d'affaires of the Republic in England sends a memo detailing the latest news he has received with respect to the efforts of the Spanish government, agitated by the émigrés, to send 6,000 more men to reinforce the troops stationed on the island of Cuba in order to proceed with the expedition.

On September 15 the chargé d'affaires informs of the steps taken to verify the number of rifles received by the Spanish government from its contracts, showing that the number has risen to 30,000 sent to Santander, El Ferrol, and La Coruña. On December 1 he is sent a reply, charging him with communicating any additional news he acquires, which will be sent directly to the minister of war.

On September 17 the chargé d'affaires of the Republic in England sends the reports for that month, including one which discusses the question of a blockade of Veracruz by Laborda's squadron, and expressing his fears that in doing so, England would recognize it and would use it as an excuse to interfere in our affairs. The descendants of the Canary Islanders were most despondent when we heard of the defeat of the Spanish at Tampico, thereby ending the invasion.

Meanwhile the Mexican poets were tireless in composing sonnets and fables celebrating their victory over Spain.

A crow looked down
On a tired mule
And believing it dead
It's mine! It said
And most assiduously
Pop! He thrusts his head
Up inside a filthy place
Into some innards
The mule feels something
And how he stands up! Hurry!
And the stupid crow dies
Smothered and starving
The moral of this little fable
Is for he who ventures
Into matters when perhaps
The mule is not dead.

There are not only fables, but also songs written for officers in the army, such as the following:

What do we flaunt? I am the first
To wave the flags of Mars
Bring then the blade and braids
Clothe my stubborn fist in iron
Aye? Tis not bad for an officer, a heart
And great esteem from the motherland
Adorned in classical functions
Acting brave with warlike gestures
MORE! What is that sound that thunders in my ears?
TO ARMS! Now cry the watchtowers
The enemy invades our sands
By my faith these are no lies
The scene is enough to fear for ANAHUAC
I RENOUNCE IT, and will never more see its shores.

The captain general of the island of Cuba, Francisco Dionisio Vives, sent his troops under the command of Brigadier Barradas, and this Spanish division occupied Tampico, Altamira, and other nearby cities. This news brought jubilation to the descendants of the Canarian colonists, since we were the object of persecution by the Mexican government who considered us to be Spanish sympathizers.

General Santa Ana commanded his army to fight, and to our great dismay we heard that the Spaniards had been defeated and General Barradas had surrendered. On September 20 the following surrender agreement reached the San Antonio town council:

1. Tomorrow at nine o'clock in the morning the Spanish forces will evacuate the fort of la Barra with their weapons and to the sound of drums, and will deliver both weapons and ammunition to the Mexican army, under the leadership of General Manuel Mier y Terán, second in command of the army. These troops will move to Tampico de Tamaulipas together with their officers, who will retain their swords.

2. At six o'clock in the morning on the following day, the entire Spanish division in Tampico de Tamaulipas will march under the orders of General Terán, and will surrender their weapons, flags, and ammunition in the outlying area of Altamira; officers may retain their swords.
3. The Mexican army and government solemnly swear to respect the lives and personal property of all members of the invading division.
4. The Spanish division will march to the city of Victoria, where they shall remain until they set sail for Havana.
5. Permission is herein granted to the Spanish general to send one or two officers to Havana in order to secure transportation to convey their forces to said port.
6. The Spanish general will be responsible for covering the cost of maintaining his division while they remain in the country, in addition to the transport costs.
7. The sick and wounded men who are unable to march will remain in Tampico until they can be transferred to the Mexican army hospital, where they will be attended at the expense of the Spanish division, which will leave behind the necessary surgeons, orderlies, and soldiers to care for them.
8. The Spanish division will be provided with the baggage and provisions necessary for the march, which will be paid for by said division according to the current prices in the country.
9. The colonel of the Spanish division is charged with carrying out the provisions of this surrender with respect to the troops in la Barra, and will allow the safe passage of the commander in charge at the point called Doña Cecilia.
10. General Mier y Terán will name two officers who will facilitate these operations with respect to the previous article.

The preceding agreement is drawn up and signed by the undersigned on the aforementioned date.

Pedro Landero
José Ignacio lberri
José Antonio Mejía
José Miguel Salmón
Fulgencio Salas
I hereby ratify this surrender.—Antonio López de Santa Ana
I hereby ratify this surrender.—Isidro Barradas

Proposal from the Spanish general. On the arrival of any Spanish forces belonging to General Barradas's division, they will not be permitted to disembark, and they will be advised of this agreement.

Additional articles

Proposal from the Mexican general.—The general in command, officers, and troops belonging to General Barradas's division solemnly swear never to return, nor to take up arms against the Mexican Republic.

II. Failure of the Invasion and Consequences

All our hopes were swiftly dashed upon hearing that the Spanish expedition, despite initially conquering a few towns and cities, had been swiftly defeated by the Mexican army and had retreated to Cuba, thus ending the attempt to invade and reconquer New Spain. Meanwhile colonists from the north continued to arrive, some as genuine settlers and others who came disguised as professionals: doctors, businessmen, etc., to whom the corrupt governor of the state of Texas was selling authorizations. The great stampede began in 1830 when the Mexican government saw the failure of Spain's pretensions toward its old territories in New Spain, and further opened the gates to foreigners from the North in order to avoid future Spanish expeditions. The Mexicans clearly preferred to take the risk of someday losing Texas to the North Americans than to be governed by Spain again.

So on February 10, 1830, the state government of Coahuila and Texas issued Decree 118, in which it was announced that since the Texas region lacked attorneys, any citizens over the age of twenty-five could hold such positions, provided that they possess the necessary expertise, as decided by the congress and, if necessary, a consulting body of the government. The relevant credentials would be arranged in accordance with Decree 103.

The first Anglo-Saxon attorney was admitted by Decree 151 on September 24, 1830, which granted "a letter of citizenship to the attorney Tomás Gefferson Chambers, whose title, after approval by the Court of Justice, will permit him to practice law in this state."

CHAPTER 7

Cholera

This failed attempt at an invasion by Spain only served to increase the hatred of all things Spanish by the Mexican people, instigated by the government though various legal provisions. They claimed that the root of all evils was the ignorance of our people caused by the flaws in our colonial education, as well as the determination of some individuals to perpetuate the defects and preoccupations that had chained down the Mexican people for so many years. For this reason, the government publicly questioned whether it was actually worth reestablishing relations with Spain. According to many in the ruling class, this would unleash a horde of Spaniards from the lowest classes, with no morals, who would spread their pride and fanaticism throughout the country, together with their political intolerance and their hatred of foreigners; in a word, all of the defects and preoccupations that had closed off Spain to the growth and progress of the rest of Europe.

More and more Spanish settlers were persecuted as enemies of the public good, accused of using every means at their disposal to disturb the peace and ceaselessly stoke the fires of discord.

The alarming news reached San Antonio that the country was stricken with cholera morbus. The first cases appeared in the town in September 1833.

The symptoms of the illness were:

First. Vomiting and evacuations of white matter similar in appearance to rice water.

Second. A strange alteration of the appearance of the hands and the legs.

Third. A special metallic sound to the voice.

Fourth. Cyanosis, or a lividness and mottling of the skin, which cooled until the body was completely icy, together with cold sweats, without the patient being aware of the cold.

Fifth. Weak pulse and loss of physical and moral strength.

Sixth. Cramps and spasms.

Seventh. Lack of urine production.

These are the general symptoms, but I should also add that when blood is removed from the veins, it appears black, sticky, and clotted. The doctors in San Antonio say that their chemical experiments have shown that the proportion of free carbon is twice as high as in healthy blood, and the colored material is four times greater. In a meeting with the town's doctors, they told us that the water, albumin, and fibrin in the blood disappear almost completely, giving it a tar-like consistency. Left untouched, it rarely separates into serum and coagulates, but instead is transformed into a dark crimson substance similar to gelatin, with no well-defined scabs. When the doctors opened up the arteries, they found only small amounts of coagulated blood, with the same characteristics as the contents of veins, instead of being bright red in color as is normal.

My grandmother told me of many remedies and cures for cholera, which also affected the people of the Canary Islands when they lived there. On the basis of this, a group of descendants of Canary Islanders and myself drafted a document to distribute among the inhabitants of the town to help people avoid, and if necessary cure, this terrible disease.

Our older relatives told us that the following factors predispose us to cholera: fear of disease, excessive spiritual work, deep meditations and worrying, excessive studying, lack of proper warm clothes, moving from a warm place to a cold place, putting on damp clothes, walking with bare feet, sleeping in the open air, untidiness of clothing and bedrooms, and dirt and filth in patios, hallways, and furniture.

Among the foods that we consider to be harmful are stews with sauces and strong spices, salads, salted or old meats, pork, rabbit, goat, duck, pork skins, sausages, chorizo sausages, all spiced meats, fresh or dried fish, particularly catfish and *mestiapiques*,[46] milk, fresh cheese and butter, damp and wind-producing vegetables such as green beans, cabbages, turnips, lettuces, green peas, purslane, spinach, prickly pears, and fruit, and other irritating foods like green chili. All kinds of wine and liquor, and also fermented drinks such as *chichi*,[47] *charape*,[48] and beer containing alcohol.

To prevent the illness it is crucial to employ good hygiene in the body and living quarters; one should bathe frequently when there is good weather, change clothing or wash it regularly, and keep oneself warm with flannel. Cleanse and fumigate the house regularly with lavender, chamomile, bay leaves, rosemary, costmary, or any other aromatic herb, sprinkle vinegar or boil it in the rooms, and if possible fumigate with chloride.

Curing the illness is essentially based on helping the afflicted as soon as symptoms appear: they should take a half bowl of the compound called three lyes, or simply lime water, since both medicines when properly applied have the same effect.

Allow me to describe the method for preparing it, since it may someday serve as a remedy if this document is publicly disseminated.

Formula: two quarters of superior powdered *tequesquite*,[49] two quarters of powdered ash, two quarters of new lime. Lime water is made by adding one spoonful.

The three ingredients are mixed together and then added to a pint of ordinary water, stirred, and left to rest; oak ash is the best kind of ash to use. After letting it rest in water, half a bowl can be administered to the patients every fifteen minutes. A paste of lime and water should also be made immediately, and used as a poultice for the stomach and belly, the soles of the feet and the palms of the hands, which is removed once dry and replaced, until the patient feels restored. The lye or lime drink should be administered to the patient until the nausea and evacuations have passed.

If the body becomes chilled or begins to suffer cramps, it should be rubbed with a cloth or blanket wherever it feels cold until it has warmed up again. The areas afflicted by cramping should be covered with an ointment made of the following: one bottle of spirits, an ounce of tobacco, two ounces of ground mustard, half an ounce of camphor, and an ounce of powdered Spanish flies. If Spanish flies are unavailable, an infusion can be made with a handful of salt and a mashed head of garlic, and in the absence of spirits, use mescal.

Some of the patients who have been cured with the lyes or lime water later suffer from urine retention; to return this to its natural course the following poultice should be applied to the stomach: half a pound of mallow flowers, half a pound of elderflowers.

These are cooked and ground into a paste, then fried in rose oil, with a quarter ounce of Castilian saffron. The mixture is strained through a cloth and applied to the body.

The following diet should also be followed: During the first three days of illness, the patient should not be given more than one bowl of cold *atole*,[50] well cooked and thin, every two or three hours. Broth can be very damaging and should only be fed to the patients after two or three days. Painful experience has shown that the patients are not safe from relapse; it is necessary to maintain a rigorous convalescence. In the beginning of this period of recovery, nothing should be eaten beyond three half-bowls of thin corn atole per day, taken in the morning, at midday, and in the evening of the first and second days; on the third day the same regimen should be followed, with the addition of a few spoonfuls of cold moistened bread, and so on, gradually introducing solid foods until complete recovery has been achieved. The patient should be warmly wrapped, and should remain in bed for three days, and in their bedchamber for at least another eight days without going into the open air. Care should also be taken not to get them wet, to keep up the body temperature and above all to ensure the repose of both body and spirit.

CHAPTER 8

I. The Regulations for Becoming a Colonist

The years have passed, and the arrival of more colonists has aggravated all our problems.

The governor of the state, José María Viescas, continued to grant citizenship papers to foreigners, and charged the American colonists vast sums of money for the right to settle here. To illustrate this, on September 25, 1830, he used Decree 152 to award citizenship to Diego Grant, who had falsified his name from James Grant to make it sound Spanish. But then he went just too far; the Anglo-Saxon population needed priests from their religion, and so through Decree 183 of April 23, 1830, he granted a license for the building of a church to the Protestant minister Henry Doyle, who was well known in San Antonio, having lived there for various years exercising his ministry.

Such was the scandal that erupted in the town after this authorization, that a few days later, on April 25, the governor found himself forced to sign instructions which altered the allotment of land to new colonists requesting it under the Colonization Law of March 24, 1825. These instructions appeared to be an attempt to calm our protests at the freedom being granted to the Anglo-Saxon settlers. However, in practice the situation remained the same, or worse.

I will now detail the first five articles, which recognize and are intended to prevent the illegal entry of foreign colonists (without success, of course).

> First Article. According to the agreements that each empresario or colonist has made with the government, and considering the Colonization Law of March 24, it shall be the commissioner's obligation to examine most scrupulously the certificates brought by foreign colonists, issued by the authorities of

their homelands and attesting to their Christianity, morality, and good behavior, as established in article five of the aforementioned law, without which they shall not be admitted into the colony.

Second Article. In order to prevent false certificates, none shall be accepted by the commissioner unless the empresario first provides a written report attesting to their legitimacy.

Third Article. Each and every one of the foreign colonists must solemnly swear to submit to the federal constitution of the United States of Mexico, to the individual constitution of the state, and to the general and specific laws of the country that they are adopting as their homeland.

Fourth Article. Land titles will be issued to the new settlers on behalf of the State and in accordance with the Law and all legal formalities, and on determining the situation of adjacent plots, if such plots exist.

Fifth Article. No land will be granted to any colonist who is settled or who wishes to settle within a limit of twenty leagues from the border with the northern United States, or ten leagues from the coast, unless the interested party is in possession of a special order from this government, and the prior approval of the supreme leadership of the Federation.

This gave rise to a wily trick in the northern states, whereby Protestant colonists were baptized by an Irish Catholic priest before coming to Texas. They remained devout Protestants, but carried a certificate from the priest whom they had paid verifying that they were legally Catholics.

II. Benjamin R. Milam and James Bowie

Even José María Viescas, however, did not dare to sign one truly important decree, which was left to Rafael Ecay y Musquis. This was Decree 159, from October 5, 1830, which granted citizenship to James

Bowie and allowed him to establish a store selling wool and cotton fabric.

James Bowie, Moses Austin and his son, and Benjamin R. Milam, who was granted citizenship on April 25, 1835, were among the adventurers from North America who fought the hardest to establish Texan independence, from the very day they settled here.

James Bowie came from the north and lived and died in San Antonio, during the famous battle of the Alamo. Today he is one of the heroes of U.S. history. He was born in Logan County, Kentucky, in 1796. At eighteen years of age he left home and went to live in one of the settlements of Canarian colonists on the outskirts of New Orleans. After some time there he was granted Texan citizenship, and in 1830 he invested $15,000 in land in Texas and took up residence in San Antonio.

On April 25, 1831, he married a dear friend of mine, Ursula Veramendi, daughter of Gov. Juan Martín Veramendi y Olargive, who remained governor until February 7, 1833. It was a great romance. Ursula was considered one of the most beautiful women in the South.

The wedding was the most important social event in San Antonio for many years. According to Father Refugio de la Garza, who officiated the ceremony:

> It was celebrated in the church of San Fernando de Béjar on April 25, 1831, and they were married according to canon law, since James Bowie had previously converted to Catholicism. The marriage banns were published after the three solemn masses on September 11, 17, and 24, and as no canonical impediments were found, they were married twenty-four hours after the final bann. The wedding was celebrated publicly with a wedding mass in the church of San Fernando de Béjar. James Bowie, native of Louisiana (the official mistakenly entered the last state where he had lived in the United States as his place of birth), legitimate son of Raymond Bowie and Albina Yons, was married to Miss Ursula Veramendi, native of

this town and legitimate daughter of Juan Martín de Veramendi and María Josefa Navarro. José Angel Navarro and Juan Francisco Bueno stood as witnesses. In the presence of the witnesses, I hereby sign.

During one of James Bowie's expeditions against the Indians, Ursula Veramendi moved from their ranch to her parents' house in San Antonio. That tragic summer the cholera epidemic broke out, and Ursula, her two children, her parents, and several servants died. Bowie never recovered from this blow.

This year, 1833, the state of Texas has 84,294 inhabitants. Only 12,000 of these are Spaniards, harshly persecuted by the Mexican government together with the descendants of the first Canarian colonists, who have never hidden our sympathies with Spain.

III. Thoughts of Independence and Legalization of the English Language

The towns of Goliad, Austin, Trinidad de la Libertad, and Nacogdoches, together with the capital, San Antonio, all belong the Party of Béjar. The majority of the inhabitants of Austin and San Antonio are foreign colonists, although the greatest agitation for independence can be found in Austin. In both towns the laws of the state have fallen apart. The San Antonio town council called a meeting of all of the magistrates in their party, unbeknownst to the state government, and together they chose several representatives to travel to the capital of the state and the federation in order to present their idea of forming an independent territory, thus leaving the Mexican Federation and joining with the lands occupied by the United States.

The state immediately sent civil servants to investigate. However, these are corrupt bureaucrats who sold themselves to the colonists and downplayed the significance of these events to the distant authorities in the capital of the Mexican Republic.

Toward the end of last year, 1832, the attacks by savage Indians to our town of San Antonio and its surroundings meant that the normally fertile lands did not produce the crops and seeds that they normally would. This calamity could not be prevented, except through a formal campaign using respectable force which would bring peace, once and for all, by forcing the errant tribes to submit to the laws of the Republic and form a single society with the rest of the inhabitants of these lands. But as I said, the wild Indians have been making constant attacks on our ranches, and their owners have joined forces with the small group of soldiers that protects them, and have shown them the bravery of the Texan people by pursuing the Indians to the hills of San Saba. They must understand that Texas cannot be insulted by such impunity, and for this reason the border fighters have banded together to form a group of three hundred men, with the goal of fighting the war to its bitter end.

During this year, 1833, the situation has become unsustainable. The governor of the state, Juan Martín de Veramendi, sent a report dated January 6 to the president of the Republic, Manuel Gómez Pedraza, and to the illustrious gentlemen, Generals Santa Ana, Moctezuma, and Cuesta, informing them that "the disorder of the Republic has reached such heights that the constitution, which has been the anchor that has saved the Republic from shipwreck during many political tempests, is now insufficient, since it has been destroyed and infringed upon a thousand times. It is no longer looked upon with respect, and in order to return to the constitutional path it will be necessary to take a few steps away from it."

He continued:

> When the constitution of a nation has lost the prestige that sustained it, and when it is easily disregarded, it cannot provide for the happiness of its people, who need new and firmer guarantees. For this reason our constitution must be reformed. Dispensations and citizenship, however, continued to be granted to all those who requested and could pay for it, without taking into account the

danger of the invasion of colonists from the north. In this way, on January 6, 1834, Tomás Gefferson Chambers was exempted from the examination required by the decree of December 22, 1830, thereby allowing him to practice law in the state based solely on the qualifications and certificates he presented. All of them, according to popular rumor, were falsified.

The English language was finally legalized. It was only logical. The Anglo-Saxon avalanche was unstoppable. Today, April 17, 1834, the supreme government of the state of Texas published a law that further developed article 192 of the constitution and detailed a plan to improve the administration of justice in Texas.

The text was in Spanish and English.

The second article established that all civil and criminal matters were to be judged by juries in the manner and form established by law. It names three types of criminal trials: verbal, for the correction or punishment of minor crimes; informative summaries, for the swift investigation of the crime and the criminal in more important cases; and plenary, for the definitive resolution and sentencing of these cases.

Section 6 elaborates the administration of justice in civil cases. In trials: verbal and conciliation. In written trials. The eighth section deals with the execution of justice and executive proceedings.

By far the best news we Canary Islanders received during those turbulent years was on June 6, 1834, when we learned from a town council employee that a June 2 ruling had ordered the confiscation of all the land belonging to the former marquis of Aguayo. This man was hated by the Canarian colonists since his lies to the governor and to the king himself had caused our ancestors to leave the Canary Islands and settle in these distant lands.

At long last the Canary Islanders saw justice served against an all-powerful figure, the marquis of San Miguel de Aguayo, who had caused such harm to our ancestors by tricking them into coming so

Gobierno Supremo

DEL ESTADO LIBRE DE

COAHUILA Y TEJAS

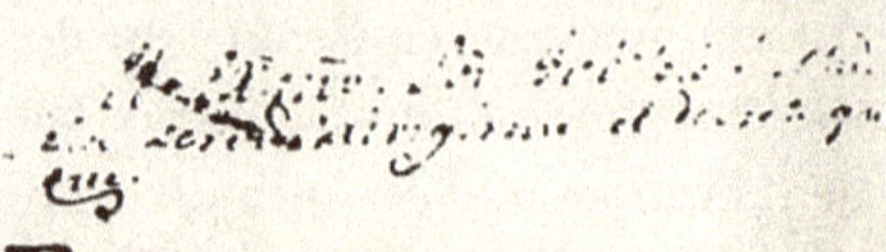

El gobernador del Estado de Coahuila y Tejas á todos sus habitantes—SABED: que el congreso del mismo ha decretado lo que sigue.

„Decreto num. 159. El congreso constitucional del Estado libre independiente y soberano de Coahuila y Tejas ha tenido á bien decretar lo siguiente:

Se concede al estrangero [illegible] la carta de ciudadano en el supuesto de que tenga verificado el establecimiento de tegidos de lana y algodon que ofrece poner en el Estado.

Lo tendrá entendido el gobernador del Estado para su cumplimiento, haciendolo imprimir publicar y circular. Dado en la ciudad de Leona-Vicario á 30. de setiembre de 1830.=*Ramon Garcia Rojas*, diputado presidente.—*Mariano Garcia*, diputado secretario.= *Vicente Valdez*, diputado secretario suplente.

Por tanto, mando se imprima, publique, circule y se le dé el debido cumplimiento. Leona-Vicario 5 de octubre de 1830.

Rafael Eca y Músquiz

Santiago del Valle
Secretario.

del Estado libre

DE COAHUILA Y TEJAS.

El Gobernador del Estado de Coahuila y Texas, á todos sus habitantes SABED: *que el congreso del mismo Estado ha decretado lo que sigue.*

El Congreso Constitucional del Estado libre, independiente y Soberano de Coahuila y Texas, deseando proveer lo conveniente á la felicidad de sus comitentes y llenar el encargo que tiene por el articulo 192 de la constitucion, decreta el siguiente.

PLAN PARA EL MEJOR ARREGLO DE LA ADMINISTRACION DE JUSTICIA EN TEXAS.

Seccion 1.ª

Art. 1.º Texas se constituye en un circuito judicial que se denominará *Superioridad Judicial de Texas*.

Art. 2.º Todos los asuntos civiles y criminales, se juzgarán por jurados en el modo y forma que se prescribe por esta ley.

Art. 3.º El circuito, se divide en tres distritos, que son los tres Departamentos de Texas.

Art. 4.º La Superioridad Judicial, se compone de un Juez Superior, un Secretario, y un Sherif para cada distrito judicial; y para las causas criminales el Juri, y un Promotor.

Art. 5.º La Superioridad tendrá sesiones cada cuatro meses en las cabeceras de los tres distritos, debiendo ser en el de Bejar los primeros lunes de Enero, Abril y Agosto. En el de Brazos, los primeros lunes de Febrero, Mayo, y Setiembre; y en el de Nacogdoches, los primeros lunes de Marzo, Junio y Octubre.

Art. 6.º Para los asuntos civiles, habrá en cada municipalidad un tribunal por cada juez de primera instancia compuesto del mismo, un sherif subalterno, y el juri. Sus sesiones serán el cuarto lunes de cada bimestre del año.

Art. 7.º Tanto en lo criminal como en lo civil, el juri se compone de doce jurados, y la opinion conforme de ocho de ellos, se tendrá por la resolucion del juri.

Art. 8.º En cada comisaria de policia habrá un

of the free State

OF COAHUILA AND TEXAS.

The Constitutional Governor of the State of Coahuila and Texas to all its inhabitants, KNOW YE: *that the Congress of the same state has decreed the following.*

The Constitutional Congress of the free, Independent and Sovereign State of Coahuila and Texas, desirous to provide for the happiness and prosperity of their Constituents, and to comply with the obligation imposed on them by the 192 article of the Constitution; Decree the following:

A PLAN FOR THE BETTER REGULATION OF THE ADMINISTRATION OF JUSTICE IN TEXAS

Section 1.st

Article 1st. Texas shall be formed into one Judicial Circuit, which shall be denominated *The Superior Judicial Court of Texas.*

Art. 2d. All causes civil and criminal shall be tried by juries, in the manner and form prescribed by this law.

Art. 3d. The Circuit shall be divided into three Districts, which are the three Departments of Texas.

Art. 4th. The Superior Court shall be Composed of one Superior Judge, one Secretary, and one Sheriff, for each judicial District; and in Criminal cases, the Jury and one Prosecuting Attorney.

Art. 5th. The Court shall hold its sessions every four months in the Capitals of the three Districts, commencing in that of Bexar, the first Monday of Jan. April, and August: In that of Brazos, the first Monday of Feb. May and Sept. And in that of Nacogdoches, the first Monday of March June and Oct.

Art. 6th. For the trial of civil causes, there shall be in every Municipality a Tribunal for each *Primary Judge*, Composed of the Judge, a *Subaltern* Sheriff, and the Jury. Their Sessions shall be held every two months of the year, commencing on the fourth Monday of the month in which the session ought to be held.

Art. 7th. In all cases both civil and criminal, the Jury shall be composed of twelve men, who shall be sworn, and the joint opinion of eight of them shall be considered the decision of the jury.

Art. 8th. In every Commissary's District there

o Supremo
tado libre
UILA Y TEJAS.

Para que tengan su puntual y debido cumplimiento los decretos de 21 de febrero y 4 de abril del corriente año, y segun disponen los articulos 7 y 6 de dichas leyes para la enagenacion de todas las fincas del [illegible] he venido en dictar las providencias que siguen.

1.º Para que los acreedores de que habla el art. 7 de la ley de 21 de febrero del presente año, disfruten de la gracia que dicha ley les conceda, ocurriran oportunamente al gobierno, quien haciendo una declaracion de los creditos que son notoriamente privilegiados, los admitirá en pago de las posturas, bajo la fianza de mejor derecho y con las condiciones y restricciones legalmente establecidas.

2.º Conforme se fueren remitiendo á este gobierno los inventarios y valúos por los comisionados al efecto, se harán las divisiones respectivas de las referidas fincas, las que se publicarán por medio de avisos que se fijarán en los parajes publicos de los pueblos, á cuyo fin se remitirán á los gefes de los departamentos el número de ejemplares necesarios.

3.º Desde la fecha de los avisos de que habla el articulo anterior que será el dia de la publicacion en esta capital hasta concluidos treinta dias, podrán los interesados hacer posturas, dirigiendolas al gobierno por escrito ó presentandose por si ó sus agentos á la secretaria, expresando la porcion á que se interesen.

4.º Si cumplido el termino prefijado para las posturas entendiese el gobierno hallarse en el caso de que habla el articulo 1.º de la ley de 4 de abril de este año, usará de la facultad que allí se le concede; y no siendo así, se designará el dia y hora del remate de cada porcion con la unica formalidad de fijarse carteloness en los parajes publicos de esta capital.

5.º En la hora señalada, para la almoneda, se admitirán á los interesados las pujas y mejoras que hagan, y el gobierno hará uso de las facultades que por las leyes citadas se le confieren á efecto de determinar los plazos que se pidan para el pago de las fincas, los que serán en proporcion al interes que se advierta en las posturas, asi como resolverá en el acto del remate las qüestiones que suscitien los postores por las gracias que les concede el art. 7. ya citado.

6.º Los pagos que se ofrescan al contado constituiran las mejores posturas sobre [illegible] y los creditos privilegiados, se reputarán como tales.

7.º Para recibir en plazos las porciones rematadas, los interesados afianzarán suficientemente con hipoteca general de todos sus bienes y especial de la finca que reciben, dando, á demas fiador llano por los bienes muebles y semovientes que rematen anéxos á la misma finca.

8.º Los primeros pagos ya sean totales ó parciales, se harán en la tesoreria del Estado, de donde sacarán los certificados correspondientes á efecto que de en su vista, se estiendan á favor de los compradores los documentos que acrediten su propiedad; y los demas que los deudores deben verificar al cumplimiento de los plazos, lo harán en las administraciones principales de las rentas en los respectivos departamentos, de quienes recibirán los certificados correspondientes.

Monclova 2 de junio de 1834.

far from everything they knew and loved.[51] The marquis's creditors, led by the president of the council dealing with his estate, managed to bring his assets to auction and to sell them with deeds granted in Mexico City on September 9, 1825, to the English companies Baring Brothers & Co., and Staples & Co.

CHAPTER 9

I. Confusion and Disorder

Once it became known in the northern states how easy it was to settle in Texas, either secretly through the northernmost parts of the territory, or by paying off the authorities, the influx of huge numbers of colonists led the governor of the state of Coahuila and Texas, Francisco Vidaurri y Vilaseñor, to issue a decree on June 24, 1834. This decree called for an emergency session of congress on August 11 in order to "pass measures for the preservation of the federal system; to restore the disturbed public order through announcements which invoke religious sentiments, which have not yet been lost; and to avoid any disruption these events may produce in the interior of this state."

The situation was one of utter confusion. The news arriving from Monclova, the state capital, and from Mexico City, the federal capital, was contradictory. The most absolute confusion reigned throughout the land. Proof of this can be seen in two decrees from the governor of the state, from July 23 and 24, 1834. The first stated: "The uniform desire of the nation has been expressed through the unanimous vote of citizens from the majority of the states; in recognition of this, the state of Coahuila and Texas hereby sacrifices its opinion in the interest of the public good, and recognizes General Antonio López de Santa Ana as president of the Republic. We swear to obey all his acts of governance that are in accordance with the constitution and the general laws of the land." In contrast, the decree passed the following day, June 24, declared that "the state does not recognize as legal any governmental actions taken as of May 31 by the president of the republic, Antonio López de Santa Ana, and will not recognize any subsequent actions until the noble bodies of the union are able to freely exercise their functions."

This uncertainty emanating from our leaders is causing a growing impression of misrule, not just among the North Americans but also among Mexicans themselves and among the descendants of the Canary Islanders, who wish only for peace and order. We want an end to political corruption, and we want to feel that we are being truly governed.

The latest news to reach San Antonio is that the governor of Coahuila and Texas, Francisco Vidaurri y Villaseñor, author of the above decrees, has been removed from his position by the Mexican authorities and that Juan José Elguiazábal has been named in his place. On August 31 he addressed the populace in the following manner: "Obedient to the will of the nation, the state of Coahuila and Texas will occupy the position that providence has provided for it in the Mexican Republic. The entire state recognizes the eminent president Antonio López de Santa Ana. What more should be done to reestablish public order? Nothing more than exercising the civic virtues inherent to the Texan character."

II. The First Anglo-Saxon Bank

The most important decree in recent years was passed on April 25, 1834, and covered the following main points:

1. The acceptance of a proposal by Benjamin R. Milam that within a period of three years he will explore and make navigable the Colorado River of Texas, as far as the mine village, dredging it of mud, and clearing out the palisades and other obstacles that currently impede navigation.

2. Accordingly, Benjamin R. Milam was granted the exclusive rights to navigate the aforementioned river with boats and steamships, for a period of ten years.

Once a North American had been granted this absolute permission to navigate the Colorado River, the first major step toward the invasion of Texas had been taken. The next step was to buy boats and weapons that could be transported downriver for attacking Texas from the south, and by land from the north.

This required money, but it had to be easily and legally available. And so on April 30, a few days after the decree above, the second crucial step was taken by the North Americans. Authorization was granted to Samuel M. Williams to establish the Commercial and Agricultural Bank.

During this year, the evidence of Anglo-Saxon supremacy in Texas has become more than clear. The number of North Americans in the state is now 30,000, compared to the 8,000 Mexicans and descendants of the Canary Islanders.

Texan independence, fomented by North America, is now unstoppable—the very state they had recriminated Spain over, and on the basis of which they achieved their independence.

There is a final decree from May 8, 1835, that fruitlessly attempts to stem the relentless tide of Anglo-Saxons taking up public offices. In this decree it establishes that:

1. The government is authorized to grant citizenship papers to all those foreigners who have legally obtained this right in accordance with the federal constitution, the state constitution, and the colonization laws.

2. Henceforth, those not born within the territory of the Republic may not be employed by the State, nor be admitted into the popular assemblies, nor into any other proceeding for which the laws require citizenship, unless they are in possession of the documents described in the first article.

The unrest in Texas is growing. There is talk of independence, and possible war with Mexico.

On November 7, 1835, a convention in Austin declared the people of Texas to be at war with Mexico. The declaration reads as follows:

DECLARATION OF THE PEOPLE OF TEXAS IN GENERAL CONVENTION ASSEMBLED

Whereas, General Antonio Lopez de Santa Anna, and other military chieftains, have, by force of arms overthrown the federal institutions of Mexico, and dissolved the social compact which existed between Texas and the other members of the Mexican confederacy; now the good people of Texas, availing themselves of their natural rights, Solemnly Declare:

1st. That they have taken up arms in defense of their rights and liberties, which were threatened by the encroachments of military despots, and in defense of the republican principles of the federal constitution of Mexico, 1824.

2nd. That Texas is no longer morally or civilly bound by the compact of union; yet, stimulated by the generosity and sympathy common to free people, they offer their support and assistance to such members of the Mexican confederacy as will take up arms against military despotism.

3rd. That they do not acknowledge that the present authorities of the nominal Mexican Republic have the right to govern within the limits of Texas.

4th. That they will not cease to carry on war against the said authorities while their troops are within the limits of Texas.

5th. That they hold it to be their right, during the disorganization of the federal system, and the reign of despotism, to withdraw from the union, and to establish an independent government, or to adopt such measures as they may deem best calculated to protect their rights and liberties; but that they will continue faithful to the Mexican Government so long as that nation is governed by the Constitution and Laws that were formed for the government of the Political Association.

6th. That Texas is responsible for the expenses of her armies, now in the field.

7th. That the public faith of Texas is pledged for the payment of any debts contracted by her agents.

8th. That she will reward by donations in land, all who volunteer their services in her present struggle, and receive them as citizens.

These declarations we solemnly avow to the world, and call God to witness their truth and sincerity, and invoke defeat and disgrace upon our heads, should we prove guilty of duplicity.

B. T. Archer, President

CHAPTER 10

Independence, the Alamo, and Complete Anglo-Saxon Dominance

The government's reaction was another memorandum, three days later on November 10, which read: "The colonists established in Texas have recently given the most unmistakable testimony of the extremity of their wickedness, ingratitude, and agitated spirits; forgetting the great debt that they owe to the Supreme Government and to the Nation that so happily took them under its wing and granted them fertile lands to cultivate and all the resources necessary to live with comfort and abundance, they have risen up against this very government and taken up arms against the nation. The pretext of upholding a system that the vast majority of Mexicans wish to change is simply a way to disguise their criminal intentions of dismembering the territory of the Republic."

In spite of this, on March 2, 1836, the convention met once again in Washington and declared independence. On March 17 the constitution was finally approved and signed.[52]

Colonists continued to arrive in Texas, now daring to settle without permission in San Antonio, and clamoring for independence.

The American Benjamin Milam, granted the exclusive right on April 25, 1834, to navigate the Colorado River for ten whole years, soon revealed his true purpose in these lands. On December 5, 1835, he invaded San Antonio with more than 300 men. The history of this town records no bloodier battle. We defended it house by house, and Milam himself perished in the battle. The invaders managed to take the town's main streets by surprise and then seized the Plaza de Armas and the surrounding streets. I can clearly remember how our house served as a shield for our family, despite the attackers' attempts to break in. With the death of Milam and the other leaders and the arrival of reinforcements from Laredo, the dreadful nightmare ended.

When I reached nineteen years of age, in 1832, I married John Smith. He was a North American who had settled in San Antonio a year earlier. He was close friends with James Bowie and Stephen Austin. In 1834 Austin, a fierce fighter for independence, as I have already mentioned, told us that the moment was ripe for Texan independence, although not through violence. He always said that he preferred dialogue to violence, and together with James Bowie and my husband, he had drafted a constitution for independence from Coahuila. This document was presented by Austin at the general Mexican Congress. The government's response was to throw him into prison for sedition and disturbance of the peace on January 3, 1834, where he remained until September of that year. Once Austin was freed, it was clear that all possible options for dialogue had been exhausted and the American colonists understood perfectly that there could be no peaceful agreement with the Mexican government.

During Austin's imprisonment, my husband and James Bowie met frequently with the colonists to draft a declaration of independence.

The North Americans ruled in Texas. They called themselves Texians, and directed all of their efforts toward obtaining independence. On March 2, 1835, they held a general assembly in Washington and declared the independence of Texas.

The document they drafted was designed to topple the Mexican government, which did not respect their rights as free men but instead preserved the fundamental bastions of tyranny.

This petition, and the defense until death, if need be, of the independence of Texas as a free nation of the world, was justified in the following way:

1. The Mexican government created colonization laws and invited North Americans to populate Texas under the assurance

that they would be allowed to enjoy the same freedom and republican institutions that they had been accustomed to in their homeland, and which they had won at the cost of much bloodshed.

2. These promises were not fulfilled, on account of the political changes implemented by General López de Santa Ana. After twelve years of settlement in Texan territory, this man offered them the choice of abandoning their lands and homes, acquired with so much effort, or submitting to the most detestable of tyrannies: military and religious despotism.

3. As a way of avoiding this declaration of independence by Texas, a document had been presented to the government which proposed a constitution for Texas as a state independent from Coahuila; however, this document was disregarded and its spokesperson, Stephen Austin, was thrown into prison.

4. On multiple occasions we were ordered to hand over our fellow citizens, and military detachments were sent to detain them for trial, with complete disregard to the laws and authorities. Our flourishing Texan businesses had been ruined by confiscations and government-led piracy.

5. Our worship of the Almighty had been obstructed, while the Mexican government sustained a dominant national religion whose worship better served the earthly interests of the priests than the glory of God.

6. The Mexican government was in no way stable, and the country was the object of an interminable series of military revolutions, which only served to highlight the fact that all its governments were corrupt and tyrannical.

In the light of this dismal situation, it was futile to expect any hope of a solution from the government. Governments dominated by the military were incapable of remaining independent and governing for themselves.

During the thirty-three-day siege of the Alamo mission, Antonio Cruz Arocha left to ask Sam Houston for help. That same day my husband joined them, passing through the enemy lines with thirty-three men to aid in the defense of the fort. The following day, Colonel Travis, fearing that Santa Ana's soldiers had killed Antonio Cruz Arocha, ordered my husband to go in search of Sam Houston, since he knew the land well. This order saved his life.

Several days later, we learned from a letter written by a Mexican officer and published in the newspaper *Lima de Vulcano* on April 5 "that of the captains, Travis, the commander-in-chief, died bravely on the forecourt next to a cannon with a rifle in his hand." Only six people survived: two women, two Anglo-American children, a black servant belonging to Colonel Travis, and a Mexican woman.

On March 7 General Santa Ana published a proclamation in San Antonio: "People from Béjar, return to your homes and take up your domestic labors. Your town and the FORTRESS of the Alamo are now under the protection of the army of the republic, consisting of your fellow citizens, and you can be sure that no groups of foreigners will return to interrupt your peace or attack your existence or properties; the supreme government has placed you under its protection and will watch over your prosperity."

We did not trust this proclamation from Santa Ana, myself in particular, as I had been married to an American since before the declaration of independence. Like nearly all of the Canary Islanders, upon hearing of Santa Ana's march toward the Alamo I fled with my husband and children to the mule ranch, far to the south near the Río Cibolo, and there we stayed.

We only returned to San Antonio on May 25, 1836, when we heard that Houston had defeated Santa Ana at the San Jacinto River.

Life resumed in San Antonio filled with great hope. We were an independent state, and organization was needed so that we would not fall into the tyranny we had fought so hard against.

It was agreed that we were to be a republic and that the president would be elected for only three years.

Our lives changed, and so did society. Mexican names were abandoned, and Spanish words were eliminated: Béjar became Béxar, or Bexar, San Antonio. We considered ourselves to be different.

My husband John Smith was elected mayor of San Antonio on September 19, 1837, and remained so until March 9, 1838, and on January 8, 1840, he was chosen once again, this time staying in office until January 1, 1841. He was later elected as representative of Béjar in the congress of the republic in Washington-on-the-Brazos, where he died in 1844.

The problems of the descendants of the Canary Islanders, however, did not end with Texan independence and the consolidation of the Anglo-Saxon majority. We were now very much a minority, and German and French colonists outnumbered us. We had certain historically recognized rights going back to the founding of the town and the construction of the irrigation canals. These rights were not always respected by the North Americans, and in the minutes of the San Antonio town council, Diary A, June 22, 1844, there is record of a protest by the descendants of the Canary Islanders because the German immigrants were watering their gardens from the San Pedro, or mother, canal, which had been built by our ancestors and therefore gave us exclusive water rights.

Before I end my diary, I would like to mention something curious that happened this year. A newspaper has been established, the first in the United States, which expounds on new, so-called communist ideas. It was founded by one Adolph Douai, who was a great friend of a German man called Karl Marx. This man uses his newspaper to oppose slavery in Texas and participation in the civil war.

I know Mr. Douai. He is a friend of my second husband James B.

Lee. We often meet in our house to speak of his ideas, which are revolutionary but interesting, although perhaps more apt for developing in poorer countries than ours. Time will tell if I am right or not.

Now, at the age of seventy and close to death, I must bring this diary, this continuation of my aunt María's work, to a close.

I hope that someday this narrative will help Canary Islanders to understand how much we have achieved here in Texas since the first islanders arrived so long ago.

Afterword

FRANCISCO MARÍN LLORIS

In 1986 the Royal Economic Society of Friends of Gran Canaria decided to publish a book that it considered to be of great importance, both in itself and in relation to the work of diverse experts in Canarian history. It represented an important contribution to the study of the history of the Canary Islands, and revealed a unique and hugely intriguing episode of the adventures of the islanders in America. This book, *Fundación de San Antonio de Texas* (The Founding of San Antonio, Texas), was written by Armando Curbelo Fuentes, a prestigious attorney and a tireless researcher into the history of the Canary Islands' relationship with America. The volume opened with a prologue by the unforgettable historian Antonio Rumeu de Armas.

Armando Curbelo was not satisfied with this first book, and continued his research in the archives of the Canary Islands, of Seville, and of the United States, and also made several trips to San Antonio. These were not just fact-finding visits, but they also helped him to get a feel of the environment in which the islanders' experiences in the United States unfolded. The result of this considerable effort was a second book, edited by the city government of Teguise, Lanzarote, and containing an introduction by the prestigious Gran Canarian historian Antonio de Béthencourt Massieu. This book, which you hold in your hands, was a detailed study of the period when native Canary Island families inhabited and governed San Antonio—today San Antonio, Texas—right up until it was annexed to the United States following the Battle of the Alamo.

The Royal Economic Society of Friends of Gran Canaria has the fortuity to edit a new book by Armando Curbelo, one that elaborates on his previous volume and keeps the introduction by Antonio de Béthencourt Massieu. This book highlights the important links between the Canary Islands and the history of many places throughout America, including the United States. It was presented on November 29, 2007, at an event in the conference hall of the Royal Economic Society of Friends of Gran Canaria, during activities organized by the American Chamber of Commerce in the Canary Islands, led by Gran Canarian Juan Verde, for a visit to the island from a delegation of representatives from American businesses.

Sources

Archival Sources

Archivo de Bejar (B.A.), San Antonio, Texas

Real orden (Royal order). Aranjuez, May 22, 1784.

June 14, 1785, number 84, and response with number 842, March 17, 1784.

September 6, 1789.

12-7-1792. *Diligencias contra Ignacio Flores* (Proceedings against Ignacio Flores), number 94 and Sp. Ar. C-1, 147/.

1800. *Lista de presentes* (List of those present), March 12 and April 21, 3, and 16.

Quarterly VIII, 216317.

Census, Mission Espada, December 31, 1793.

Quarterly VIIIO, pp. 318–19.

1784.

See Dun Apache Relations, *Quarterly* XVI, pp. 253–54.

Josefa Granados's will from January 9, 1787, and Bethencourt's will from January 5, 1779.

July 23, 1749. *Mederos ante el tribunal* (Mederos in court).

2-2-1773.

See 1793, Record 89.

October 23, 1794, and see also December 20, 1790.

Archivo General de Indias (A.G.I.), Seville, Spain

Guadalajara 1710–1738; 67-1-37, pp. 1, 6.

Guadalajara 178, Marquis of Casafuerte to the King, September 1, 1731.

Miscellaneous file 331.

67-4-38, pp. 257–376.

Archivo General de la Nación (A.G.N.), Mexico City, Mexico

Austin, Municipal Government, p. 297, note 2; and *Real despacho autorizando la asignación de tierras* (Royal order authorizing the assignation of land), pp. 338–43, both in *Quarterly* VIII. *Cartilla de partición* (Division Record), *Leal contra Padrón* (Leal versus Padrón), B.A. 1733, 60; and *Provincias internas* (Internal provinces), vol. 32, from reports, 1731.

Biblioteca del Ministerio de Asuntos Exteriores, Madrid, Spain

Canarian Museum
Document collection of Millares Torres, vol. 1.

Parochial Archive of the Cathedral, Mexico
Testaments, book 5.

University of Texas Libraries, Austin
Box 20 - 1 7, L.S. in E. July 19, 1749.
Volume 18. Box 2 c. 17, pp. 1–35.
Volume 18. Box 2 c. 15, September 1747, pp. 20–30 v., 20–32.
Volume 19. Box 2 c. 17, January 15, 1748, pp. 1–14 v.
Volume 19. Box 2 c. 17, July 19, 1749, pp. 7, 8.
Volume 20. Note 9, D.S. in E. July 19, 1749.
D.S. in E. July 19, 1749, pp. 1–2v. 3 - Liv, 86 a 90-122 v.- 123 v.-130-131 v.-142- 145 - 148 - 149 v. 151, 152.
Volume 20. Box note 2 c. 17, c.c. July 21, 1749, pp. 1–24.
Volume 20. Box 2 c. 17, D.S., pp. 100–109 v. in E 6 - 2 1775.
Volume 30. D.S. in E. July 19, 1749, pp. 19 v.–20 and 21.
Volume 30. Box 2 c. 17, Volume 22, D.S. with cc January 1, 1750, pp. 2–2 v.
Volume 31. D.S. with D.S. January 13, 1757, pp. 1–1 v., c.c. in E. July 19, 1749, pp. 22 and 22 v. 26 and 28.
Page 17, Mexico 30. January 1750.
D.S.E. July 19, 1749, 2 v. - 17 v.

U.S. Library of Congress in *Quarterly* VIII

Books and Articles

Buck, Samuel M. *Yanaguana's Successors: The Story of the Canary Islanders' Immigration into Texas in the Eighteenth Century*. San Antonio, Texas: Naylor, 1949.

Chabot, Frederick. *With the Makers of San Antonio; Genealogies of the Early Latin, Anglo-American, and German Families with Occasional Biographies, Each Group being Prefaced with a Historical Sketch and Illustrations.* San Antonio, Texas: Artes Graficas, 1937.

Curbelo Fuentes, Armando. *Fundación de San Antonio de Texas: Canarias, la gran deuda americana.* Las Palmas: Real Sociedad Económica de Amigos del País, 1986.

Glick, Thomas. *The History of the San Antonio Texas Irrigation System.* San Antonio, Texas, 1972.

Núñez y Domínguez, José de J. *Un Virrey Limeño en México, don Juan de Acuña, Marqués de Casafuerte.* Mexico, 1927.

Rivera Cambas, Manuel. *México Pintoresco, Artístico y Monumental.* Mexico, 1880.

Endnotes

1. Town councils, or municipalities.

2. The Black Legend is a style of subjective historical writing that demonizes Spain, its people, and its culture in an intentional attempt to damage Spain's reputation.

3. María Curbelo was born in Teguise in 1717, daughter of Juan Curbelo and Gracia Perdomo Umpiérrez. Her first marriage was to José Bueno de Rojas, and her second was to Cristóbal Santos Coy. She died in San Antonio in 1803. She was the last of the original settlers from the Canary Islands. She was known in San Antonio as Aunt Canary.

4. A military fort.

5. Several members were from Lanzarote—Juan Leal Goraz, Juan Álvarez, and Juan Curbelo—and two were from Gran Canaria, Antonio Rodríguez Mederos and Juan Niz, his father-in-law. Salvador Rodríguez was from Tenerife.

6. Juan Leal Goraz was the leader of the expedition when it left Tenerife and the first elected president of the San Antonio cabildo.

7. The Canary Islanders, from the moment they founded Villa de San Fernando de Béjar (later known as San Antonio, Texas) and after they established the cabildo, always distinguished between the "founding colonists from the Canary Islands and the other residents" who had lived before them in the fort of San Antonio, and were nearly all family members of the soldiers of the fort.

8. Juan Antonio Pérez de Almazán was captain of the San Antonio presidio upon the arrival of the Canary Islanders. Charged with presenting them with their lands, he was the highest military authority in the area. He was captain of the presidio until July 1733, when the viceroy marquis of Casafuerte replaced him due to the continuous conflicts he had with the Canarian colonists.

9. An old Spanish unit of area, equivalent to the amount of land that can be planted with a fanega (a Spanish bushel) of grain.

10. Manuel Rivera Cambas, *México Pintoresco, Artístico y Monumental* (Picturesque, Artistic, and Monumental Mexico) (Mexico, 1880, pp. 335–36); José de J. Núñez y Domínguez, *Un Virrey Limeño en México, don Juan de Acuña, Marqués de Casafuerte* (Mexico, 1927, p. 87); and the Parochial Archive of the Cathedral, Mexico (Testaments, book 5, p. 174).

His term of office as viceroy lasted for eleven months, five years, and two days, from October 15, 1722, to March 17, 1734.

Don Juan de Acuña y Bejarano, first marquis of Casafuerte, was born in Lima, Peru, and baptized two months after his birth in the city's cathedral on May 9, 1658. Philip V rewarded his services to the crown by naming him marquis by royal decree on July 12, 1708, published by the royal office on February 27, 1709. He died in Mexico on March 17, 1734, and was buried in the San Cosme church in Mexico City, with the following inscription: "Juan de Acuña, Marquis of Casa Fuerte, died as viceroy of this kingdom, on March 17, 1734. He is buried in this Presbytery."

On another tombstone is the following inscription: "Here rests the famous Marquis, enlightened in war and in peace, for all his responsibilities, that which he deserved did not let him but do what was right: No one was more glorious in war, nor more applauded in government, no less pained than long-suffering, bound in the weariness of his rest. Greater than great was he, and his greatness inspired him to noble kindness. He was studied for his discipline. And he was so far from luxury and ostentation, that in his greatness he rests alongside lesser men."

11. Armando Curbelo Fuentes, *Fundación de San Antonio de Texas: Canarias, la gran deuda americana* (Las Palmas, 1986), p. 32ff.

12. Ibid., p. 58ff.

13. Ibid., p. 65.

14. Named governor general of the province in July.

15. Curbelo Fuentes, *Fundación de San Antonio de Texas*, p. 42ff.

16. José de Urrutia was captain of the presidio of San Antonio de Béjar from 1734 to 1738. The fifth son of the marriage between José Urrutia and his first wife, Rosa Flores y Valdéz, he was also chief justice of Villa de San Fernando.

17. The indigenous inhabitants of the Canary Islands.

18. An archaic unit of measure, the distance between the tips of the thumb and the index finger when they are held as far apart as possible.

19. A Spanish bushel, used for measuring quantities of grain.

20. On July 9, 1746, the same day King Philip V died, Francisco de Güemes y Horcasitas Gordan y Sáenz Villamalinedo, count of Revillagigedo, took up the position of viceroy of New Spain. He ended his term on November 1, 1755.

21. Juan Banul, a native of Brussels, was a master blacksmith and a member of the expedition of the First Marquis of Aguayo. He settled in San Antonio in 1719 and married Adriana García, who was of Flemish origin. She was the second wife of Manuel, a son of Lanzarote native Juan Leal, who was born in Lanzarote in 1728 and arrived with the expedition of Canarian colonists. Curbelo Fuentes, *Fundación de San Antonio de Texas*, p. 43.

22. José el Canario, as he is referred to in the University of Texas archives, did not arrive in San Antonio with the Canarian founders. Sometime before 1749 he married Polonia Granados, daughter of Juan Rodríguez Granadillo from Lanzarote. This occurred after the expedition had reached Veracruz and before they began the overland voyage to San Antonio. Curbelo Fuentes, *Fundación de San Antonio de Texas*, p. 58.

23. The prosecutor Andreu was aware of a document sent to the viceroy of New Spain on September 1, 1749, by several officers and noncommissioned officers regarding the possible replacement of the governor and the pressure being exerted by the missionaries. This had no doubt been suggested by Pedro del Barrio in the face of the threats in A. Rodríguez's written declarations.

24. This demonstrates how the report was prepared in bad faith, since it implies that the governor ruled against the missions because he was an interested party in the case, when in fact he was simply a governor fulfilling his duty and intervening with the full weight of his authority.

25. José Curbelo, son of Juan Curbelo and María Enríquez, was born in Lanzarote in 1711. He married Rafaela García.

26. Curbelo Fuentes, *Fundación de San Antonio de Texas*, p. 43.

27. Pedro del Barrio y Esquiella, governor of the Marquisate of the Valley of Oaxaca and later governor of the province of Texas.

28. Cristóbal de los Santos Coy, son of Diego Santos Coy and María

Farias. He was married to María Curbelo, who was born on Lanzarote in 1713. He arrived in San Antonio with his parents, Juan Curbelo and Gracia Perdomo Umpiérrez, and was the town's schoolteacher.

29. Curbelo Fuentes, *Fundación de San Antonio de Texas,* pp. 83 and 84.

30. María Jesús Curbelo Delgado, daughter of José Antonio and Josefa, born in San Antonio in 1813. She was the first descendant of a Canary Islander to convert to Protestantism and the first to marry an Anglo-Saxon. Her first marriage was to John W. Smith, the first Anglo-Saxon mayor of San Antonio, and her second was to James B. Lee. Frederick Chabot, *With the Makers of San Antonio.*

31. Agustín de Ahumada y Villalón, marquis of Amorulas, was viceroy of New Spain from November 10, 1775, to February 5, 1760.

32. Joaquín Montserrat, marquis of Cruillas, was viceroy of New Spain from October 16, 1760, to August 23, 1776.

33. Glick, *The History of the San Antonio, Texas, Irrigation System* (San Antonio, 1972), pp. 43 and 44.

34. Ibid., p. 45. On Huizar, see Arnessen, "The Primitive Art of Territorial Measurements and Their Practice in Texas," *Southwestern Historical Quarterly* 29 (1925), and Manan A. Haig, *San Antonio's Mission San José* (San Antonio, 1968), pp. 215 and 217.

35. An old Spanish term for a plot of land that receives rotating access to irrigation.

36. General Library of the University of Texas at Austin, Volume 18, Box c. 17. D.S. in notebook, September 15, 1749, pp. 29 and 30.

37. Ibid., pp. 20 and 32.

38. Ibid., Volume 20, Box 2 c. 17, July 21, 1749, pp. 1–24.

39. Ibid., Volume 29, Box 2 c. 17, D.S. 100–109, V. E62 1775.

40. *Deformación del Heredamiento de Tenoya, Año 1506,* Zárate. Canarian Museum, document collection of Millares Torres, Vol. 1, pp. 26 and 27. "It appears that lands granted and distributed in the Tenoya gorge have need of this water, and there is no way to irrigate more than nine lots; according to the witnesses and the information, it would appear that the most that we should irrigate is every twenty days, and only the amount of water required in the heat of summer or as needed."

41. Enrique Nery, baron of Bastrop, was born in Holland in 1757. He was a widower, with five children. He died in El Saltillo and, according to his last will and testament, had the following properties

in San Antonio: twenty-four plots next to the Apache Pass, two plots in the area called Tío Jerónimo next to the river, seven plots on the lands of José Labaume, a stone house in the corner of the plaza, and two or three parts of the bridge. He also owned properties in Holland that were confiscated as a result of his revolutionary activities. He was the indisputable leader of the Anglo-American colonists.

42. N.A. Verified in B.A., January 11, 1720.

43. N.A. Verified in B.A., September 1789.

44. An archaic Spanish unit of weight.

45. During this time the Mexican government allowed *empresarios*, or speculators, to acquire large tracts of land if they promised to bring in settlers to populate the region and make it profitable. Each empresario agreed to settle a specific number of Catholic families on a defined land grant within six years.

46. A type of fish.

47. A fermented beverage made from corn.

48. A liquor fermented from agave syrup.

49. A mineral salt containing compounds of sodium chlorate, sodium carbonate, and sodium sulfate, used in Mexico since pre-Hispanic times as a food seasoning.

50. A drink made from corn flour.

51. Curbelo Fuentes, *Fundación de San Antonio de Texas*, pp. 23–28.

52. Washington-on-the-Brazos, a town founded in 1834 near the Brazos River. The declaration of independence was signed here, and it was the capital of the republic from 1842 to 1846.